100
WONDERS OF INDIA

ISBN: 978-93-5194-129-3

© Roli Books, 2015
First published in 2007
This resized edition published in 2015
Second impression, 2019
Roli Books
M-75, Greater Kailash-II Market
New Delhi-110 048, India
Phone: +91-11-4068 2000
Email: info@rolibooks.com
Website: www.rolibooks.com

Main Text: Nirad Grover
Additional writing by: Malini Saigal, Malavika Chauhan,
Rupin Dang, Hari Dang, Razia Grover, Sreelata Bhatia,
Komilla Raote, Sudhir Sahi, Sanjay Singh Badnor, Dileep Prakash,
Brinda Gill, Himanshu Joshi, Raaja Bhasin, Shonar Joshi,
Yash Saxena, Nikhil Devasar, Devendra Chauhan, Karni Singh

Editor: Monica Arora
Design: Nitisha Mehta
Cover design: Sneha Pamneja
Layout: Naresh Mondal
Production: Naresh Nigam
Maps by: Anis Khan

Printed and bound at Sundeep Press, New Delhi

100
WONDERS OF INDIA

The Finest Treasures of Civilisation and Nature

Lustre Press
Roli Books

INDIA

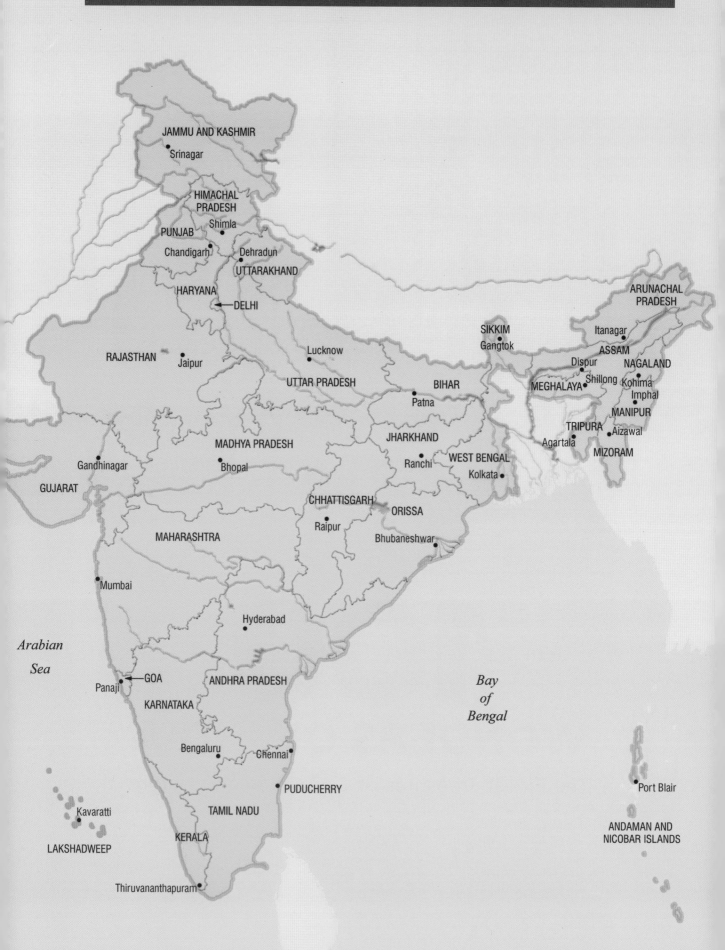

Preface

It is said that India is a continent more than a country. There is much merit to that, if all the components that go into the making of history, as well as geography, are considered.

A vigorous civilisation that has spanned at least 4,500 years is bound to have left monumental marks in its march. And if UNESCO's list of 830 World Heritage Properties is any criteria to go by, the fact that 26 of these are in India—less than those of only six other countries—is tangible proof of the creative genius, and industry of this ancient land's people, and of the gifts bestowed on it by nature.

Man-made wonders in this book are selected from a vast matrix of religious and secular genres and styles of architecture and art, the one common denominator being that they are frozen in time and space, except for two unique train journeys. Thus the showcase, with the primaeval lines of Bhimbetka's prehistoric rock art at one end and the stunning curves of the modern Lotus Temple at the other, includes palaces, paintings and public places; mosques, museums and mansions; citadels, cathedrals and carved caves; temples, tombs and towers; sprawling cities and solemn stupas.

In the natural section are wonders from the country's astoundingly varied landscapes. Rising from the white beach sands of Lakshadweep Islands in the Arabian Sea to the white Himalayan snows of Mt. Kanchenjunga, the third highest peak in the world, these are scattered across a host of habitats including torrential streams and calm rivers, desolate deserts and teeming wetlands, rolling hills and misty mountains, coral reefs and jagged cliffs, and forests ranging from tropical to alpine, within which live amazing creatures of the wild, including, of course, the majestic tiger.

Through the pages of this book, written in lucid language and splashed with lavish photographs, come take a journey into the wonder that is India.

Contents

NATURAL

Muted colours of peace and tranquillity

The Ajanta murals are the finest examples of early Indian art

MAHARASHTRA

• Ajanta

• Mumbai

*Arabian
Sea*

State and capital:
Maharashtra, Mumbai
(514 km)

Convenient access:
Road to Ajanta, air,
rail to Aurangabad

Accommodation:
Budget to high-end

Best season:
November to March

Also worth seeing:
Aurangabad, 108 km
SW, Ellora caves,
132 km SW

Buddhism first found artistic expression in India on a canvas of breathtaking beauty at Ajanta, in the state of Maharashtra, in western India. Excavated around a horseshoe-shaped ridge on the Deccan plateau, overlooking the deep Waghora River gorge, 30 caves built as *viharas* and *chaitya* halls by Buddhist monks contain the finest examples of early Indian murals, sculpture and rock-cut architecture. While the earliest date to the second and first centuries BC, a second group belongs to the fifth and sixth centuries, and the final to the

seventh century. The latter is known for its sculptural art, particularly the Parinirvana, a seven-metre-long figure of the reclining Buddha with his eyes closed as disciples celebrate his attainment of *nirvana* (enlightenment). After 700 years of inhabitation by monks and artisans, the caves appear to have been suddenly abandoned, perhaps in favour of the nearby ones at Ellora. Accidentally discovered under layers of thick vegetation by a British officer out on a tiger hunt in 1819, Ajanta is now one of UNESCO's World Heritage Sites.

Patronised by Hindu kings,

Ajanta's paintings are unparalleled in the history of Indian art. In particular, Indian religious philosophy—inward looking vision, peace and tranquillity—finds expression through them. Their artists achieved an unusual mastery in technique on a wide canvas of subjects, in composition and use of colour. The first six caves belong to the more austere Hinayana Buddhism that eventually faded out of India by the fifth century. Here, the Buddha is depicted only symbolically through sculptural motifs, such as the bodhi tree under which he preached and

of the most famous murals of Ajanta, such as the *Padmapani* (Lotus Holder), the Bodhisattva of Compassion, surrounded by celestial airborne figures. Of the innumerable *Jataka* tales, one shows the Buddha as Prince Mahajanaka who despite being tempted by Queen Shivali, a dancing girl, and palace maids, has the ritual bath before renouncing the world to become an ascetic. The maximum wall paintings are in Cave 17, where the Buddha is seen in his previous births in the form of various animals, including a monkey, a buffalo and an elephant. Another compelling rendition shows him putting forward his begging bowl when his son Rahul, tutored by his mother Yashodara, asks him for his rightful inheritance.

The mural paintings of Ajanta are not frescoes, for they were not painted on wet lime plaster. Instead, a binding medium of glue was applied to a thin coat of dried lime wash. Between this surface and the stonewalls, were two layers of plaster made of natural materials such as mud, rock-grit, vegetable fibres and grass. All murals are dense compositions in rich, but currently muted shades of green, brown, black, ochre and blue. Except for blue where a foreign substance—*lapis lazuli* from Afghanistan—was used, all the colours were made from natural pigments derived from materials such as lamp soot and lime. It was during the fifth to sixth centuries that painting techniques, which until then had been passed down orally, were put on paper. Shading and perspective making are evidence of a sophisticated skill and understanding of art even in those early times.

Facing page: Aptly titled The Dying Princess, *a touching painting in Cave 16 depicts the Buddha's conversion of his half-brother Nanda, with his wife swooning with grief at the instance of Nanda's leaving on horseback, accompanied by musicians and attendants, to become a monk.*
Below: *The caves are numbered serially, as one approaches them from the east, and not according to the dates of their excavation. Often square in shape, the* viharas *have different sizes and elements. Some are undecorated while others are ornately styled; there are those with porches and those without.*

attained enlightenment; the wheel of life; or the lotus flower that symbolises the law of cause and effect. A frieze in Cave 10, depicting a prince worshipping a bodhi tree, is considered to be the oldest mural in all the caves.

The largest body of paintings belongs to the fifth and sixth centuries when the Mahayana form of Buddhism had evolved and Buddha began to be represented in human form. Mythical creatures, Buddhist gods and scenes from the Sakyamuni's life are shown, along with the natural flora and fauna. Narrative episodes from the *Jatakas* (legendary tales from the life of the Buddha) are depicted on a large scale. There are scenes of court life and the Buddha's previous incarnations in the form of Bodhisattvas, as well as glimpses of daily life, forests, palaces and hermitages.

Buddha depicted in the form of various animals

Aptly titled *The Dying Princess*, a touching painting in Cave 16 depicts the Buddha's conversion of his half-brother Nanda, with his wife swooning with grief at the instance of Nanda's leaving to become a monk. Cave 1 has some

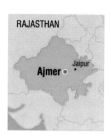

A Sufi shrine with a healing touch

Chishti's Dargah at Ajmer is revered the world over

State and capital:
Rajasthan, Jaipur
(132 km)

Convenient access:
Road, rail to Ajmer,
air to Jaipur

Accommodation:
Budget to high-end

Best season:
October to March

Also worth seeing:
Adhai din ka Jhopra,
Taragarh Fort,
Anasagar Lake

Right: More than 700 years following the Saint's death, the number of his followers continues to multiply.

Facing page: Shops sell items for offering at the Dargah outside the Shah Jahani Gate.

Above: A sufi saint; Sufism is a mystic form of Islam wherein one of the devotional practices is the repetition of divine words or lines from religious literature.

Khwaja Moinuddin Chishti came to Ajmer from Persia in 1191, during the reign of the Hindu King Prithviraj Chauhan. Better known as Khwaja Garib Nawaz (Uplifter of the Downtrodden), he set up his own Sufi doctrine known as the Chishtiya Silsila (Order) and began to spread his message. The sultans of Delhi's Slave Dynasty and, subsequently, the Mughal emperors became his followers and staunch patrons. Due to the patronage received from Emperors Akbar, Jahangir and Shah Jahan, the Khwaja's popularity rose to great heights. Although he passed away in 1233, it was only 150 years thereafter that the Sultan of

the first of the great gates, which was constructed by Sultan Ghiyasuddin Khilji, in the second half of the 15th century. Akbar was the first Mughal emperor to visit Ajmer, and it is believed that he came on foot after his son Jahangir was born. Akbar had a mosque constructed within the complex in 1571, and is said to have donated a massive *deg* (cauldron) for the purpose of cooking food for pilgrims. Later, in 1638, Shah Jahan raised a beautiful mosque made of marble. He also built a gate, known as the Shah Jahani Gate. However, the most impressive gate, now the main entrance to the mosque, is the Nizam Gate built by the Nizam of Hyderabad in 1915. Another striking

Rajab, the seventh month in the Muslim calendar. The primary reason for this mass gathering is the belief that during this time the divine grace or spirit of the Saint himself is said to linger around the cenotaph, granting wishes and bestowing blessings. *Qawwali* (Sufi devotional music and song) sessions held at the Mehfilkhana are a popular part of Urs. These begin in the evening and continue through the entire night. The traditional *mehfil-i-sama* (formal term for a *qawwali* session) has a strong Mughal feel to it and strict protocol is observed. Dressed in saffron robes, sitting under a canopy held up by silver stilts, the Diwan (Religious Head) of the Dargah

Mandu built a tomb and a dome over his grave.

The Dargah (Tomb) of the fabled Khwaja at Ajmer is one of the most important of all Sufi shrines in the subcontinent. Though a treasure trove of edifices, dating from the 14th to the 20th century, it is more renowned for its powers of healing and wish fulfilment, attracting scores of pilgrims from India and abroad.

One of the earliest and most prominent structures in the complex is the 23-metre-high Bulund Darwaza,

building is the majestic Mehfilkhana (place of intimate gatherings for artistic performances) built by Nawab Bashir-ud-Daulah Sir Usman Jah of Hyderabad, in 1891.

The Urs Fair

One of the most well-known aspects of the Dargah is the annual Urs Fair. Hundreds of thousands of pilgrims congregate to Ajmer to participate in this six-day event held to commemorate the death anniversary of the Saint. The Fair takes place during the month of

presides over the *mehfils*. The silver doors of the Jannatti Darwaza (Gateway to Paradise), a special entrance that leads to the inner sanctum and which usually remains closed most of the time, are thrown open. Pilgrims passing through the Gateway are supposed to secure a berth in heaven. The Fair concludes with the *Qul ki Rasam*. At this ceremony the entire Dargah, including the sanctum sanctorum, is washed with rose water and then wiped dry by women using their tresses.

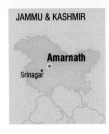
A sage, a mendicant and a silver mace

Located at a height of 3,888 metres in the Greater Himalayas, with no road leading to it, Amarnath is physically tough to reach and there is more than one fable relating to its discovery. According to the first, the Cave emerged when the ancient Sage Kashyapa drained the then underwater valley of Kashmir through a number of rivers and rivulets. Subsequently, Bhrigu, another of Hinduism's scriptural sages, on a visit to the Himalayas discovered the holy Cave. The more widely accepted story, however, credits the find to a Muslim shepherd named Buta Mallik who happened to meet a mendicant while on the pastures. The mendicant gave him a sack of coal and upon reaching home he discovered that the sack, in fact, contained gold. Overjoyed, Mallik rushed back to thank his benefactor but on the spot of their meeting discovered the Cave, which became a place of pilgrimage ever since. To date, a percentage of the donations made by pilgrims are given to the descendants of Mallik, and the remaining to the trust which manages the shrine. The shepherd community is also the guardian of the shrine and the pathway leading to it. A ceremonial five-day trek called the *chhari yatra* for the seasonal opening of the Cave is led by the head priest who belongs to the village of Ganeshpuri and is supposed to be a descendant of the priest who accompanied Mallik on his discovery of the shrine. Presently kept at Srinagar at the venue of the Dashnavi Akhara (sect), the *chhari* is a silver mace believed to have been handed over by Shiva to Kashyapa as a symbol of *shakti* (power) with the command that it be carried to Amarnath every year.

Before paying obeisance, pilgrims take a dip at the Amravati stream and procure *prasad* (blessed food) consisting of *bhang* and *dhatura* (intoxicating herbs). Shouting 'Bam bam bhole!' (Hail Shiva), they collect water and white clay from the Cave walls and follow it up with a hearty vegetarian spread.

A stalagmite of staggering proportions

The cone of ice in Amarnath Cave waxes and wanes with the moon

State and capital:
Jammu & Kashmir, Srinagar (141 km)

Convenient access:
Road to Baltal, Chandanwari, air to Srinagar (heli-services up to Amarnath), rail to Udhampur, Jammu

Accommodation:
Tents during trek and at Amarnath

Only season:
July-August

Also worth seeing:
Pahalgam, 45 km SW (walk starts from here), Sonamarg, 14 km from Baltal

Top: The ice lingam of Shiva inside the cave.

Facing page: Located at a height of 3,888 metres in the Greater Himalayas, with no road leading to it, Amarnath is physically tough to reach.

The legend goes that Shiva, the Destroyer of the Hindu Trinity, on being constantly nagged by his consort Parvati agreed to narrate the secrets of immortality and creation of the universe. Seeking a place where no one could eavesdrop, the God forsook his ride, Nandi the Bull, at Pahalgam or Bailgaon (Bull village), released the moon from his hair at Chandanwari (*chanda* means moon), shed the garland of Sheshnag the snake at its namesake place, departed from his son Ganesha at Mahaganesh Parvat (mountain) and at Panjtarni quit the five elements he was Master of, that is, earth, water, air, fire and sky. With his wife Parvati, he finally reached Amarnath Cave, and to ensure that no one dare listen to the posterity mantra, he created Kalagini (the Ring of Fire) which ensured the area was devoid of life. Finally, sitting on a deer skin rug with Parvati, he narrated the immortal secret not knowing that there were two pigeon eggs under the mat.

The mantra registered with the unborn birds and it is said that ever since they hatched, they have had eternal life. Many visitors today report seeing a pair of white pigeons near the cave.

Tucked away at the farther end of the Lidder valley, the mouth of the huge hemispherical hollow is 45 metres wide and 27 metres high. Extending 18 metres into a rugged cliff face of white Mesozoic dolomite, the cave tapers down to a width and height of nine and 4.5 metres, respectively, at its deep end. The object of reverence within is a massive shivaling (phallus symbol identified with Shiva) made of ice. The deity is actually a stalagmite, which waxes and wanes with the phases of the moon—on the full moon day of August it attains a maximum height of 4.25 metres—and is formed out of water seeping down in sub-zero conditions from Ramkund Lake directly above the cave. Beside it are similar formations identified as Parvati and Ganesh.

Ashoka the Great's engraved ideology

Rock edicts and pillars spread his message of peace

An ambitious lad at the head of a rag-tag army, a crafty Brahmin instigator and a debauched king of a malcontented kingdom were the key characters in the establishment of the Mauryan Empire in northern India in the fourth century BC. The young man was Chandragupta Maurya, of uncertain, perhaps tribal origin. Growing up in an age dominated by Alexander's incursions into the Punjab, Chandragupta set his sights early on the Nanda kingdom based in Magadha (present-day eastern Uttar Pradesh and Bihar). The Brahmin Kautilya, sworn enemy of King Dhana Nanda ably assisted him. Gathering up an army fired by guts and promises of glory, Chandragupta wrested Punjab from Greek control and swept eastwards, conquering satellite states and outlying provinces of the Nandas, before capturing the capital, Pataliputra, in 326 BC. Through treaty, war and alliance, he bequeathed to his successors an empire that stretched from Afghanistan to Gujarat, through till Central India and Bengal.

Inscriptions in local languages

Chandragupta's famous grandson Ashoka (269-232 BC), was a man of war turned towards peace. Unable to bear the bloody aftermath of the war against Kalinga (modern Orissa), Ashoka foreswore violence, embraced Buddhism, and resolved to spread the light of his philosophy of *Dhamma* (broadly defined as enlightened, responsible coexistence) amongst his subjects. Ashoka propagated his message of peace, charity and humane governance through 14 rock edicts, many cave edicts, and numerous free standing pillars throughout his land. Inscribed in Brahmi, origin of most Indian scripts, the edicts are in local languages—sometimes in more than one language in an area—and written in direct informal prose. Besides enshrining Ashoka's humanitarian ideology, which was to become the cornerstone of Indian philosophy and religious thought, these inscriptions are the earliest intelligible historical records from ancient India.

Tapering shafts of symbolic elements

The highly polished, beautifully carved Ashokan pillars in sandstone are examples of a fully developed art, the initial stages of which are nowhere to be found. Moreover, the wonderful high polish of Mauryan stone was not seen again in the subcontinent for many centuries. This suggests a strong influence of imported craftsmanship from Achaemenid or West Asian lands as a result of the surge of trade, diplomatic and artisan traffic in the wake of Alexander's military expedition to India. Notable among the pillars are the ones at Sanchi, Sarnath, Rampurva and Lauriya Nandangarh. Each is a tall, tapering shaft, without a base, but capped by a gently arched bell of lotus petals, carved in a stylised, Iranian fashion and crowned by seated or standing animals, over a narrow carved frieze on a drum below.

The symbolism of the pillars has been widely debated. Could they be rooted in tree worship, or do they represent the cosmic axis, the stone shaft that joins the heavens to the earth, in the same way that a king, ordained by the gods, is connected to his people? Or were they early phallic symbols of a nascent Shaivaite philosophy? The pillar at Sarnath, a sacred Buddhist spot, has four lions seated back to back on a drum with a carved frieze of four animals: a bull, a horse, a lion and an elephant separated by four *chakras* (wheels). The lion was a symbol of the Mauryan dynasty and the four smaller animals represent the four cardinal directions in Indic philosophy. The *chakra* has always been an important symbol of cosmic law in Upanishadic thought, whereby the *chakravartin* (king) is one who upholds this cosmic order. Buddhism also reveres the wheel as the symbol of the Buddha's first sermon on the 'Turning of the Wheel of Law'. Thus the four solemn lions gazed sternly in the four directions, emphasising the divine authority of the Mauryan lion, the righteous *chakravartin*, to rule the four corners of a vast empire.

The same pillar capital now stands as the National Emblem of the modern Republic of India.

Above: An edict in Brahmi script on the Ashokan pillar at Sarnath, where the Buddha gave his first sermon, frowns upon the causing of schisms in the Buddhist community. Brahmi is considered the progenitor of all writing systems in South Asia.

Left: The capital of the Sarnath pillar is now the National Emblem of India

Facing page: Unlike later columns, the pillar at Vaishali, an important town in the fourth century BC, is crowned by only one lion capital facing north, possibly indicating the direction in which the Buddha made his last journey to Kusinagara, where he died.

An ode to the Bah'ai Faith

The Lotus Temple is a nine-sided expression of worship

The Bah'ai Temple has received prestigious international awards for excellence in religious art and architecture, structural design, excellence in outdoor illumination and for being one of the most finely built concrete structures.

Christened the Lotus Temple because of its extraordinary shape of an unfurling 27-petalled lotus flower, the House of Worship of the Bah'ai sect in India was designed by an Iranian architect Fariburz Sahba and opened to public in 1987. The Bah'ai faith with over five million followers worldwide, originated in Persia in the early 19th century. The message of the founder Baha'u'llah was 'One World, One Faith',

signifying the spiritual and social unification of the human race, and accordingly, the temple is open to all faiths and cultures. There are no religious icons in the plain central hall and no rituals. Short 15-minute prayer services from all faiths are recited or chanted through the day. It is basically a place for meditation, peace and tranquillity.

The lotus is the Indian national flower and a popular symbol in most Indian religions, representing the

emergence of purity and perfection from stagnant, muddy waters. It also symbolises detachment from material preoccupations. This inspiration for the architect resulted in perhaps the most spectacular of all the seven existing Bah'ai temples in the world. Though the designs are different, all temples have a central dome and nine sides, the figure 9 symbolising unity in the acceptance of the nine major world faiths, which feature in the message of the

involved, the implementation of the design was achieved because of the traditional craftsmanship and means of construction available in India. The architect himself marvelled at the rare combination of traditional skills, empathy for a spiritual undertaking, and patience displayed by the Indian workforce in executing the extremely difficult project. Women carried as much as 20 kilograms of concrete at a time in baskets on their heads, upto the highest level, as the structure was first cast in reinforced white concrete on the site. The following task of cladding it in white marble was immensely complex too, because of the need to cover curved surfaces on both sides of the petal. Working in minimal workspace due to the closeness of the freestanding petals to one another was also a challenge. The concretising process of the petals had to be completed in one continuous operation of 48 hours in order to avoid weak jointing, while the steel reinforcing for the petals was galvanised to prevent rusting and rust stains on the white marble. nine arches ringing the tranquil prayer hall, which seats about 2,500 persons, hold up the exquisite superstructure. Skylight filters in through a discreet system of glazing at the apex of the inner petals and on partial surfaces of the remaining two rings. Ventilation and cooling follow traditional techniques; fresh air is cooled as it passes over the nine pools of water and is then drawn in through basement openings, eventually exiting through a vent in the central dome.

The beautifully landscaped lawns on the 26-acre site surround the building. Attracted both by its beauty and the humanist philosophy of the Bah'ai faith, millions visit the House of Worship each year—the maximum-recorded visitors in a single day have been about 1,50,000.

founder. The flower rises in three concentric circles of nine petals each, the upper two rings curving inwards and upwards, pointing to heaven, as it were, and embracing the central dome. The lowest ring curves downwards as canopies over the nine entrances. At the ground level, surrounding the structure, are nine pools of water, like the leaves of the flower, reflecting the luminous flower of the superstructure itself. A library and other ancillary functions are located on a series of terraces on either side of the main steps, almost camouflaged by landscaping. The temple is clad in pristine white marble from Greece, which was specially cut in Italy to the specified curvature and thickness of each component of the petals. There are virtually no straight lines in the main structure.

A triumph of traditional craftsmanship

A team of about 800 engineers, technicians, artisans and local labourers worked on the project, which took 10 years in designing and implementation. When it was built, it was one of the most complicated constructions in the world, and while modern western engineering expertise helped to arrive at the precise geometrical calculations

The baroque Basilica of Bom Jesus

In its chapel lie St Francis Xavier's miraculously preserved remains

GOA

• Panaji

Arabian Sea

State and capital:
Goa, Panaji (10 km)

Convenient access:
Road, air, rail to Goa, boat from Mumbai

Accommodation:
Budget to luxury

Best season:
November to March

Also worth seeing:
Se Cathedral, cruise on Mandovi River, Mangeshi Temple, 9 km SE

Though the small state of Goa on the western coast of India traces its history to the third century BC, much of her extant architecture and culture reflects 450 years of Portuguese rule. This period commenced with Afonso de Albuquerque wresting control of the port in 1510, and today, even 45 years after the Portuguese have left, their influence on its culture remains deeply embedded.

Under its European rulers, Goa became the political and ecclesiastical capital of all Portuguese possessions in Asia and acquired the grandeur of an imperial city. Travellers praised its secular and religious architecture. Among these is the Basilica of Bom Jesus, one of the holiest places of worship for Catholics in Asia, owing to the revered relics of St Francis Xavier preserved here in a beautiful mausoleum.

Francis Xavier was born on 7 April, 1506, in Spain. Having an intellectual bent of mind, he pursued academics and learning, received priesthood, served the sick and taught the gospel. He travelled to the East, reaching Goa in 1542 and returning again after further travels. Falling ill on a voyage to the Far East, he died on Sancian Island, near China, in December 1552 at the young age of 46. His body was buried on the Island after being coated with lime to precipitate its decomposition that would enable the bones to be taken to Malacca.

But in February 1553, when it was exhumed, the body was found to be miraculously life like. It was taken to Malacca for burial in the Church of Our Lady of the Mount. After four months, when his successor had the body exhumed again, it had not shown any change. It was subsequently conveyed to Goa, where it was received by the people in March 1554 and placed in St Paul's College till 1613, following which it was taken to the Professed House of Bom Jesus. Following the canonisation of the Saint in 1622, an exquisite silver coffin was crafted for his body, within which it is presently placed in the chapel in the transept, on the southern side of the Basilica.

The mausoleum lies in a chapel with gilded columns

The Basilica of Bom Jesus ('Good' Jesus) is dedicated to Infant Jesus and regarded as one of the finest examples of baroque architecture in India. Built during 1594-1605, out of blocks of the locally quarried reddish laterite stone, it has a three-storeyed façade. The 'IHS' monogram, symbolic of Jesus Christ, enclosed with angels and decorative motifs, is engraved on the highest square of the façade. Inside, the richly gilded main altar has the figure of Infant Jesus, above which the large statue of St Ignatius Loyola, founder of the Order of Jesuits, gazes at a medallion higher up. Above the medallion are fine figures of the Holy Trinity. The main altar is flanked by two decorated altars in the transept, one dedicated to Our Lady of Hope and the other to St Michael. On the right of the main altar, in a chapel with gilded twisted columns, floral decorations of wood, and paintings depicting scenes from the life of the Saint, stands his mausoleum. Gifted by the Duke of Tuscany, Cosmas III, the shrine was fashioned by the Florentine sculptor Giovanni Batista Foggini (1653-1737) in over 10 years. Its parts were packed and transported to Goa, where they were assembled in 1698.

The rectangular base of the mausoleum, made of reddish-purple jasper, is decorated with white marble carvings. Above this is another large rectangular section, with extensively worked bronze plaques in the centre of each side, each of which depicts a scene from the life of St Xavier. The third section of the mausoleum is a marble balustrade, which supports the carved silver casket in which lie the sacred relics of the body.

Public expositions

Once every 10 years there are public expositions of the undecomposed relics. The first exposition was held in 1782, and the last in 2004, during which an estimated 2 million devotees came to seek blessings. After the public exposition of 1952, it was decided that the body be placed in a crystal urn, and the public should no longer be allowed to touch it directly.

Top: The vestry of the Basilica.
Right: The relics of St Francis Xavier attract devotees to Goa from all over.
Facing page: The large statue of St Ignatius Loyola, founder of the Order of Jesuits, gazes at a medallion higher up.

Bhimakali

Shimla

Sacred Shaktipeeth of Goddess Kali

Bhimakali Temples are sanctuaries of the Bushahr rulers of Rampur

State and capital:
Himachal Pradesh,
Shimla (184 km)

Convenient access:
Road to Sarahan, air,
rail to Shimla

Accommodation:
Budget to mid-range
(in Rampur)

Best season:
April-May, September
to November

Also worth seeing:
Raja Bushahr Palace,
Kinnaur tribal region, E

*Above: View of the
Bhimakali Temple.*

*Facing page top: The
silver doors of the
inner courtyard are
inserted in dry stone
masonry, while the
timber construction
is decorated with
delicate floral and
geometric motifs.*

Golden finials representing the sun and the moon pierce the skies from the roofs of the Bhimakali Temple's main shrines, whose wooden structures have withstood the test of time. In this temple-palace configuration, the typical building style and technique of Himachal Pradesh, called *kath kona* (timber with stone bonding), finds its most magnificent expression. The Bhimakali Temples are regarded as one of the 51 sacred Shaktipeeths (places where the temples of the Goddess Durga have special significance) in India. They are believed to be the original shrine of the Goddess, and the last in the Satluj Valley to be served by Brahmin priests.

Perched atop the western Himalayas, the cluster of several structures lies on the legendary Hindustan-Tibet route at Sarahan. Jacaranda trees abound in summer in the valley of the gushing Satluj River deep down below, while the steep mountain slopes above

Sarahan are covered by deodars and birch upto the snowline. The Temples are the personal sanctuaries of the erstwhile ruling Bushahr family of Rampur, which was one of the biggest princely states in these hills. A centre of livestock, wool, shawls, blankets and dry fruit trade with Tibet, Rampur is located at a height of about 1,000 metres.

Entry to the complex is past a narrow winding street leading to its blank outer walls. Inside it, one is greeted by sloping slate roofs peaking at the centre and curving at the ends, in a mix of Hindu and Buddhist styles, emulating the lofty peaks that frame them. Of the four main temples, each dedicated to an important deity, the forbidding Bhimakali, one of the fierce forms of Durga, occupies the two main ones. Decorative panels compose their overhanging balconies while carved wooden skittles hang from the eaves. The tilting stature of the original temple owes itself to an earthquake in 1905. Within the

four storeys of the older building are the priest's room, a kitchen, shrines and store rooms, all connected by narrow, straight staircases. It is said that there once existed an underground passage linking the shrine chamber with the priest's village, so that in disturbed times he could steal in and continue to perform the daily ritual of prayer. Human sacrifice to appease and please the dark Bhimakali was carried out in a small cell inside, while another cell served as a watchtower. The second of the two main shrines, earlier only one storey high, now has an elaborate superstructure with a two-tiered enclosed verandah and four pent roofs capped by a circular one. The Maharaja made these additions in 1930 when the deities inside the old shrine building had to be shifted to the new one. Here, on the second floor, the daunting Goddess dwells as a wedded woman, while on the third floor, she is portrayed as a maiden.

19th century repousse work on silver doors

The complex is actually a combination of a palace and temples. The temple of Narasimha (a form of Vishnu) at the south-eastern entrance is the only stone structure, and the only shrine built in the conventional *shikhara* (tower) form. A highly decorated metal door opens into the first courtyard and the king's palace. The queen's palace, also a double-storeyed building, stood on its right, segregated from the other buildings but connected to the king's palace by a staircase used exclusively by the him. Across another courtyard and above the next gateway is the rebuilt Ram Mandir, enshrining an image of the legendary hero of the epic *Ramayana*. The silver doors leading into this courtyard are a splendid example of mid 19th century repousse work, depicting mythological subjects and various Hindu gods.

It is more than likely that even in an entire lifetime one may not get to be part of the principal festival of the Goddess. For the Udyapan Jag, as it is called, comes around not before 100 years or more of the previous one—the last Jag took place in 1904, and the one before it 280 years earlier. The entire pantheon of deities from the surrounding mountains was brought to pay respects to Bhimakali during the six-month celebration of 1904, during which 600 goats were sacrificed.

Below: A silversmith taps out repousse designs at Sarahan.

Petroglyphs from the Mesolithic period

Bhimbetka's primaeval paintings

On a train journey in 1958 to Bhopal in Madhya Pradesh, archaeologist V.S. Wakankar made an immediate note of what would have seemed to be mere rock formations to the untrained eye but were, in fact, rock shelters and caves in the distant hills. Returning to the site, armed with a professional team and tools, Wakankar found almost 600 natural dwellings, once occupied from the Paleolithic era onwards. Although

this was a momentous discovery on its own, it turned out to be an exceptional one when paintings were discovered in the caves dating back to over thousands of years, made by those who had once resided in them. The earliest paintings reflecting a primitive, hunting-gathering way of life, can be traced back to the early stages of the Mesolithic period (about 12,000 years ago). Following this is art created when a sedentary,

agricultural culture was in place, and thereafter come the pictures clearly made during the historical period.

Surrounded by the Vindhya and Satpura Hills, Bhimbetka is tucked into a dense forest of *sal* and teak, with craggy overhanging rocks and dried leaves for ground cover. Branches extend from knotted trees, the sound of gushing water mixes with the sound of wind whooshing through the caves, some of whose

MADHYA PRADESH

State and capital:
Madhya Pradesh,
Bhopal (45 km)
Convenient access:
Road to Bhimbetka,
air, rail to Bhopal
Accommodation:
Budget to luxury
in Bhopal
Best season:
November to March
Also worth seeing:
Mosques of Bhopal,
Bhojeshwar Temple,
28 km NW

interiors have smooth surfaces in a variety of textures suggesting that they once might have been under water. The setting is primaeval and the area's richness in wildlife has led it to be declared a wildlife sanctuary.

Scenes from everyday life in a variety of colours

The selection of 15 odd caves easily accessible via a concrete path bear myriad painted tales of hunters and their game, men and their families, childbirth, rites, rituals and ceremonies, warriors and chiefs. The figures of animals are well etched while those of humans are like typical line drawings of young children. Hunters wear head dresses and ornaments, children are shown playing and running, women

grinding and preparing food, musicians playing drums and families getting together for honey collection and sacred rituals. Animals seem to be a favourite theme with the artists: there is a whole array of wildlife ranging from bigger beasts like elephants, tigers and bison, as on the 'Zoo Rock', to smaller fauna like deer, rabbits, fish, frogs, lizards, peacocks and other birds. Domestic animals are in plenty too and include grazing buffaloes.

The paintings are simple yet convey movement and fluidity. The emotional impact of the scene comes through by using insightful techniques. For instance, in trying to convey fear, the size of the wild animal, as it tears after a petrified

hunter, is greatly exaggerated. The fact that various hues of red, green, yellow and white still survive is partly because the drawings are often tucked away in niches and deep recesses, and also due to the remarkable durability of the paint. Crushed haematite (iron oxide) was used to procure red while green was derived from chalcedony. These powders were possibly mixed with some kind of resin or gum from trees, vegetable dyes, roots and animal fat to impart long lasting as well as waterproof qualities. Fanned twigs combined with animal hair must have served as brushes. At times, one can discern that the same surface has been used as the 'painting board' for different artists at different periods.

Shrines of power and prestige

Bhubaneshwar's temples propitiate Shiva

State and capital:
Orissa, Bhubaneshwar

Convenient access:
Road, air, rail to
Bhubaneshwar

Accommodation:
Budget to high-end

Best season: October
to April

Also worth seeing:
Orissa State Museum,
Khandagiri Jain caves,
Konark 65 km SE,
Puri 60 km SW

Bhubaneshwar became the capital of the kingdom of Kalinga (Orissa) in the seventh century under the Shailodbhava rulers, and remained so under successive dynasties till the 13th century. A ruler's temporal prestige and power was directly proportionate to the magnificence of religious edifices he ordained, and Bhubaneshwar became the 'City of Temples', dotted with over 7,000 shrines clustered in groups around the Bindusagar Tank. This Tank is said to contain water from every river in India, and its environs are particularly propitious. The dominant deity is Shiva. In this profusion of sacred spaces it is possible to see the complete development of the splendid Orissan version of the North Indian temple style.

The Orissan style

Two distinct elements appear in the temples. The first is a curvilinear towered sanctuary, also known locally as the *rekha deul,* with the traditional ribbed *amalaka* (disc-shaped crown) and *kalasa* (finial). The tower is broken into horizontal bands with carved *amalaka* motifs in the four corners. Through the centuries, the tower became higher

and more complex, with miniature replicas of itself at the corners. The second element is the square *mandapa* (porch hall) in front of the *rekha deul,* known locally as the *jagmohan,* roofed with a pyramid of horizontal elements. Later temples, such as the Lingaraja, added a *nata mandir* (dancing hall) and *bhog mandir* (hall of offerings for the priests and devotees).

Exquisite sculpture is another notable element in Orissan temples, testifying to a centuries old tradition of stone carving, which is kept alive till today. The sculptural forms do not however overwhelm the walls and are focussed on the principal divinities visible in elevated and decorated wall niches. Gracefully poised, with gentle smiles, these deities are carved in deep stone relief. Subsidiary figures of musicians, warriors, devotees and lovers are more exuberant, and the niches are surrounded by delicately etched patterns of lotus stalks,

petals and scrollwork. A common feature of temples in Orissa is that the interior walls are fairly stark, while the exterior walls are lavishly decorated. In later temples, more attention is paid to architectural mouldings than the sculpture.

From the Parasurameshwara to the Lingaraja Temple

The best-preserved temple of the early phase (mid seventh century), the Parasurameshwara Temple contains all the elements of the Orissa style. The *jagmohan* is a later addition as can be seen by its ungainly juncture with the *rekha deul.* The double-storeyed flat roof is a prelude to the multi-layered *deul* of later temples, such as the Lingaraja. Each side of the *shikhara* (temple tower) is divided into three sections

by a central projection, each housing a sculpted divinity including a pot-bellied Ganesha, one of the most beloved of Hindu gods, associated with good fortune, and his son Kartikeya, the God of War, on his peacock.

The Vaital Deul Temple (late eighth century) is dedicated to Goddess Durga. It has a rectangular sanctuary with a vaulted roof reminiscent of Buddhist *viharas* (monasteries). The interior carvings of the *mandapa* suggest a Tantric bent to the rites. A gem of Orissan art, the Mukteshwara Temple (late 10th century) displays finely detailed sculpture, especially in the expressions and attire of female figures. An interesting feature of the surface decoration is the *bho* ornament, which consists of an arch with a *kirtimukha* (ferocious lion-like threshold guardian), flanked by two dwarf-like figures.

However, the most outstanding temple is the 11th century Lingaraja, with its ribbed, towering 31 metre high *deul* dominating the city skyline. The gigantic Lingaraja was constructed over several centuries and as rituals became more complex, it was enlarged. The new additions were higher than the earlier *jagmohan*, and created an uneven silhouette, unusual in medieval temples. Vertical and horizontal divisions mark the exterior walls and organise the profusion of deeply carved figures, floral patterns, animals, and divine beings. Swaying female figures appear in a variety of poses, and gracious, sweetly smiling divine beings preside over exuberant processions. An unusual motif is the rampant lion springing over a crouching elephant, which may have been a royal emblem.

Only about 500 of the original temples remain. Their monumental sculpted forms, in the older southern part of the planned city, tower over the surrounding rice fields, kept green by the fertile delta of the Mahanadi River skirting Bhubaneshwar.

'Rural Hub' in red clay

Bishnupur's terracotta temples resemble thatched huts of Bengal

Right: Significant temple construction at Bishnupur continued from the late 16th century to the 19th century. Though at first glance, the temples look quite similar to each other, closer inspection reveals individuality in form. Within the overall resemblance to the structure of thatched rural huts in Bengal, there exist three sub-styles: the chala is characterized by curved roofs and cornices, the ratna by towers and the daalan by its flat tops.

Facing page: The Shyama Rai Temple has vaulted verandahs on all sides. Triple-arched entrances with curved cornices on top lead into the Temple. The sculptural decoration is chiefly of scenes from the Ramayana and stories related to Krishna.

Even though temples are aplenty in India, what is interesting is the diversity in style and architecture. Standing apart are the delightful temples of Bishnupur, in the Bankura district of West Bengal. A most unassuming little town, it has a collection of about 30 such temples scattered around the countryside, making it a perfect excursion by foot or cycle.

Bishnupur was once the capital of the Mallas, who ruled this area for 1,000 years, and were feudatory chiefs under the Mughals during the 16th century. One of the kings, Bir Hambir, notorious for his greed, turned a new leaf under the influence of the Vaishnava movement (the worship of Vishnu), sparking off a sudden proliferation of temples in the 17th and 18th centuries dedicated to the Preserver. Because there was not much stone in this part of the country, the rulers decided to make the best of what they had in abundance—red clay, and at times laterite. The nature of this unusual material, and the reigning political and religious influences of the time, gave birth to the curiously attractive temples of Bishnupur: structures largely resembling the thatched rural huts of Bengal, with an icing of Bengali, Oriya and Islamic styles.

From the dominant Muslim empires of the time came geometric motifs and multi-lobed arches. On later temples was an infusion of Hindu iconography of a revivalist movement within the faith. The Oriya element announced itself in the form of the *deul* (cubical shrine room). Though at first glance the temples look quite similar to each other, closer inspection reveals distinct individuality evident in the mix of curvaceous roofs, elegant towers and flat tops. Bir Hambir's pyramidical Rasa Mancha, instead of being devoted to a single deity became a congregation place of all the Bishnupur idols on the Rasa Festival. Jor Bangla, constructed by Raghunath Singh II in the mid 17th century, sets itself apart by its two domes joined together by a *shikhara* (towering superstructure). There are Radhashyam, Lalji and Nandalal, with single towers on sloping roofs and multi-cusped arches, and Madana Gopala and Shyam Rai, flaunting five towers and multiple arches. Shyam Rai also draws a second look for its brick carvings.

Krishna flirting with his *gopis*
While half a dozen temples are still in superb condition, many others have suffered from the hot and humid, temperamental Bengal climate. What strikes one is the manicured green grass dabbed by the 500-year-old crimson hues of the terracotta monuments. Since the emphasis was on Vaishnavism, the dominating theme is the Rasalila, with Krishna and his beautiful *gopis* (milkmaids) dancing away the red dust of the brick façades. Radha-Krishna themes are interspersed by Vishnu's ten incarnations, Rama fighting Ravana at Lanka, and, of course, the whole pantheon of Indian gods. Tales are depicted from the *Mahabharata* and *Ramayana*; Sri Chaitanya, the 16th century ascetic, is seen along with his devotional drummers. Nature, always an integral part of Indian art, is present in running borders of floral motifs and a profusion of rather comical, albeit lifelike, geese and ducks, elephants, horses, scampering monkeys and roaring tigers. The rulers also used these plaques to portray historic events and the life of the common people. Thus, one sees soldiers and battlefields, royal processions, dancing postures, and queens and kings in courtly ambience engraved minutely in bas-relief.

Buddha's seat of enlightenment
The Buddha meditated under the legendary Bodhi Tree at Bodhgaya

State and capital:
Bihar, Patna (117 km)

Convenient access:
Road to Bodhgaya, air
to Patna, rail to Gaya

Accommodation:
Budget to mid-range
at Bodhgaya

Best season:
November to March

Also worth seeing:
Sher Shah's Tomb at
Sasaram, Barabar
Buddhist Caves

With great spiritual personalities, surrounded as they are amidst legends, it is always difficult to imagine the details of the lives they lived. In the case of the Buddha, one is perhaps at some advantage as much of the information available of his time on earth, is fairly well documented. Four sites are considered most holy for Buddhists—his birthplace at Lumbini in Nepal; Sarnath, where he gave his first sermon; Kushinagar, where he took leave of his body, and the most important of all, Bodhgaya in Bihar, where he received *nirvana* or enlightenment.

A prince's renunciation
As per belief, disillusioned with the world, the young Prince Siddhartha of Kapilavastu in Nepal renounced his family and palace in search of the *raison d'être* behind life and a solution for its endless cycle of pain and suffering. Under the hallowed *Asvatta* (banyan) Tree, also known as the Bodhi Tree, he commenced on a spiritual journey in search of an

answer. After sitting for 49 days on the sacred *kusha* grass below, resisting all kinds of temptation, Siddhartha attained enlightenment and was thenceforth known as the Buddha. After this, he is said to have left Bodhgaya and moved on to Sarnath.

Relics mark the seven weeks spent after enlightenment
Before leaving, however, he visited seven different places over seven weeks, which now lie within the precincts of the Mahabodhi Mahavihara or the Great Temple at Bodhgaya. The first week was spent under the Bodhi Tree itself. The great Emperor Ashoka's (third century BC) children carried a sapling of the original tree to Anuradhapura in Sri Lanka, and when the original at Bodhgaya died, it was replaced in turn with a sapling brought back from Anuradhapura. Underneath the tree is a *vajrasana* (stone slab) where the young ascetic is said to have meditated and attained *nirvana*. The second week was spent at the Animeshlochana Stupa, from where

he stared unblinkingly at the Bodhi Tree. A small white temple now marks the spot. Carved stone lotuses indicate spots on the raised platform of the *Ratnachankrama* or the Jewel Walk, where he spent the third week walking and meditating. The blue, yellow, red, white and orange colours of the Buddhist flag derive from what took place during the fourth week: as the Buddha meditated on the highest laws behind existence, his body is said to have emanated these very colours. This spot is called Ratnagraha Chaitya. Sitting under the Ajapala Nigrodha Tree, the Buddha spent the fifth week in discussion with a Brahmin, explaining that it is one's deeds and not his birth that define a man. In the penultimate week, the Buddha meditated by the Muchhalinda or the Lotus Pond, abode of the Serpent King, who gave him protection. The scene has been depicted in life-like form in the middle of the pond. And finally, during the last seven days, the Buddha is said to have sat under the Rajyatana Tree of which the exact location is not known but a spot

has nevertheless been identified for worship.

The present 52-metre high Mahabodhi Mahavihara is said to have been built on top of a temple constructed by Ashoka; part of the railings that surround the temple belong to that period. An ornate *torana* (gateway) leads to the inner courtyard where a large stone with the Buddha's footprints is kept in a shrine. In the inner sanctum is his gilded statue in the *bhumisparsha mudra*, that is, with one finger pointing towards the earth.

Devotees from all corners of the world come to Bodhgaya. Some prostrate themselves, others rotate their personal prayer wheels, each turn of which is meant to absolve them of sins accrued. Butter lamps shed a golden glow on the temple, incense smoke fills the air with aroma, and soft murmurs of prayers and chanting float through the atmosphere, broken only by occasional gongs from the many international monasteries in the area.

TAMIL NADU
Chennai •

Thanjavur •

Arabian Sea

Bay of Bengal

State and capital:
Tamil Nadu, Chennai
(350 km)

Convenient access:
Road, rail to Thanjavur,
air to Tirucharapalli

Accommodation:
Budget to mid-range

Best season:
November to March

Also worth seeing:
Museum and Art
Gallery for Chola
bronzes, Thanjavur
Palace, 1 km,
Brihadeshwara
Temple at
Gangaikonda-
cholapuram,
71 km NW

Thanjavur's 'Big Temple'

The Brihadeshwara Temple's cupola had to be pushed up by an elephant

Between AD 600 and 1200, several dynasties rose and fell in South India, one of whom were the Cholas. They defeated the Pallavas in the ninth century and established the largest empire in India since that of the Guptas in the fourth century. The Chola capital was at Thanjavur (Tanjore). Surrounded on three sides by the sea, the South Indian peninsula, already rich in spices, textiles and other goods, was theirs, along with Sri Lanka. They drew from the wealth of neighbouring lands and also facilitated trade between the West, and eastern countries such as Java and Sumatra, Cambodia and

common in the region, Shiva was an equally popular deity, and the Brihadeshwara Temple, built by the great Chola Emperor Rajaraja I (AD 985-1014), is dedicated to him. This is quite evident from the number of exquisitely carved sculptures installed in the complex. Shiva's iconic symbol, the lingam, representative of strength, dominates the sanctum sanctorum, where it is a massive four metres high, and seven metres in circumference. In fact, because of its height, it became necessary to make two circumambulatory passages inside. Lingams of various sizes, numbering around 250, are found all over the

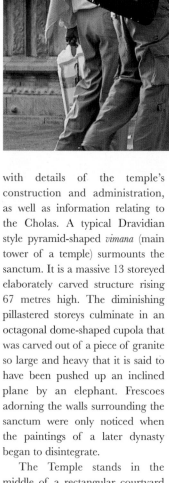

*Right: A Shiva
devotee, identifiable
by the three
horizontal lines of
sandalwood paste
smeared across
his forehead, sits
in a niche in the
Temple wall.*
***Facing page top &
bottom:*** *Some of the
structures, such as
the entrance porch
with an overhanging
eave, are later
additions. While
the gateways, walls,
columns and other
surfaces are
embellished with
sculptures that evoke
wonder at their
execution, there is a
collection housed in
the museum of rare
Chola bronzes,
which is equally
breathtaking.*

Malaysia. Architecture, arts and literature touched new heights of excellence. The Pallavas before them had already erected some great temples, and now, the Cholas, whose empire flourished under an efficient administration, lavished their wealth on architecture, excelling the feats of their predecessors. The Brihadeshwara Temple at Thanjavur is one of the finest examples of their accomplishments. A World Heritage Site, it is also called the 'Big Temple' by the local people.

Omnipresent Shiva

Towering spires and monumental gateways make this temple, literally and metaphorically, soar over most other temples of southern India. Though the worship of Vishnu was

temple complex—in the surrounding walkway and in smaller shrines. On all, flowers placed on top, a dot of turmeric, and vermilion or white paste applied on the forehead of the deity express the fervour of worshipping devotees who come in hundreds each day. Apart from the lingams, Shiva's status as Nataraj, the God of Dance, is made apparent by sculptures of numerous dancing maidens in various positions of the classical Bharatanatyam style. The granite Nandi, mythical bull mount of Shiva, guards the entrance to the shrine. Weighing over 25 tons, it is reputed to be the largest Nandi sculpture in India.

The Temple's elephants

The sanctum stands on a high basement whose walls are inscribed

with details of the temple's construction and administration, as well as information relating to the Cholas. A typical Dravidian style pyramid-shaped *vimana* (main tower of a temple) surmounts the sanctum. It is a massive 13 storeyed elaborately carved structure rising 67 metres high. The diminishing pillastered storeys culminate in an octagonal dome-shaped cupola that was carved out of a piece of granite so large and heavy that it is said to have been pushed up an inclined plane by an elephant. Frescoes adorning the walls surrounding the sanctum were only noticed when the paintings of a later dynasty began to disintegrate.

The Temple stands in the middle of a rectangular courtyard surrounded by smaller shrines,

the treasury, museum and library. A real baby elephant stands delightfully at the entrance, receiving offerings in kind from the faithful and even acknowledging them with a knock of its trunk on their head. Preceding the sanctum is an ante chamber and an incomplete multi-columned *mandapa* (temple hall).

Thanjavur was a prominent Hindu site under the Cholas, and important even later, when it came under Maratha rule in the 16th-17th centuries. Today, the area around it is known as the rice bowl of Tamil Nadu but the Brihadeshwara Temple, piercing the sky with a gilded finial donated by the king Rajaraja I himself, remains Thanjavur's most brilliant showpiece.

RAJASTHAN

Jaipur

Chittorgarh ○

Symbol of Rajput valour

Chittorgarh Fort stands tall in defeat

State and capital:
Rajasthan, Jaipur
(309 km)

Convenient access:
Road, rail to Chittor,
air to Udaipur

Accommodation:
Budget to mid-range

Best season:
November to March

Also worth seeing:
Mauryan and Gupta
period remains at
Nagari, 20 km NE,
Bassi Wildlife
Sanctuary,
25 km NE, Udaipur,
112 km SW

Above: Aerial view
of the Fort.
Facing page: The
Tower of Victory.

Not perhaps the most stupendous as far as its physical remains are concerned, Chittorgarh nevertheless seizes one by its exceptionally turbulent and tragic past. The area of Chittor in Rajasthan passed into the hands of the Sisodia clan of Rajput kings in the eighth century and remained with them till the 14th century. During this time, the Fort was built and added onto by each successive ruler as much as it was destroyed by each of its three invaders. The first invasion in 1303 was by the Delhi Sultan Allauddin Khilji, who, it is said, enamoured by the legendary beauty of Queen Padmini, sacked the Fort in order to claim her. Realising that the odds in battle were heavily stacked against them, the Rajput women committed themselves to the flames of a huge pyre (an act known as *jauhar*), while the men, donning the robes of martyrs, rode out stoically to face death at the hands of the Khilji army. In 1535, Bahadur Shah, the Sultan of Gujarat, invaded Chittor, precipitating for the second time the same grim sequence of events. This time Queen Karnavati initiated the *jauhar*. The final blow came from the Mughal Emperor Akbar in 1568,

resulting in the third and last *jauhar* and martyrdom.

Battlements enclose an eclectic mix of monuments

The present Fort lies along twelve kilometres of a hilly outcrop, occupying almost 280 hectares of land. A kilometre-long road zig-zags its way to the top through seven gates, passing on its way monuments of respect dedicated to brave warriors who fell during the third battle. Within exist façades of palaces and rooms, the biggest structure is that of Rana Kumbha's palace with its own elephant, horse stables and temple. It is thought that one of the *jauhars* took place in its cellars. Padmini's palace, where Allauddin is supposed to have seen the beautiful Queen, now bereft of its interiors, is beautifully situated, surrounded by a large pool. A more recent contribution, the Fateh Prakash Palace (1930) houses the Fort museum. Two regally imposing towers draw attention with their varying designs and decorative elements. On the surface of the nine-storeyed, 37 metres high Vijay Stambha (Tower of Victory) built by Rana Kumbha to commemorate his victory over Mahmud Khilji in 1440 are depictions from the Indian

epics *Ramayana* and *Mahabharata*. The second, embellished by sculptures of Jain *tirthankaras* (teachers), is the 22 metres high Kirti Stambh (Tower of Fame). A Jain merchant built it at an earlier date as a homage to the *tirthankara* Adinath. Both have narrow staircases leading to the top floor.

Chittor also gained fame for a different reason as the home of the 16th century saint-singer Meera Bai, who openly expressed her absolute love for the Hindu god Krishna to whom she felt spiritually betrothed, even though she was wedded to Prince Bhojraj, son of Rana Sangha, one of Chittor's great rulers. A temple is dedicated to her in the precincts of the Fort and her compositions are still sung all over Rajasthan.

Splendid views of the country-side where the legendary battles are said to have taken place are available from vantage points on the circular road running around the ruins of the Fort. Looking down from the precipice, one can also see the vast tank of the ancient Gaumukh reservoir which derives its water from a spring through the mouth of a carved cow. Way below is the lower (new) town, which houses most of Chittor's current population, leaving only a few of the hereditary settlers within the actual Fort area.

Travelling on the 125-year-old 'toy train'

The Darjeeling Himalayan Railway climbs 1,750 metres without a single tunnel

From 325 metres above sea level at New Jalpaiguri (NJP) to 2,077 metres at Darjeeling, the Darjeeling Himalayan Railway (DHR) 'toy train' takes you on an 88-kilometre journey across the picturesque mountain terrain of the Eastern Himalayas. And on the eight-hour climb, at an average speed of 10 kilometres per hour, there is enough time to savour the scenery, glimpse the culture, and appreciate the bold and ingenious

engineering techniques that created the first and most outstanding hill passenger railway in India. That it is still fully operational after 125 years and retains most of its original features, specially the B Class steam locomotives that power the train, is testimony to this. Constructed in over three years in 1881, the railway was purchased and integrated into the Indian State Railways in 1948, and accorded the World Heritage status in 1999.

Loops and Z reverses

The train basically follows contours of the Hill Cart motor-road and criss-crosses it over 150 times. Though there are no manned railway crossings, the motor traffic is disciplined and comes to a halt when the train gives its sweet whistle. The ascent begins at Sukna, with the views of the river fading away, and the flat plains giving way to the wooded lower slopes of the mountains. Here, the gradient of

Mahanadi station, the river of the same name originates as a waterfall with a 45-metre drop. Now the gradient eases and the train chugs west into Kurseong station (1,482 metres), through the town bazaars, skirting the front of shops and market stalls on a busy stretch of road. There are some splendid views of the plains from the heights near the town.

Highest station in India

Thereafter, the grade stiffens slightly upto Tung, and on to Sonada (2,000 metres), following which you are cruising on the easiest section of the climb, passing through magnificent forests for about 10 kilometres to Ghum, at 2,256 metres, the highest station of the Indian Railways and the second highest station in the world. There is a museum at Ghum on the first floor of the station building with larger exhibits in the old goods yard, and on a clear day, Mt Kanchenjunga stands majestically in the backdrop. Though it is the steepest short gradient of the journey, only a six-kilometre descent to Darjeeling (2,077 metres) now remains. And as a grand finale, on this final section the line traces an arc along Batasia, the most famous of all the loops. With the train on a curve and Kanchenjunga in the backdrop, Batasia is a photographer's dream.

line, it represents the ascent of another of the conical spurs which are common in the locality. Proceeding past it, the train encounters another Z reverse before Gyabari station (1,072 metres). Just beyond it, the fourth and last Z reverse is negotiated and the gradient becomes slightly easier. The story goes that in the gorges below, a Nepalese headman in charge of the labourers working on the road shot a large Himalayan bear. Possessing no lead for bullets, it is said, he used copper coins.

A stream called the Mad Torrent marks the half-way distance to Darjeeling, and at the 43rd kilometre point, the train passes a precipitous rock-face where the road was blasted out, in some places for a depth of 15 metres. Near

State and capital:
West Bengal, Kolkata
(575 km to New
Jalpaiguri)

Convenient access:
Road, rail to New
Jalpaiguri, air to
Bagdogra

Accommodation:
Budget to mid-range
at New Jalpaiguri,
budget to high-end
at Darjeeling

Best season: February
to November

Also worth seeing:
Mirik hill resort town,
49 km SE, Kalimpong,
51 km E, Gangtok,
94 km NE

the railway changes dramatically. The first water stop is at Rangtong and also the first Z reverse—unlike most hill railways, the DHR does not have a single tunnel, but employs the unique system of loops and Zs. It has three loops and five Z-type reverses. The Z reverse technique is used to climb up the side of steep hills, and it is here that the steepest grades on the railway are found. At Chunabhati (670 metres), after the first loop, dense jungles throw deep shadows on the mountainsides. Tindharia station, considered to be above the Terai fever level, is the site of the workshops, first built in the late 19th century. After a zigzag outside this station comes Agony Point, the fourth loop. Generally regarded as the most sensational spot on the

Top & above: *The train employs a fleet of 17 working locomotives and the Ghum Museum-based Baby Sivok loco. Its 13 steam engines were built between 1889-1928, in Scotland, and the four diesel engines were manufactured at Bengaluru in 2000.*

Remains of 4,500-year-old cities

Dholavira and Lothal attained high sophistication in town planning

GUJARAT

Dholavira

Gandhinagar

Lothal

Arabian Sea

State and capital:
Gujarat, Gandhinagar

Convenient access:
Road to Dholavira and Lothal, air to Bhuj (for Dholavira), Ahmedabad (for Lothal), rail to Gandhidham (for Dholavira) Bhurkhi (for Lothal)

Accommodation:
Budget, high-end

Best season:
November to March

Also worth seeing:
Nal Sarovar Bird Sanctuary, Modhera Sun Temple, Jain temples at Patan, Velavadar Wildlife Sanctuary

Right: Kiln fired bricks, smoothened and tightly joined were a hallmark of Indus Valley architecture. While about 12 towns came up on the coastline of the Gulf of Cambay, none of them became a scientific port like Lothal, which had a 64-roomed warehouse on a high plinth connected to the dockyard.

One of the world's oldest civilisations, along with the Mesopotamian, Chinese and Egyptian, is known as the Harappan (after Harappa, one of its major cities) or Indus Valley (after the broad plain of the Indus River where it lay) Civilisation. Flourishing between *c.*2600 and *c.*1700 BC, spanning 1.3 million square kilometres across north-western India and much of Pakistan, it covered an area comparable in size to that of western Europe. During its heyday, it was also the largest of all four civilisations. Earlier it was speculated that the vast spread of Indus Valley centres succumbed to successive waves of Aryan invasions. However, this theory is now almost entirely discarded, and the most likely reason for its decline and final extinguishing is ascribed to environmental disasters or decline in trade and commerce.

Extraordinary town planning

Not only did this period see the emergence of the first urban societies in South Asia, what is remarkable is that such a high level of sophistication in town planning, crafts and culture was not to appear again till 1,000 years after its demise. The major cities of the period were Harappa, Mohenjodaro, Kalibangan and Ganeriwala in present day Pakistan, and Rakhigarhi, Lothal and Dholavira in India. Excavations at some of these sites are still in progress.

Dholavira (locally known as Kotada), discovered in 1960, is situated on Khadir *bet* (island) in the Kutch region of western Gujarat. Not quite part of a tourist agenda, this low plateau area, which gets surrounded by water during the monsoon, attracts only the odd curious traveller or those interested in ancient cultures. Around 100 hectares of its dwellings have so far been unearthed. Of these, 48 hectares comprise the main city area whereas, the sporadic structures outside may have been occupied by agriculturists or merchants. The main city is divided into the acropolis, middle town, and lower town and a stone and brick wall, five metres at the base etch its boundary. In comparison, the wall of the citadel is much thicker, probably because it was the abode of the rulers. The middle town, also spacious and well fortified, seems to have been occupied by the more prosperous members of the society. Broad streets, equal in measure, were laid out on a north-south grid, and a large area may have served as an open-air stadium for ceremonies or sports. This tendency to plan out the cities to the last detail, giving importance to sanitation and drainage, was a trademark of the entire Indus Valley culture.

A special find at Dholavira is a massive inscription of 10 signs in the as yet undeciphered Harappan script. The signs, made in gypsum, were arranged on a big wooden board, which must have fallen at some point, and although the wood decayed over time, the order of the signs embedded in the sand remained intact. While plenty of pottery, beads, tools, seals and

weights have been discovered, the most important aspect of Dholavira may well be its remarkably extensive and efficient drainage and water harvesting systems. Massive wells and reservoirs, along with small and big drains, unearthed in every part of the city and beyond were obviously crucial in a desert town to save rainwater or trap it from nearby rivers.

Decimal system in prevalence

Lothal was one of the earliest dockyards in the world to utilise knowledge of tides, currents and waves for sluicing ships at high tide into the basin. Bricks were made to resist the impact of salinity, gates to protect the town from being swept away, and walls to prevent silting of the shores. It is speculated that inundations at Harappa and Mohenjodaro may have been a factor contributing to the construction of high platforms and walls at Lothal in order to safeguard against a similar situation.

Beads found at Lothal are as minute as 0.25 millimetres—three hundred such beads weigh only one gram. Baked bricks were made following a strict ratio of 1:2:4 and the precision and quality of the materials used for lining the drains were excellent. The decimal system

seems to have been operational—weights discovered are in units of .05, 0.1, 1.2, 5, 10, 20, 50, 100, 200 and 500, with each unit approximating 28 grams. This indicates a highly developed commercial system, the reach of which extended to far away regions like Mesopotamia.

Left: An excavated structure from the upper town of Lothal located close to the warehouse so that an eye could be kept on the stored goods. This area was occupied by the well-to-do residents, their mansions and private baths.

Jaipur

● **Mt Abu**

State and capital:
Rajasthan, Jaipur
(465 km)

Convenient access:
Road to Temples, air to
Udaipur, Ahmedabad,
rail to Mt Abu

Accommodation:
Budget to high-end
(at Mt Abu)

Best season:
Year round

Also worth seeing:
Achalgarh Fort, 8 km,
climb Guru Shikhar
peak for view, 15 km

The opulent Dilwara temples

Ornate ceilings have a cosmological import

Jainism was founded in the sixth century BC by Mahavira, considered to be the last in a line of *tirthankaras*, (saints who facilitate the crossing of the soul from one life to the next). Like Buddhism, founded in the same century, Jainism believes in non-violence. By profession, most members of the Jain community were traders and financiers, many of whom became politically important in the courts of the Rajput rulers of Rajasthan, where the community was originally based. The extravagance lavished on their temples is a mark of the enormous wealth they controlled and which they uninhibitedly spent on their religious buildings. The Dilwara group is located just outside the hill of Mount Abu, Rajasthan's only hill station, whose added attractions are a lake and several old 19th century stately mansions.

Striking sculpted walls and corbelled ceilings

Among the most outstanding of five temples are the Adinatha Vimala Vasahi (1032) and the Neminatha Luna Vasahi (1230), built in pristine white marble quarried in Makrana. The first takes its name from its founder, Vimala Shah, a minister in the royal court. His picture, greets visitors in the entrance porch. The temple is dedicated to the first of the Jain *tirthankaras*, Adinatha, seen inside the main shrine, which is an open cell. The temple originally had a closed and an open *mandapa*. A third was added about a century later, along with a double-colonnaded corridor and 58 smaller shrines running around the court-yard in which the main shrine is built. In each of the subsidiary shrines is a copy of the main image. Though the columns of the temples have carved embellishments, it is the exquisitely sculpted walls of the shrine and *mandapas*, in particular

the corbelled ceilings, which hold your attention. Carved in precise and minute detail are human and animal figures.

The Luna Vasahi Temple

The Luna Vasahi Temple, built by two wealthy merchant brothers in honour of their dead brother Luna, is dedicated to the 22nd *tirthankara*, Neminatha. Based on the Vimala Vasahi Temple, it lives up to its visual appeal. Images depict horsemen, soldiers, elephants, musicians and dancers, scenes from the lives of the *tirthankaras* and cosmological themes. Patterned stone screens enclose the entrance porch where sculpted portraits of the patrons and their wives can be seen. There is also a *kirti stambha*, a large black stone pillar, on the left of the temple, built by the Maharaja of Mewar. Especially remarkable in the Luna Vasahi Temple is the dome over the open *mandapa*. Designed like a lotus, it is seemingly upheld by 16 brackets shaped as seductive maidens, connecting the intervening ornamental carved pillars. The female figures are known as Vidhyadevis, or the Goddesses of Knowledge, each one holding her own symbol. The dome

interior displays 11 concentric rings, symbolising the cosmic cycles of the universe. Some rings have a circular procession of horsemen, birds or elephants, musicians, dancing maidens, and some consist of bud-like pendants. Other spaces, also seen in the Luna Vasahi Temple, include the Navchowki, with a composition of nine rectangular ceilings; and the Hastishala (Elephant Cell), a later addition featuring a row of sculpted elephants.

Craftsmen paid in gold and silver

A third temple, dedicated to Parsvanatha, the 23rd *tirthankara*, is built in grey stone. Its central tower soars above the other temples, and like the others, it has carved columns and an ornate ceiling.

It is believed that the craftsmen who created these buildings were first paid in silver, equal to the value of the weight of marble shavings each day. Gold was later offered if they could chisel deeper, making the carvings sharper and more refined. The Dilwara temples, as indeed all the elaborate Jain temples of the country, present a puzzling dichotomy. On one hand, is the extravagant and ostentatious display of wealth in the religious edifices, and on the other hand, the religion encourages extreme austerity in the personal lives of its followers.

Above: The overwhelming ornamentation is reinforced by the repetition of motifs.
Facing page: Ceiling interior of the Luna Vasahi Temple.

Krishna's refuge by the sea

Dwarka's mythological and historical origins remain underwater

GUJARAT

Gandhinagar

• Dwarka

Arabian
Sea

State and capital:
Gujarat, Gandhinagar
(478 km)

Convenient access:
Road, rail to Dwarka,
air to Jamnagar

Accommodation:
Budget to mid-range

Best season:
November to March

Also worth seeing:
Rann of Kutch, Palitana

'The sea, which had been beating against the shores, suddenly broke the boundary that was imposed on it by nature. . . . I saw the beautiful buildings becoming submerged one by one. In a matter of a few moments it was all over. The sea had now become as placid as a lake. There was no trace of the city. Dwarka was just a name; just a memory.' (Arjuna speaking in the *Mahabharata*)

Dwarka, the legendary city of the *Mahabharata* and the *Puranas*, lies on the north-western tip of the Kutch peninsula in Gujarat, overlooking the Arabian Sea. Legend has it that it was founded by Krishna, when he and his people fled Mathura, on the banks of the Yamuna, to escape the repeated attacks of Jarasandha, King of Magadha, whom he had angered. Regarded as one of Hinduism's holiest cities, Dwarka's

name derives from the Sanskrit *'dwar'* meaning 'door'. After Krishna's death the sea is said to have closed over the city and Krishna's Yadava clan moved north to Hastinapur. The modern city of Dwarka is considered the seventh in line, built after the previous ones had all been inundated. Existing shrines and temples date to the 10th - 11th centuries, and a considerable amount of the architecture can be credited to the patronage of 19th-century Gaekwad rulers.

Lineage goes back to 1520 BC

Though Dwarka's mythological antecedents have never been accredited as fact, the search was on for the lost city since the 1930s. It was only in the early 1980s that the Marine Archaeological Unit of the Indian Institute of Oceanography accidentally stumbled upon the

remains of a ninth-century Vishnu temple underwater. Further explorations, lasting over 10 years, revealed two more Vishnu temples and the eroded remains of the walls of an ancient township. A highly technical means of dating established its lineage to about 1520 BC. Further finds of Syrian and Cypriot anchors, coins and pottery, and other tools of a later date support the theory of a thriving port city and trading centre. From its discernible outlines, Dwarka was a planned fortified city built on reclaimed land and extending more than a kilometre from the shore alongside a river. There were distinct residential and commercial areas, palaces, plazas, a road system and public service utilities.

Dwarka's reputation as a spiritual centre was recognised as far back as *c*.AD 800 when the great sage Shankara accorded it the position of one of the four great *mathas* (centre of education attached to a temple and hospice) of India, facing the four cardinal directions. The 12th century philosopher Ramanuja, and the saints Kabir and Guru Nanak also came here. The Bhakti saint Meera Bai, a 16th

century princess from Chittor, who devoted her life to composing and singing hymns of Lord Krishna, spent the last years of her life in Dwarka.

Dwarkadeesh Temple is the focal point

The pilgrimage centre is naturally known for its temples, destroyed by Muslim armies in the 11th-15th centuries and rebuilt time and again. Of these, the most renowned are the Rukmini Temple (12th century) and the Dwarkadeesh (Lord of Dwarka) Temple (16th century), also known as Jagat-mandir (Temple of the World). The Rukmini Temple, dedicated to Krishna's wife, is a small structure built on the typical temple plan. Though, not in very good shape, much of the original sculpted surfaces, particularly on the columns and sanctuary entrance, can still be seen. The Dwarkadeesh Temple is the magnet of the city. It rises high through a series of open balconies on five storeys and enshrines an image of Lord Krishna. One side of this magnificent, ornately carved granite and sandstone structure

borne on 72 pillars from a high plinth faces the sea. Events from Krishna's life, especially his birthday, are celebrated with much pomp and splendour here, though non-Hindus cannot enter without special permission.

The splendid view from Dwarka's lighthouse over the Arabian Sea on one side and the historic city on the other is breathtaking. Subterranean views of this historic site can be expected as the proposal for an underwater museum takes tangible shape. The island of Bet lies to the north of Dwarka, where Krishna is

believed to have lived with his family and where Lord Vishnu slayed a demon. Many of Dwarka's artefacts have also been discovered here.

Above: A woman collects water from Bet Island, where many archaeological remains have been found.
Left: Bathing ghats at Dwarka.
Facing page: An ancient temple jutting out onto the Arabian Sea is indication that much more of Dwarka's hoary past lies unrevealed under the waves. Pilgrims throng the many shrines of the city.

Shiva's dark home

Elephanta Caves are deep journeys into the spiritual world

MAHARASHTRA

Mumbai
Elephanta

Arabian
Sea

State and capital:
Maharashtra, Mumbai
(22 km off-shore)

Convenient access:
Road, air, rail to
Mumbai, boat to
Elephanta Island

Accommodation: Day
rooms at Elephanta,
budget to luxury in
Mumbai

Best season:
November to March

*Above: Carved into a
niche, the massive
triple-headed Shiva's
left and right profiles
depict the female and
male aspects.*

*Facing page: One of
the guardian figures
sculpted at the
entrance to the main
sanctuary. The pillars
are squat and
tapering with
cushion-like capitals.*

Named by the Portuguese owing to the presence of a stone elephant (now at the Victoria Gardens, Mumbai), Gharapuri or Elephanta was constructed by the Rashtrakuta kings who ruled *c.* AD 757-973. Over time, it exchanged hands, scraping through the inevitable destruction that was to be the fate of majority of India's art, until the British restored the caves to some extent.

While some may only observe the surface meaning of panels of Indian religious art, to others, including the artists who created them, they are deeper journeys into the spiritual world. Thus, it is not uncommon to find some of the most outstanding examples, in areas until recently inaccessible, suggesting the makers' intention that one must pay the price of hard labour to witness the divine. Elephanta, almost cut off from the mainland of present Mumbai, must have remained safe in its anonymity, beckoning only ardent devotees and seekers. Today tourists are deposited by ferry to the island where a climb of 100 odd steps brings you to the caves.

The rock-cut Trimurti

The caves look unassuming and plain from outside and as one stands in the bright sunlight, peering at the inkiness within, there is no indication of what to expect. It is only after the first few steps, as one's eyes adjust to the dark interior, do the sculptures depicting the great Shiva (the Destroyer in the Hindu Trinity) in his many aspects materialise out of the gloom. Each is remarkable in size and beauty. But, unquestionably, the most splendid of them all is the monolithic Trimurti, breathing almost lifelike out of the rock.

The Trimurti, standing 5.45 metres tall, has three visible faces. The one on the left is of Uma, the life giving *shakti*; on the right is Rudra, the Destroyer's terrible aspect; and finally, in the middle, is the benign and serene Swarupa, the true self of Shiva. Keeping guard from their many niches are the *dwarapalas* (gatekeepers), depicted in gigantic proportions so as to indicate the size and force of the one they protect. Forbidding yet graceful in body, these sculptures are no less artistic than the main panels.

Episodes from Shiva's life

In the imagery of Kalyanasundara or the marriage of Shiva and Parvati, one meets the bride's father Himalaya, along with the Moon God Chandrama, and two others of the holy Trinity, Brahma (the Creator) and Vishnu (the Preserver). On another panel, Shiva receives Ganga on his head, breaking the impact of the River Goddess before she touches the earth. A different panel depicts him playing dice with Parvati, where the latter seems peeved at having lost to the Lord, accusing him of using unfair means. Shiva, according to the myth, plunges existence into darkness until Parvati retracts her accusation, once again dispels chaos with peace, whereupon Ravana lifts Kailash at one end. While elsewhere in the cave Shiva stands in his most alluring aspect of Ardhnareshwar (half man-half woman). The figure of the dancing Nataraja (another form of Shiva), 'a synthesis of science, religion and art' is well known all over the world for its symmetry and dynamism. Here one sees it face to face in a larger-than-life depiction.

MAHARASHTRA

Ellora

Mumbai

Arabian
Sea

State and capital:
Maharashtra, Mumbai
(412 km)

Convenient access:
Road to Ellora, air,
rail to Aurangabad

Accommodation:
Budget to high-end

Best season: October
to March

Also worth seeing:
Bibi ka Makbara in
Aurangabad, 24 km SE,
ruins of Daulatabad,
15 km SE

*Top left: A stone panel
shows the abduction
of Sita by Ravana,
from the Hindu epic
Ramayana.*

*Top right: Ellora caves
are more carved than
constructed.*

*Facing page:
Generations of
artisans chipped and
chiselled the last
detail of the
Kailashanatha Temple,
planned as per
the principles of
Vastushastra, the
ancient Hindu treatise
on architecture.*

Grand grottoes of Ellora

The finale of rock-cut architecture

Formerly known as Elapura, Ellora lay on the thriving trade routes between Ujjain and the west coast, in the time of the Rashtrakuta and the Western Chalukya dynasties, between the seventh to the ninth century. Essentially, Ellora is a two-kilometre-long basalt escarpment, chiselled into 34 caves of Buddhist, Hindu and Jain affiliation. Prosperous merchants and nobles, kings, determined clergy and an active laity sustained three centuries of rock excavation to make Ellora's grand grottoes. This was the time when Hinduism was crystallising into an orthodox Puranic pantheon governed by Brahmanical ritual, and Buddhism was on the wane. Preceding Gupta and Pallava dynasties had seen the emergence of stone architecture and formal Hindu temples. The Ellora caves mark the glorious finale of rock-cut architecture in India. Temples of the ensuing centuries were not to be sited on dramatic or somewhat isolated rocky ridges such as at Ajanta and Ellora.

The Ellora caves fall into three distinct groups and are numbered from the left. The Buddhist caves (1–12) date from the Chalukyan period. The first nine resemble *viharas* (monasteries) and are filled with images of the Buddha, Boddhisattvas and related figures. Cave 10, named for Vishwakarma, the celestial architect, contains a teaching Buddha image before a votive stupa, within an imposing *chaitya* (stupa) hall.

Hewn around the same time, the Hindu caves (13–29) are the highpoint of Ellora's aesthetic development, carrying forward Pallavan rock-art tradition from Mammallapuram with intense, detailed renditions of mythological scenes. Cave 16 is somewhat a misnomer, as the magnificent Kailashanatha Temple is hewn free of the surrounding cliffs, in an unparalleled feat of Herculean stonework. The Jain caves (30–34) date from the last phase of Ellora, around the ninth century, and are simpler than the others. The finest in the group is Cave 32, also called Indra Sabha, a monolithic shrine with carvings of elephants, lions and *tirthankaras*.

The gigantic Kailashanatha Temple

Now a UNESCO World Heritage Site, this mammoth complex was commissioned by the Rashtrakuta King Krishna I in the eighth century. A deep rectangular trench was dug in the cliff, isolating a block of stone over 30 metres high and 60 metres wide. Working patiently from top down, masons displaced approximately 85,000 cubic metres of rock to create a multi-layered structure with columns, halls and spires; in effect, a peninsular version of Mount Kailasha, the abode of Shiva in the lofty Himalayas.

A rock-cut wall and entrance way screen the Temple. Once through the monumental gateway, the sheer scale of the conceiver's vision is overwhelming. A 7.6-metre-high plinth raises the structure out of the yawning pit. From this plinth emerges the flat-roofed *mandapa*, seemingly supported on 16 richly carved columns in groups of four. Two gigantic pillars and two elephants appear in the foreground, while a larger than life Nandi bull stands guard in a tall, graceful pavilion. The main shrine is surmounted by two towers. It was once covered in white gesso plaster to emulate the snow-capped peaks of Kailasha, and the temple friezes painted in polychrome colours. Subsidiary shrines, chapels and galleries exist in the side walls, and a perambulatory path scooped out of the surrounding cliff face.

The exterior walls of the complex are richly decorated with niches, pilasters, windows and cornices as well as images of deities, amorous couples, animals and other motifs. On the east of the Nandi shrine is a relief depicting a 10-armed Shiva, watched by his consort Parvati, destroying the demon Andhaksura. Another large, dramatic relief shows Ravana shaking Mount Kailasha, much to the fright of attendants, animals and sundry maidens. Even Parvati appears distraught and leans towards her Lord, while an unperturbed Shiva uses his big toe to subdue the multi-armed and multi-headed demon.

Prose in red sandstone

Fatehpur Sikri is an expression of Akbar's eclecticism

State and capital:
Uttar Pradesh,
Lucknow

Convenient access:
Road, air, rail to Agra

Accommodation:
Budget to luxury
in Agra

Best season:
November to March

Also worth seeing:
Taj Mahal and other
Mughal monuments
of Agra, 35 km NE,
Keoladeo Bird
Sanctuary, 25 km NW

A palace city, built in red sandstone between 1571-85, Fatehpur Sikri was conceived by Akbar, the great emperor of the Mughal dynasty. A man of exceptional administrative and artistic enlightenment, Akbar moved his capital 35 kilometres southwest of Agra to the environs of Sikri, a small village. It was here that the Sufi saint Salim Chishti had predicted that an heir would be born to the childless emperor and it was in the saint's hermitage that Salim, heir to the throne was born thereafter. In gratitude, and perhaps for other strategic reasons at the time, Akbar swiftly started construction of his new capital atop a long ridge, encompassing the saint's abode as a pilgrimage spot.

Fatehpur Sikri embodies the secular and eclectic philosophy of Akbar. Astutely aware of the advantages of gaining Hindu allies during his ambitious policy of enlarging the empire, he entered into a matrimonial alliance with his most formidable Rajput adversaries. It was Jodha Bai, his Hindu queen, who gave birth to Salim, and she and his Muslim wives had their independent 'palaces' in the complex. Akbar's tolerant attitude to all religions was freely expressed in his advocacy of Din-i-Ilahi, a catholic philosophy that challenged Islamic orthodoxy. He built a special room at the end of the large mosque, where he encouraged private discourse with persons of various religious persuasions.

It is the architecture of Fatehpur Sikri that expresses the Emperor's eclecticism. Skilled craftsmen from all over India fashioned the city as an ensemble of styles resonating with traditional elements from diverse regions. From Rajasthan, Gwalior and Gujarat, they brought the typical *chhajja* (overhang), the roof outlined with *chhatris* (umbrella-shaped small pavilions), the trellised partitions—most exquisitely crafted in Salim Chishti's tomb—and ornate serpentine brackets, typical of Jain architecture. Function, orientation, aesthetics and topography dictated the location of buildings. Independent structures, alternating with courtyards, were strung along a subtle system of multiple axes in a geometric grid. All the main structures were placed at right angles to one another on the cardinal axes. Among them were the Diwan-i-Khaas (Hall of Private

Above: View of the great mosque: the towering Buland Darwaza is on the left and Salim Chishti's Tomb in the centre.

Audience), the king and queens' private residences, and the mosque. Service areas at the periphery of the hierarchic layout surrounded public areas like the Jami Masjid (Friday Mosque), Diwan-i-Aam (Hall of Public Audience) and the courts. Secular buildings lay north-south while the mosque was necessarily on the east-west axis.

Tansen set candles alight with his musical brilliance

Among the more fanciful elements of the plan is the Panch Mahal, a receding five-storeyed watchtower of open-sided pavilions. As per anecdote, in the Pachisi Court, a large rectangle designed like a chess board, witnessed courtiers or slave girls moving as pieces of chess directed by the emperor himself, who sat on a raised platform in the centre. Here, too, the legendary musician Tansen, one of the nine jewels of Akbar's court, would perform and, could even set the candles alight with the power of his

music. There is also a Hawa Mahal (Palace of Wind), the Khwabgah (House of Dreams), where Akbar would entertain the women of the harem, and the Hiran Minar (Deer Minaret), a circular tower spiked with elephant tusks, reputed to have been built over Akbar's favourite elephant's grave.

The great mosque, standing at the highest point of the ridge, is the crowning glory of the complex, its grandeur enhanced by the mighty Buland Darwaza or Gate of Victory, commemorating Akbar's military campaigns. A wide flight of steps sweeps up to the majestic 54 metres high arched entrance to the mosque. Directly opposite it stands the tomb of Salim Chishti, a splendid white marble structure shining like a pearl in the vast courtyard.

Fatehpur Sikri was built in a remarkably short period of seven years, and abandoned as suddenly as it had blossomed. During its short 14 years of occupancy, it overflowed

with intellectual and artistic activity. However, distance from the far-flung corners of the empire where intermittent rebellion was rife, compelled Akbar to move his capital again. Some say it was a lack of adequate water that was the cause of Sikri's abandonment. Whatever the reasons, its architecture and planning, today in a pristine stage of conservation, clearly reflect the vision of a mastermind, at once a politician, an administrative genius and a humanist.

Above left: The Anup Talao (Peerless Tank), with a seating platform in the centre, was a pleasure site. Beyond, the building with the cupolas, is the Diwan-i-Khaas (Hall of Private Audience) where the emperor met with important people.

Above right: Detail of a façade displaying a latticed screen, recessed arch, geometrical and floral patterns and brackets.

Facing page: Sufi saint Salim Chishti's Tomb, originally built in sandstone, was later clad in marble. Within is a mother of pearl canopy inlaid with sandalwood.

The fine heritage of a financial district

The ramparts of Mumbai's Fort area were replaced by elegant edifices

State and capital:
Maharashtra, Mumbai
(earlier Bombay)

Convenient access:
Road, air, rail to
Mumbai

Accommodation:
Budget to luxury

Best season:
November to March

Also worth seeing:
Gateway of India,
Chhatrapati Shivaji
Maharaj Vastu
Sangrahalaya

Above: The statues of
Justice and Mercy
stand on top of the
Mumbai High Court
building. Designed in
the Gothic Revivalist
style by J.A. Fuller,
it was completed
in 1878.

Facing page: Aerial
view of Convocation
Hall of Mumbai
University. The
Gothic style building,
designed by Sir
George Gilbert Scott
and funded by the
wealthy businessman
Sir Cowasjee
Jehangir, has a
remarkable circular
stained glass window
on the front façade,
around which are
arranged signs
of the zodiac.

Though it would seem far-fetched to anyone standing near the nine-metre-high ornamental Flora Fountain, a fort of stone and mortar, skirted by a moat, stood in the heart of what is now Mumbai's core commercial and financial district. In the early 18th century, a solid basalt wall ran from the seafront near today's Lion Gate towards Kala Ghoda, turning northward to Chhatrapati Shivaji Terminus (CST), and then southward, skirting the western edge of Ballard Estate to touch the eastern sea shore. This wall was reinforced with bastions, equipped with cannons, and punctuated with watch towers that guarded the access to its inner space. Apollo Gate, Church Gate and Bazaar Gate, the three entry points, closed at sunset. While the ramparts of the once protected settlement have long been demolished, they still wield an invisible presence and live on in the term 'Fort' that continues to define the area and appear on letterheads and boards of offices located here.

Unlike other strongholds of Maharashtra built by the Marathas, Deccan Sultans or the Portuguese, the Mumbai Fort was built by the British, who acquired the H-shaped Mumbai Island and six other islands (collectively known as Mumbai) in 1661 as part of the dowry of Portuguese princess Catherine of Braganza on her marriage with King Charles II of England. The East India Company rented the islands from His Majesty in 1668 at a modest 10 pounds a year, fortified Mumbai, and thus founded a base that blossomed into a prosperous city.

First motion pictures at the erstwhile Watson's Hotel

Though strengthening of the enclosing structures continued, stable and secure political conditions by the mid-19th century implied that the walls no longer served a purpose. Finally in 1862, Sir Bartle Frere ordered the ramparts to be demolished, thus opening out a space for conscious urban planning, in turn promoting construction activity, which was encouraged by a boom in trade and commerce. The 1870s saw the rise of a circular complex of edifices of a uniform and elegant style with decorative keystone heads centred on a central garden in front of the Town Hall built in 1833. Along the curving road that sweeps across from the Gateway of India till the CST (earlier Victoria Terminus, built in1878), emerged a vista of decorative European pediments, sculptures, fretted window screens, grills, capitals and keystone heads, as also elements of Indian architecture. Walking along this path one passes the stately Elphinstone College, the small and beautiful David Sassoon

Library, the grand Army and Navy Building and the erstwhile Watson's Hotel, where the Lumière Brothers introduced motion pictures in India in 1896. To the west of this row, overlooking the Oval Grounds, are the Neo-Gothic Secretariat (now City Civil and Sessions Court), Convocation Hall and University Library, the High Court, Public Works Department, the Central Telegraph Office, followed by the imposing commercial bank quarters. Crossing the Flora Fountain junction to DN Road, there is much to notice: the striking Canada Building with horses in bas-relief, the *haveli*-styled Badri Mahal and the dome and corner entrance of the Bombay Mutual Life Building. Plaques on many of these provide information on their style and date of construction.

Architectural styles identified as Neo Gothic, Neo Classical, Indo-Saracenic, Art Deco and others which are amalgams of these and more have thus become the heritage of Mumbai's business precincts. A visual unity is apparent as the architects had to follow guidelines that entailed keeping to a certain height and making provision for an arcade on the ground floor to offer people protection from the elements. Working within these regulations, each designer responded with individual plans in various stone materials.

Bijapur's Gol Gumbaz

The city of minarets has the largest uninterrupted floor space under a tomb

KARNATAKA

Bijapur

Bengaluru

Arabian Sea

State and capital:
Karnataka, Bengaluru
(630 km)

Convenient access:
Road, rail to Bijapur,
air to Belgaum

Accommodation:
Budget to mid-range

Best season:
November to March

Also worth seeing:
Mihtar Mahal, Jami
Masjid, Ibrahim Rauza,
Bara Kaman
mausoleum

About the time the Mughals were extending their dominance and cultural influence over North India, 1,500 kilometres from the great imperial cities of Delhi and Agra, Bijapur, situated at the heart of the Deccan plateau, was evolving its own distinct character with elements borrowed from lands far away in western Asia.

Yusuf Adil Shah, the founder of Bijapur, arrived at Bidar from Turkey in 1461 as a slave. Slowly, his abilities propelled him to become the Governor of Bijapur province, and when the Bahmani kingdom split in 1489, he established himself as an independent ruler. His

successors styled themselves as 'Shah' and governed Bijapur for almost two centuries. As each ruler responded to the needs of his subjects and a growing capital city, as well as dictates reflective of imperial status, Bijapur soon turned into a strongly fortified and planned urban centre graced by fine buildings constructed with the locally abundant dark brown stone. In the heart of the city was the citadel, which housed palaces, mosques, tombs, gardens, and a mint encircled with considerable walls and a moat. The growing city was further protected by another wall reinforced with almost a hundred bastions. A vast

network of waterworks constructed around the structures were typically crowned with bulbous domes resting on foliated drums; tall, slender ornamental minarets; beautifully carved bracketed eaves; and a crescent finial surmounting the spires, to denote the Adil Shahis' Turkish origin.

The Sultan lies buried under a 60-metre-tall dome

Undoubtedly, the *pièce de résistance* of Bijapur's medieval marvels is the Gol Gumbaz, the monumental tomb of Sultan Muhammad Adil Shah (r. 1626-56), the seventh ruler of the dynasty. Set on a platform amidst lush green lawns, the immensity of the massive mausoleum—surmounted by a dome that is credited with covering the largest such uninterrupted floor space in the world—is instantly tangible. Each side of the square tomb is 63 metres on the outside, with walls three metres thick and 34 metres high. The dome is 44 metres and 38 metres in diameter, on the outside and inside, respectively, and summits at over 60 metres from the ground. Supported by an ingenious matrix of eight imposing pointed arches, it covers 1,704 square metres. Indeed, the Gol Gumbaz's master-builder must have had as much courage as he had skill to attempt a building of such gigantic proportions.

Though the Sultan did not live to see the completion of his grand project, an inscription on its entrance arch states that the edifice retains the mortal remains of Muhammad Adil Shah, who on his death became 'an inhabitant of Paradise and a Particle of the Firmament'. He lies buried in the centre with his family, the cenotaphs on a raised platform and their interred bodies in a crypt below the vast umbrella of the dome. Apart from the simplest of markings on the western *mihrab* wall, the enclosing walls are shorn of ornamentation.

Views from the 'Whispering Gallery'

The sides of the tomb have a set of three arched recesses and the central recesses bear fretted stone screens with openings. Sculpted brackets support the eaves, above which are an arcade and a parapet. Within each of the seven-tiered octagonal towers at the four corners, a flight of steps ascends to the gallery at the base of their apex domes. Often called the 'Whispering Gallery', this is the tomb's second engineering marvel after its sheer size. Its unusually fine acoustics cause the slightest tap on the wall to resound 12 times in the wall across. Peering down from the gallery the cenotaphs far below appear remarkably tiny, affording a true sense of the dizzying height.

Stepping out of the gallery, at the base of the dome open to sky, one sees Bijapur's low sky-line spreading out below. Tombs, minarets and the city walls blend with recent constructions. Visible in the distance, a small tomb akin to the Gol Gumbaz was built as its precursor, to ensure that the final structure would stand the test of time and design.

Above & left:
Located at the edge of the city, Ibrahim Rauza, the tomb of Ibrahim Adil Shah II, has aesthetically laid out corridors and latticed stone screens.
Facing page: The Gol Gumbaz employs no camouflaged support, proving the technical ingenuity of the builders.

PUNJAB

• Amritsar

Chandigarh •

State and capital:
Punjab, Chandigarh
Convenient access:
Road, rail, air to
Amritsar
Accommodation:
Budget to high-end
Best season:
November to March
Also worth seeing:
Changing of Guard at
Indo-Pakistan Wagah
border, monuments at
Amanat Khan village

Gilded in gold

The Golden Temple is the centre of Sikhism

For thousands of residents of the city of Amritsar in northern Punjab, the day is incomplete without a visit to the Harmandir Sahib, more popularly known as the Golden Temple—the holiest of Sikh shrines in the world. Shopkeepers in the vicinity raise their shutters in the morning only after having paid obeisance at the Temple. The Temple's origins lie in a small pool, which was enlarged into a tank by the fourth Sikh Guru Ram Das (1534-81), and renamed Amritsar (Tank of Nectar). Subsequently, the city, which sprung up around it came to be called by the same name. However, it was the fifth Guru Arjan Dev (1563-1606) who laid the foundation of Harmandir Sahib, in the late 16th century. Set at the core of the tank, it was provided with gateways on all four sides, symbolising Sikhism's openness to all four Hindu castes and generally to people of all faiths and races. Since then, the Temple and the town have been razed and raised many times. In the 18th century, the Persian King Nadir Shah, Mughal ally Massa Rangar, and then Afghan predator Ahmad Shah Abdali attacked and ransacked the Gurudwara (Sikh temple). During the reign of Ranjit Singh, the great Sikh king, the shrine was nurtured, enlarged and bestowed with wealth. The last tragic event in the Temple's chequered history was in 1984, when the Indian Army stormed it to root out Sikh terrorists who had established themselves in its precincts. Today, none of this tumultuous past finds echo in the sounds of daily activities. What one hears, walking around the complex, is *kirtan* (singing of sacred hymns) from inside the sanctum sanctorum, the Akhand Paath (a continuous recitation of the Guru Granth Sahib, the Sikh Holy Book, from beginning to end) and other renditionings of the scriptures.

Gilded upper storeys

A fortified wall with 18 gates surrounds the temple complex. Its main entrance known as the Darshani Deorhi is from an ornate archway embellished with inlay work. The rosewood doorway bears verses from the Granth

Sahib. In the toshakhana (treasury) on top of the entrance lie exquisite artefacts like umbrellas, fly whisks, a headband, spades, door panels and pillars, made in gold and precious stones. Ranjit Singh and his family donated most of these—the King's sword is part of the treasury. While a white marble circumambulatory pathway surrounds the tank, pilgrims can walk up to the Harmandir Sahib via a narrow causeway, to offer prayers, receive blessings and *karha prasad* (sacramental food made of flour). Topped with a dome shaped like an inverted lotus, the building has three levels. The lowest storey is in white marble, while the two upper storeys are gilded with gold leaf—which is how the Temple gets its name—gifted by Ranjit Singh. The Granth Sahib is laid on a throne below a jewelled canopy on the ground floor, and beside it, the

Akhand Paath carries on, delivered unceasingly by different priests in three-hour shifts. It takes two complete days to read the full text once.

Resting place of the Holy Book

Facing the temple is the five storeyed Akal Takht, the supreme spiritual and temporal seat of the Sikh religion. It is in this building, believed to have been completed by the sixth Guru Har Gobind in 1609, that the gurus held court and issued commandments, and from here that today the religious governing body of the Sikhs declares writs for the community. At night, the Granth Sahib is brought to 'rest' at the Akal Takht and taken back before five in the morning in a silver and gold palanquin to the Harmandir Sahib.

Apart from Harmandir Sahib, there are various other shrines within the complex. Three venerated *ber* (jujube) trees which, predate the temple, have anecdotes associated with them. A nine storeyed tower is in remembrance of Baba Atal, a son of the sixth Guru, whereas, bathing at the innocuous looking Athsath Tirath, made in the shape of a cot, is supposed to be as good as visiting 68 holy Hindu shrines of India. A semi-circular stepped marble podium near the southern entrance salutes the martyrdom of the warrior Baba Deep Singh, who died defending the Temple against the forces of Ahmed Shah Abdali. No gurudwara is complete without a community kitchen and here, at the golden centre of the Sikh faith, the *langar* doles out free meals for approximately 30,000 visitors daily.

Above & below:
The interior walls are decorated with sculpted wooden panels, intricate gold and silver ornamentation, frescoes and stained glass.
Facing page top:
View of the Golden Temple.
Facing page bottom:
Originally written in the Gurmukhi script, the Sikh Holy Book is 1,430 pages long and consists of sayings of Sikh, Hindu and Islamic saints, in the form of 5,000 hymns set as classical Indian melodies.

The guardian of Gwalior

The flamboyant Fort controlled the routes to Central India

MADHYA PRADESH
Gwalior
Bhopal

State and capital:
Madhya Pradesh,
Bhopal

Convenient access:
Road, air, rail to
Gwalior

Accommodation:
Budget to high-end

Best season:
November to March

Also worth seeing:
Tansen's Tomb, Jai
Vilas Palace, Sarod
Ghar Music Museum

*Top & right: Massive
round towers act as
reinforcing buttresses
to the eastern façade
of the Man Mandir
Palace.*

Its huge fortress dominates the city of Gwalior, 100 metres above the plains on a sandstone cliff, surrounded by mighty, 10-metre-high turreted walls. In the medieval period, this was one of the most impregnable forts in India, guarding the approach to the hinterlands of Central India. According to legend, a Rajput prince, Suraj Sen, who was cured of leprosy by the hermit Gwalipa after

drinking the waters of a pond here, founded the Fort in the 10th century. In gratitude, the prince built a fort, calling it Gwalior after the hermit.

The Fort's chequered history is replete with battles and a succession of Hindu, Muslim and British rulers. In 1232, it witnessed the mass suicide of Rajput women who immolated themselves rather than suffer the ignominy of capture

when, after a gruelling 11-month siege, the Fort fell to the Muslim invader, Iltutmish.

Under the Hindu ruler Man Singh of the Tomar dynasty, it witnessed its golden age, and the many palaces built by him in the Fort prompted Babur, the first Mughal, to call it 'the pearl in the necklaces of palaces of the Hind'. During the Mutiny of 1857, Rani Laxmibai and Tantia Tope, prominent leaders of the struggle, made their last stand here. Subsequently, the British handed the Fort to the Scindias, who were the last ruling family to occupy it, and whose heirs command a political following even today.

A palace for Man Singh's favourite queen

Stretching north to south across three kilometres, the Fort encloses six palaces, three temples, the Scindia School and a gurudwara. Man Mandir, the Fort's most distinctive palace was built between 1486 to 1517 by Man Singh, and is also known as the Chit Mandir (the Painted Palace) after its blue, yellow and green tiles in the form of peacocks, parrots, elephants, banana trees, ducks and crocodiles. The four-storeyed structure contains a number of halls where the King held court and the women received music lessons. Its underground chambers were later used by the Mughals to incarcerate prisoners. Man Singh also built the Gurjari Mahal for his favourite queen Mrignayani. It is said that when he asked the lower-caste Gujjar princess to marry him, she agreed, provided she be given equal status as a queen and that he would build her a palace fed by the stream from her village. Set around a court-yard, her palace contains rooms decorated with carved brackets, domes and bands of moulded ornamentation. It now houses a museum that contains Hindu and Jain sculptures, inscriptions and paintings.

The ninth-century Teli-ka-Mandir, dedicated to Vishnu, is ascribed to Telap Raj, a prime minister of the region. Though Dravidian in form, it has sculptures that are distinctly North Indian. North of the temple is the famous Suraj Kund reservoir, where Suraj Sen was mysteriously cured of leprosy. Also devoted to Vishnu, the Saas Bahu (Mother-in-Law and Daughter-in-Law) Temples, were built around the 11th century. The larger of the two is a three-storeyed structure with a flat roof, supported by intricately decorated pillars, the smaller one has an open sided porch with a pyramid roof.

Jain sculptures

On the way up to the Fort, one cannot miss the massive Jain shrines, carved into the steep rocky sides of the plateau's western face. Most notable of these seventh and 15th century sculptures are the 22 standing Jain *tirthankaras* (religious teachers), of which the largest is the 19-metre-tall Adinatha, standing on a lotus. Most of the figures, standing in recessed spaces, were defaced when Babur conquered the fort in 1527.

Right: *Numbering nearly 100, some of the Jain sculptures were simply statues whereas others harboured spaces possibly used for living.*

Hoysala temples at Belur and Halebid

King Vishnuvardhana's architect produced two jewels
fusing North and South Indian styles

Above: *The flowing
artistry on the
Hoysaleshwara
Temple façade is so
engrossing that one
scarcely notices the
lack of the bell-
shaped towers—
either they were
never made, or were
desecrated at a later
date. Friezes cover
the basement and
the lower walls, with
successive rows of
elephants, horses,
lions, scrollwork,
epic scenes, makaras
(half animal-half fish)
and geese with
foliated tails.*

The waning of Chola power in southern India in the 12th century saw the steady rise of their arch enemies the Hoysalas, with their capital at Dwarasmudra near modern Mysore. Complex mythologies and temple rituals were the order of the day and the magnificence of the monarch's temples reflected his power and the prosperity of his kingdom. The Cholas had set the standard for large temple enclosures but in a signal departure from the orthodox aesthetic norms of Chola art, the Hoysala rulers encouraged a vibrant fusion of the southern and northern elements in temple building. Instead of one main square sanctuary, there were now several *garbha grihas (*sanctums), arranged in a star-shaped plan. The plinth echoed the star-shape as well, while the towers soared upwards in a bell-shape not as curved as the north Indian *nagara* and not as straight as the south Indian *vimana,* but somewhere in between.

The material for construction was closely textured chlorite schist, which is soft when quarried, but hardens on exposure. As it lent itself beautifully to intricate carving and Hoysala structures are embellished in extraordinary detail. The sculptor's tools coalesced the stately

Chennakeshava Temple, Vishnuvardhana directed Janak Acharya to build an even more magnificent edifice to Shiva at the newly refurbished capital of Dwarasmudra, now renamed Halebid. Janak Acharya responded to the challenge by duplicating his efforts at Belur in two identical Shiva temples, each with its own Nandi shrine. A pillared corridor links the twin temples. The result of this remarkable departure from any previous norm was a monument fully carved from top to bottom. Set within a large enclosure, gateways to which were a later addition, the Hoysaleshwara Temple is approached by a broad flight of stairs, flanked by two small shrines. On the plinth is a figure of a warrior plunging his sword into a leonine beast with a ferocious head, interpreted as the dynastic symbol of the martial Hoysala rulers.

Epic scenes from the *Ramayana* and the *Mahabharata* include Rama chasing the golden deer, Rama and Sita in procession, and Bhishma lying on a bed of arrows. The myriad tales of Krishna find expression in stone, and there are also scenes of courtly life and hunting expeditions. Various divinities in panels are set in the outer walls, the finest pieces being those of Brahma seated on a goose, Shiva dancing on the dwarf Apasura, Ravana shaking the Kailash Mountain, and Vishnu in his many incarnations. Maidens, dancers and musicians attend to the deities, and above them are overhanging eaves with petalled fringes.

The dynasty collapsed in 1326, and unfortunately, so did its remarkable aesthetic style.

State and capital:
Karnataka, Bengaluru
(220-235 km from
Halebid and Belur)

Convenient access:
Road to Belur, Halebid,
air to Bengaluru, rail
to Hassan

Accommodation:
Budget at Halebid
and Belur

Best season:
November to March

Also worth seeing:
Sravanabelagola,
85 km SE, Mysore,
149 km S

*Below: Sculpture of
the* Mahabaharata *warrior Arjuna on his chariot.*

grace of the Cholas with the effusive abundance of northern sculptural styles, similar to those in the Konark and Orissa temples. To this mix was added a typically Hoysala attention to ornamentation. Curving foliate patterns tumble around the niches and windows and run in a frieze around the base of the temples.

Stone screens at the Chennakeshava Temple

To commemorate his victory over the Chola armies, the Hoysala King Vishnuvardhana commissioned his chief architect Janak Acharya to build a Vaishnavite temple dedicated to Vijaynarayan. This remarkable 12th century jewel of a monument incorporates all the

typical elements of the Hoysala style. At a later date, stone screens were placed between the pillars of the *mandapa*, perhaps to afford privacy to the noble and devout audiences of dance performances. Temples were the centres of cultural life and gods were fed, bathed, adored and entertained in equal measure. Classical music and dance were largely devotional in content and flowered under the auspices of royal patronage and religious sanction. The Chennakeshava Temple *mandapa* has a large stone-paved platform, worn smooth by dancers' feet.

Hoysaleshwara Temple is carved from top to bottom

Inspired by the success of the

Glorious ruins amidst boulders

The city of Vijayanagara was once 'as large as Rome...'

State and capital:
Karnataka, Bengaluru
(350 km)

Convenient access:
Road to Hampi, air to
Bengaluru, Hyderabad,
rail to Hospet

Accommodation:
Budget to mid-range

Best season:
November to March

Also worth seeing:
Ruins at Anegundi,
15 km across the
Tungabhadra River,
Navabrindavana Island

Below: Located in the Royal Centre, at the south-western part of the site, this domed and arched row was the stable for the king's elephants.

Remarked Abdur Razzak, Persian envoy to the court of King Deva Raya II in 1443, 'The city of Bidjanagar (Vijayanagara) is such that the pupil of the eye has never seen a place like it and the ear of intelligence has never been informed that there existed anything equal to it in the world'. Vijayanagara or City of Victory, once synonymous with a mighty empire, spread over 26 square kilometres beside the Tungabhadra River, its magnificent architecture extending and echoing the language and dimensions of the rocky landscape. Almost 125 years after Razzak's visit, Vijayanagara met its fateful end, crushed and sacked by a consortium of the Deccan Sultanates of Ahmadnagar, Bijapur, Bidar, and Golconda. Yet four and a half centuries later, its ruins of sacred and secular stone monuments at present-day Hampi dot a vast terrain speckled with huge grey-brown boulders resting on or balancing against each other, lush fields, banana groves and coconut palms.

Seven concentric enclosures

Founded in 1336 by Harihara, a prince from Warangal, Vijayanagara was fortuitously ruled by a succession of able monarchs, reaching its zenith under Krishna Deva Raya (1509-29). Royal patronage to artists, philosophers, poets, and men of letters resulted in the growth of a grand imperial capital and centre of learning. Visitors from Europe and Arabia have sketched a picture of fabulous wealth and luxury. According to Portuguese chronicler Domingo Paes (1520-22), it was 'as large as Rome and very beautiful to look at', with the king's palace enclosing 'a greater space than all the castles of Lisbon'. It appears that the city comprised seven concentric enclosures, each surrounded by massive fortifications. Between the northern and southern gates of the outer fortress was a distance of about 12 kilometres. Within were imposing gateways, palaces, wide streets lined by splendid houses, official buildings, temples, market places, complex yet efficient irrigation works, orchards and fields. The outer three enclosures contained cultivable lands, while the four inner constituted the city proper, with the royal palace at the core. From Paes

we learn that the palace stood in a grid of 34 streets and the king's apartments were made with rosewood and ivory. Of the secular buildings the Lotus Palace, queen's bath and elephant stables are examples in the Islamic style, an obvious influence from the adjacent Bahmani Empire. A vast ruined area is believed to have been an important mint, producing coins of refined design and quality for the flourishing foreign trade, and where desolate rocks bake in the sun, there once thrived thick groves of lime and orange trees.

Garuda's shrine had wheels that could turn

The demands of extensive rituals backed by the liberal flow of funds spurred the building of large, elaborate temple complexes with decorative *gopurams* (entrance gateways) and additional structures apart from the main Shrine. The lofty *gopuram* of the 15th century Virupaksha Temple dominates the landscape, marking the only medieval temple still in worship at Hampi. Rising in storeys and crowned by a barrel shaped vault, it is embellished with sculptures. The Vitthalaswami Temple complex boasts sculptured gateways, columns, brackets, panels and pillars, popularly referred to as 'musical pillars', for each one produces a different note when tapped (now disallowed to visitors). Another feature of this complex is the Garuda shrine (Hindu deities have their individual vehicles and Garuda or the Eagle is the vehicle of Vishnu). Garuda's stone temple takes on the form of a ceremonial chariot complete with four wheels and fronted by two elephants and a ladder. Though the brick and plaster superstructure no longer exists, the fine quality of mouldings, pilastered niches and overhanging eaves make it seem to be carved out of a single block. Interestingly, though the chariot was unmovable, originally it was so designed that its wheels could turn. Pilgrims believed that turning them would bring them blessings, and over the centuries the axles started wearing out; to prevent further damage, the wheels have now been permanently cemented.

Above: Built during the reign of Achyuta Raya, the Tiruvengalanatha Temple conforms to the standard style of the later Vijayanagara temples, except that it features two rectangular enclosures, one outside the other. The setting, within rocky rises and palm-fringed cultivated fields, is one of the compelling visuals of Vijayanagara.

RAJASTHAN

Jaipur

State and capital:
Rajasthan, Jaipur

Convenient access:
Road, air, rail to Jaipur

Accommodation:
Budget to luxury

Best season:
November to March

Also worth seeing:
Jaigarh and Nahargarh Forts, City Palace, Jantar Mantar, Gaitor cenotaphs

Emblems of Jaipur

Hawa Mahal and Amber Fort dominate the city's monumental wealth

Unlike other historical towns of Rajasthan that spilled out over time, Jaipur was conceived with great deliberation and exactitude. Promoted by the versatile Maharaja Sawai Jai Singh II (1700-47 AD), it is the desert state's capital and grandest city. The king, himself familiar with the intricacies of architectural planning, entrusted the design to his architect Vidyadhar Chakravarti, who laid out a square grid based plan influenced both by the ancient knowledge of the Hindu building treatise *Shilpa Shastra*, as well as Western ideas. Chakravarti divided the city into nine *chokris* (blocks), intersected by broad streets and narrow bylanes, thus eliminating the haphazardness that accompanies most modern Indian urban centres. The visit of Prince of Wales in 1876 inspired Maharaja Ram Singh to have the whole city painted pink, the customary colour associated with traditional hospitality. To maintain the integrity of this pleasing visual character the blushing façade was later made mandatory by law, thus imbuing Jaipur with a distinct identity and winning for itself the title of Pink City.

Cool viewing gallery

At the first glance itself, the pyramid shaped structure of Jaipur's Hawa Mahal or Palace of Wind with its interplay of red and pink sandstone, white borders and motifs strikes one

as unusual. Built under the auspices of Maharaja Sawai Pratap Singh (r. 1778-1803), the 15 metre high, five-storeyed frontage is like a delicate screen, less than a foot in thickness, with tiers of tiny *jaalis* (latticed windows), balconies and arched roofs. The impression created is of a massive honeycomb in pink. Architect Lal Chand Usta's intention with the screen façade was not just to create a stimulating visual but to allow women of the royal household to enjoy processions and festivities taking place on the streets below without exposing themselves. The screen along with the tiny *jharokhas* (ornate windows) also played the dual role of allowing the breeze to circulate inside, keeping interiors cool even as the sun blazed outdoors.

From the Sun Gate to the *zenana*

Standing on an arm of the Aravalli Hills on the outskirts of Jaipur overlooking Maotha Lake, Hawa Mahal and the many other monuments of the city, Amber (pronounced Amer) is the most well-known Rajput fort in India. Raja Mansingh of the Kachhawaha clan of Rajput began its construction in 1592 over an earlier fortification owned by the Mina tribe, who went on to become the guardians of the royal treasure. Over the next 150 years, the Fort was added on by successive rulers, of which Mirza Raja Jai Singh (r. 1621-27)

contributed the most. A steep 10-minute ascent on foot takes one to the Suraj Pol (Sun Gate), the main gate; the alternative is to ride up on an elephant as was done by the royalty in the days of yore. Following these are four sections. The first, Jaleb Chowk, is where returning armies were felicitated and the cavalry horses stabled. Today its galleries display cannons, firearms and antiques. Further up is the Diwan-i-Aam (Hall of Public Audience), and beyond it the royal apartments. The innermost section was the *zenana* (ladies' chambers). Of the profusion of landscaped gardens, painted and carved gateways, palace rooms, audience halls and temples, a few are particularly remarkable. Two big silver lions and a silver doorway with the image of Ganesh in coral embellish the Shila Devi Temple just outside the palace area. This shrine dedicated to Goddess Kali remains the most revered of all Kachhawaha temples with ceremonies continuing to be conducted here with much fanfare. The interiors of Jai Mandir or Hall of Victory are covered with thousands of tiny mirrors off which the reflected light of a single candle is enough to illuminate the entire space.

Above: The imposing Amber Fort was the citadel of the Kachhawaha rulers of Jaipur.

Facing page: Hawa Mahal is the iconic monument of Jaipur. Bearing 953 windows, it overlooks the busy bazaar.

A perfectly symmetrical mausoleum

Humayun's Tomb was a precursor to the Taj Mahal

Above: White marble is repeated as insets throughout the surface of the monument, elegantly offsetting its overall deep red façade.

A mausoleum in red sandstone and white marble, the tomb of Humayun, the second Mughal Emperor, was commissioned by his senior widow, Haji Begum, and completed in 1565, nine years after his death. It was designed by the Persian architect Mirak Mirza Ghiyas on the banks of the Yamuna River, and is one of the finest examples of Muslim architecture and the Mughal tomb garden. The landmark medieval building largely remained in good condition more than four centuries after it was built, although the surrounding gardens fell into decay. In 2000, the entire complex was adopted for extensive conservation by the Aga Khan Trust for Culture (AKTC) and the Archaeological Survey of India, and is now listed as a World Heritage Site.

Humayun's Tomb is a perfectly symmetrical building, conceived not as a conventional single chamber but as a complex of octagonal halls,

graves of many descendants of the great Mongol, including the learned Dara Shikoh, eldest son of Emperor Shah Jahan. It was here, too, that the last Mughal Emperor, Bahadur Shah Zafar, sought refuge from the British in 1857, until he had to surrender.

Access to the main monument is past a couple of minor tombs, and the Arab ki Sarai, (a caravan serai), supposedly named after the Arab priests brought back by Humayun's widow from her pilgrimage to Mecca. The element of symmetry in the tomb complex is emphasised by the landscaped gardens that surround the main building, a superb example of the Persian *chaarbagh* (four-quartered garden, analogous to the Garden of Paradise). Overthrown by the Afghan chieftain Sher Shah after the first 10 years of his rule, Humayun spent 15 years exiled in Persia. By the time he regained his throne in 1555, he had been deeply influenced by Persian art and architecture, bringing back Persian artisans to India whose skills refined Indian building through a brilliant fusion of the two traditions. Humayun's Tomb set the standard for a distinctive new style that culminated in its most sophisticated expression 70 years later as the exquisite Taj Mahal.

Ingenious hydraulic system

The Mughals had developed a highly ingenious hydraulic system, where water movement depended on a meticulously calculated gradient. Punctuated by pools, cascades and fountains, the irrigation network of the *chaarbagh* was both functional and aesthetic. As part of a restoration project, truckloads of earth excavated from the complex's 12-hectare site exposed the original system's narrow channels, aqueducts, terracotta pipes, fountain mechanisms, wells, siphons and copper pipes. These were repaired and reactivated, and thus after 400 years, water flowed once more through the channels of the *chaarbagh*. With the planting of 2,500 mango, lemon, pomegranate and other trees and foliage, as had originally existed, the first *chaarbagh* ever to surround a Mughal tomb in India was restored to a condition similar to its former glory.

State and city:
New Delhi
Convenient access:
Road, air, rail to
New Delhi
Accommodation:
Budget to luxury
Best season:
November to March
Also worth seeing:
Dargah of Sufi saint
Nizamuddin Auliya,
Khan Khanun's Tomb

***Below:** Lattice screens allow outside light onto Humayun's grave.*

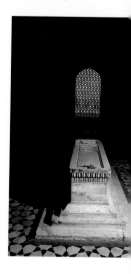

with the central one connected to the four corner halls. The edifice stands on a high red-sandstone platform cut with a line of deep arches on all four sides. Stairways lead upto the platform through the central niche of each arcaded side from the garden level below. A passage on the southern side goes down to a now musty bat-infested basement, which contains the actual grave of the Emperor.

Dormitory of the House of Timur

Wide, arched entrances, recessed between each of the four octagonal corner chambers (each with their own arched openings) lead to the central chamber. Over the cenotaph in the centre of the hall is the vaulted ceiling of the monument's great white marble dome, which is actually a double dome, a feature common to Muslim architecture in India. The outer shell rises over 38 metres, with a central finial, and is surrounded on all four sides by smaller marble cupolas sheltering the corner halls. The mausoleum has been referred to as a 'dormitory of the House of Timur' containing as it does the

The Imambaras of Lucknow

The dwelling place of the Holy Imam harks back to a rich culture

UTTAR PRADESH

Lucknow

State and capital:
Uttar Pradesh,
Lucknow

Convenient access:
Road, air, rail to
Lucknow

Accommodation:
Budget to high-end

Best season:
November to March

Also worth seeing:
British Residency
ruins, Dilkusha Garden,
La Martiniere School,
one of the oldest in
the world

Above & facing page:
The Jami Masjid
inside the Bara
Imambara is still
used for Shia rituals.

As the Mughal Empire declined, provincial outposts became stronger, and Lucknow emerged as the political and cultural centre of Awadh. It boasted the richest court in India at the time, ruled by Muslim Nawabs (provincial governors). It was during the time of Asaf-ud-Daulah (1775-95), fourth in the dynasty, that the capital was shifted from neighbouring Faizabad to Lucknow, bringing prosperity to its people. The Nawabs belonged to the minority Shia sect of Islam, among a predominantly Hindu population, and reinforced their status by building magnificent buildings, many of them religious. Among these are the two Imambaras (dwelling places of the holy Imam), constructed in a rich hybrid style. Lucknow was an exotic city then, rivalling in brilliance the classical centres of Europe. It was famous for its parks and monuments,

its cuisine, *ittar* (perfume), the delicate *chikan* needlework, music, poetry and theatre, and its elegant Urdu language. Though the city has lost much of its old-world charm now, many of its monuments still remain.

A maze of 1,024 passageways

The fort-like complex of the Bara (Big) Imambara is the largest in the world that celebrates the Shia Imam Husain. Its construction began as a food-for-work famine relief project, for nearly 20,000 workers, under Asaf-ud-Daulah in1748, and the work continued for years. Mixing crushed and pounded seashells, ground pulses, thickened syrup and jaggery reinforced the mortar. The three-storeyed main building comprises a great hall built at the end of a spectacular courtyard, approached through two triple-arched gateways. On the right of

the courtyard is the Asafi Mosque, and on its left is a five-storeyed *baoli* (stepwell), connected with the Gomti River, with only its first two storeys above water.

The Imambara's immense, vaulted Persian Hall has an arched ceiling more than 15 metres high. Remarkably, neither steel nor wood has been used in its construction, and its weight is distributed on bow-like arches. The Hall's acoustics permit the sound of a piece of paper being crumpled at one balcony to be heard at another balcony, located at the other end. It contains the tombs of Nawab Asaf-ud-Daulah, his consort Begum Shamsunissa, and the architect Qifayatullah. A staircase outside leads to the Bhul-bhulaiya, a series of rooms designed as a labyrinth, the Imambara's biggest draw. This is a maze of 1,024 passageways running through the entire building. Some of the corridors have dead ends; some terminate at precipitous drops, while others lead to entrance or exit points. At each intersection there are three wrong paths and one correct one. One can spend hours in the maze without passing through any passage twice. Though its walls are six metres thick, the mortar in

them, mixed with peanuts, lentils and water-chestnut flour is so light, that there are places where you can put an ear to the wall and hear a whisper from more than 15 metres away. Aligned along the building's centre are hidden *chor khidkees* (thief windows), from where guards had an unhindered view of the main path right through the monument. Exploring the Bhul-bhulaiya is allowed only with the help of an approved guide.

Quranic calligraphy

Located between the two Imambaras, the imposing Rumi Darwaza was built by Asaf-ud-Daulah, as a replica of the gate in Istanbul. The single-storey Chhota (Small) Imambara is modest compared to the Bara (Big) Imambara. Its building is hidden from the road by a solid gateway and can be accessed by a wide, paved pathway, flanked by gardens. Next to it is the Shahi Hammam (Royal Bath). Inlaid with white Quranic verses on a black background, the monument has a striking façade. Like the Persian Hall at the Bara Imambara, the main hall here too houses a collection of *tazias* (items used during mourning processions) and

chandeliers, the latter a collection from India, Japan, Germany and Belgium. A small display of Islamic art includes a superb piece of calligraphy in which the first verse of the Quran is worked in the shape of a dove, and a version of the entire Holy Book written in letters so tiny that the entire text fits onto a 0.09 square-metre piece of paper.

Portals and pillars lead to the Lord of the Universe

Puri's Jagannatha Temple is one of four sacred *dhams*

ORISSA

Bhubaneshwar •

Puri

Bay of Bengal

State and capital:
Orissa, Bhubaneshwar
(60 km)

Convenient access:
Road, rail to Puri, air to
Bhubaneshwar

Accommodation:
Budget to high-end

Best season:
November to March

Also worth seeing:
Konark, 35 km NW,
Bhubaneshwar,
60 km N

In the state of Orissa is located one of the four sacred *dhams* (pilgrimage places) of India (the others being at Dwarka, Badrinath and Rameswaram). Hindus believe that a visit to all four during their lifetime is desirable for a happy ending to their bodily existence, and thus, at any given time, huge numbers make their way to the coastal city of Puri, to pay their respects at the Temple of Jagannatha, the Lord of the Universe.

Legends explaining its origin abound. Fact, however, confers that the temple was built in the 12th century by King Anant Varman Choraganga Dev and completed by his grandson Ananga Bhima Dev of the Ganga dynasty. Jagannatha does not stand out as an architectural masterpiece or for its sculptural embellishments, especially if one sees it after visiting the celebrated Sun Temple at Konark in the same state. Partly, this may be due to the fact that today it stands white-washed and repaired, looking presumably quite different from its original form. Nevertheless, one of the tallest temples in India, it towers almost 65 metres above ground level, impressing onlookers with its physical stature. Surrounded by two enclosures, also of huge proportions, the temple has the customary four gates in the four directions at its outer fortification. Each portal is depicted by a different animal—Lion, Horse, Tiger and Elephant—and named accordingly. Although only Indian Hindus are allowed to enter, the building's tremendous form rising far above its surrounding walls enables a considerable view of its external features from outside.

Krishna is at the centre of many other gods

The three main deities are unique in form. Carved from margosa wood, they are Jagannatha,

otherwise known as Krishna; his brother Balabadhra; and his sister Subhadra. The first is coloured black, the second white and the third a yellowish saffron. They have short arms, no legs and large circular eyes painted on their faces. Krishna's favoured weapon, the Sudarashan Chakra (discus), is also present next to them. Outside the sanctum sanctorum, but still within the temple precincts, are 30 smaller temples dedicated to various gods and goddesses. Over the centuries, some of the most respected Indian spiritual personages, including Chaitanya Mahaprabhu and Shankara have walked through the temple. It is said that the former stood next to a column just outside the sanctum sanctorum, which is now revered as the Garuda Pillar. Another 11 metre-high pillar, standing outside the temple premises, is known as Aruna Stambha, after the figure of the Sun

God's charioteer placed on the top. Every day a flag tied to a mast, which, in turn, is attached to the Nila Chakra (blue wheel), is hoisted on top of the temple roof. Three and a half metres in height and 11 metres in circumference, the Wheel is made of *ashta dhatu*, an auspicious combination of eight different metals.

Prasada produced on a massive scale

Food is served five times to the deities from the temple kitchen. Additionally, the kitchen, one of the largest in the world, also produces fare for 30,000 people daily—during the festival period this number rises to almost 100,000. The blessed food, known as the *mahaprasada*, is vegetarian and comes in 56 (*Chappan Bhog*) varieties. It is first offered to the deities and then sold to those who wish to partake in the offering. To make

all this and other temple-related tasks possible, members of 36 traditional communities are said to render service in various capacities every day.

Amongst 24 festivals, the Rath Yatra is the biggest

The temple's annual Rath Yatra (chariot journey) is its most famous event. All three deities are pulled in their separate heavily-decorated chariots by a few thousand people to the Gundicha Temple, two kilometres away. This will be their summer abode for a week before the grand procession winds its way back to Jagannatha. Priests chant to the accompaniment of deafening drums and cymbals, devotees line the entire way, and as per tradition, as the chariots advance, the Chief Minister of the state (the king in earlier times) sweeps the path with a golden broom.

The spectacle of the Rath Yatra on the broad avenue outside the Lion Gate of the Temple. Every year new chariots are made by a hereditary community of carpenters out of the wood of specified trees from the former princely state of Dasapalla. As per tradition, the logs are thrown into the Mahanadi River and then retrieved near Puri for construction.

Citadel of moustached men and marvellous mansions

Golden battlements rise like a mirage over Jaisalmer

RAJASTHAN

Jaisalmer
Jaipur

State and capital:
Rajasthan, Jaipur
(543 km)

Convenient access:
Road, rail to Jaisalmer,
air to Jodhpur

Accommodation:
Budget to high-end

Best season:
November to March

Also worth seeing:
Royal cenotaphs at
Bada Bagh, Ludarwa,
Jaisalmer's ancient
capital, camel rides to
the Sam dunes,
Gadisar Lake

Above: As the sun traces its path over Trikuta Hill, the imposing fortifications and the pagoda-like Tazia Tower change from yellow in the morning to tawny-lion during the day, and finally to honey-gold at sunset. The imagery of changing hues inspired the famous Indian Oscar-winning film director Satyajit Ray to write a detective novel, and later make it into a film called Sonar Kella (Golden Fortress).

Facing page: The five floors of the splendid Patwon ki Haveli are now divided between the Archaeological Department, private families and craft shops.

Karna Bheel, once a famous dacoit, twirled his way into the 'Guinness Book of Records' by virtue of supporting the longest whiskers in the world. Now, his son Dhanna Ram is in the process of trying to beat the record. Both belong to Jaisalmer, and are one of the many curiosities at one of Rajasthan's oldest and most alluring forts, which also happens to be the only completely inhabited fort-city in India.

Shimmering like a golden mirage in the midst of scrub and shifting sand dunes, Jaisalmer's ramparts rise on a hill above the town below. The Fort was built in 1156 by Jaisal, chief of the Bhatti clan of Rajputs who had traditionally survived on raiding caravans carrying opium, gems and silk across the Thar Desert. Though Muslim kings trounced the Bhattis in the early 14th and 15th centuries, the remote outpost in the midst of arid wastes continued to serve as an important link on the camel trade route to West Asia. Later, with the increase of maritime activity, the town lost its importance. Nevertheless Jaisalmer remains the only fort-city in India to be still completely inhabited—where once only the ruler's family, members of nobility and caretakers of the temples resided more than 8,000 people continue to live.

Ornate havelis and temples

Within the Fort, wealthy merchants and rulers of Brahmin and Jain persuasion strove to outdo each other in making exquisitely carved havelis (mansions) and temples. The yellow sandstone lent itself to intricate carving, which, on exposure to the sun and dry heat hardened and remained well preserved. The Fort's encircling defences constitute two walls. The outer one, of dry construction without any binding mortar, had 99 bastions, on top of which were placed mammoth stone cannon balls intended to destroy the enemy with their crushing weight. The inner wall was broken by four gateways. On entering through the ornate southern gate, what strikes the eye are the milling colourfully-attired, light-eyed moustached men and Manganiyars (community of traditional Rajasthani musicians) playing songs on folk instruments. At least four wells in the fort, of which Jesloo Kuan is believed to have sprung from the arrow of Krishna, made it self sufficient.

Labyrinthine alleys meander around the 19th-century Badal Vilas Palace, 15th - 16th century Jain temples and huge mansions. Every now and then the streets open out into wide squares where hawkers peddle brilliantly coloured, woven and embroidered cloth, cushions and wall hangings, miniature paintings and old wood carvings, postcards and other souvenirs. Amongst the group of seven shrines in the core of the Fort are Parsvanatha and Ashtapadi. The Islamic influence can be seen in the addition of domes and minarets on otherwise typical Jain Hindu temple forms. Nothing catches the eye more, however, than the elaborate ornamentation that Jaisalmer's stone masons and craftsmen excelled in. The six-storeyed, early 19th-century Patwon ki Haveli and Salim Singh's Haveli are the outstanding examples. While the first was built by a powerful prime minister, the second, erected by one of the richest merchants in town, had connecting apartments for each of his five sons, 66 intricately carved balconies, innumerable finely latticed windows, beautiful murals and pillars. Typically, these mansions contained secluded women's quarters and protected inner courtyards. A hint of the new influences which had pervaded far into Rajasthan less than 100 years later is evident from the five-storeyed Nathumal ki Haveli, where a European-style horse-drawn carriage, steam engines and bicycles, along with indigenous floral, geometric and animal patterns are carved on the façade. Yet, after more than one century, Rajput customs fiercely survive in this hermetic world and many women continue to veil their faces in public.

Shahjahanabad evokes Mughal nostalgia

Old Delhi, Jama Masjid and brimming bazaars were the centre of an empire at its peak

DELHI
Old Delhi

State and city: Delhi

Convenient access:
Road, air, rail to Delhi

Accommodation:
Budget to luxury

Best Season:
November to March

Also worth seeing:
Red Fort, St James
Church, 2 km N

Right: The bazaar still bustles: the teeming main street of Shahjahanabad is lined with shops that offer a fascinating range of diverse wares.

Shahjahanabad, located on the banks of the Yamuna River in what is now known as Old Delhi, is chronologically referred to as Delhi's seventh city. The Mughal Emperor Shah Jahan built it when he shifted his capital from Agra to Delhi to fulfil his imperial and architectural ambitions. Constructed over a period of nine years (1638-49), the city was raised around the fabled Red Fort. A wall guarded by 14 gates enclosed it of which only four—the once Delhi, Turkman, Kashmiri and Ajmeri Gates—now remain. The Mughal capital was laid out with tree-lined avenues accommodating palaces, grand mansions, bazaars, bathhouses, mosques and spacious gardens.

The Moonlight Square
Shah Jahan's favourite daughter, Jahanara, designed Chandni Chowk, the city's main bazaar. Some say it was named Chandni Chowk (Moonlight Square) after the canal, shimmering with moonlit reflections, which once ran through the main street. Others say it was named after the silversmiths who worked here.

In Shah Jahan's time, the bazaar was lined with shops where you could buy anything from jewellery, silverware, rare silks and brocades to exotic animals and slaves. Today, though its canal and grand mansions have disappeared, Chandni Chowk survives as Delhi's largest wholesale and retail market, with many shops dating to the early 20th century, and some even before that. A walk through its snaking narrow alleys, arranged according to trades, is a fascinating experience. Some of these are Dariba, the silver and jewellery market; Kinari Bazaar, specialising in trousseau wear and theatrical costumes; Neel Katra (the Indigo Market), dominated by dyers and cloth merchants; and Chawri Bazaar, the wholesale paper and textbook section.

On its teeming lanes are famous eateries, family run through generations, where one can sample traditional Delhi fare: biryanis, kababs and parathas, *alu puri*, *chaat*, and sweetmeats like *jalebis* and *sohan halwa*—the oldest sweet shop dates back to the late 18th century. The great Urdu poet of the 18th-19th century, Mirza Ghalib's house is in Gali (Lane) Qasim Jaan. Begum Samru, the nautch girl who married a European mercenary and played a crucial role in 18th century power politics also had her mansion here. Other landmarks include Gurudwara Sis Ganj dedicated to the ninth Sikh Guru Teg Bahadur, who was beheaded here by Aurangzeb in 1675, and the Fatehpuri Mosque built by one of Shah Jahan's wives in 1650.

Jama Masjid, India's largest mosque

The last monument built by Shah Jahan, in 1656, the Jama Masjid was designed to be a royal statement in many ways. Commanding superb views of the city from its location on a natural hill, south of Chandni Chowk, it was also called the Masjid-i-Jahanuma (Mosque Commanding a View of the World). Its three imposing gateways, reached by a broad flight of stairs, were conceived to provide a grand spectacle for the Emperor's weekly visit to the Mosque. Built in white marble and red sandstone, it is embedded with strips of black marble, accentuating the graceful contours of its domes, minarets and towers. The central sanctuary or prayer hall is flanked by rows of arches on either side of a large doorway. Inside the hall is an exquisite pulpit carved from a single block of white marble. The four-storeyed minarets at either end of the sanctuary are embellished with projecting balconies, topped by a cupola. Visitors can climb to the top of the south minaret to gain panoramic views of Old Delhi and the Red Fort.

The Mosque was constructed at a cost of a million rupees by 5,000 masons working continuously for six years. 65 metres tall, 35 metres wide and with a central courtyard measuring 91 metres across, it can accommodate up to 25,000 people at a time. Pillared corridors topped by a dome on four sides surround the entire space. The Jama Masjid's collection of holy artefacts includes a *Quran* written on deerskin, a marble footprint, a strand of hair and the sandals of Prophet Muhammad.

Above: A sweeping flight of about 35 steps leads up to the southern gate of the Jama Masjid. Protruding galleries break the winding 130-step ascent to the top of the two 40-metre-high minarets topped by cupolas.
Facing page top: View of Old Delhi packed with houses and shops separated by a labyrinthine network of narrow lanes and bylanes, from the minaret of the Jama Masjid.

Lord Shiva's abode

Kedarnath Temple nestles in the Himalayas

UTTARAKHAND

Kedarnath

Dehradun

State and capital:
Uttarakhand, Dehradun
(240 km)

Convenient access:
Road to Gaurikund, air
to Dehradun, rail to
Haridwar

Accommodation:
Budget at Gaurikund
and Srinagar

Best season: May to
October

Also worth seeing:
6 km trek to 4,000-
metre-high Vasuki
Tal (Lake)

*Above: The minimally
decorated curved
shikhara of the
Temple, topped by a
wooden roof, rises
over the gabled,
ornamented
mandapa.*

Spread across India are the 12 *jyotirlingams* or most revered holy shrines of Shiva, the Hindu God of Destruction. While Rameshwaram at the bottom of the peninsula is the southernmost, Kedarnath is the northernmost. Additionally, in the Himalayan state of Uttarakhand, there are four *dhams* or holy shrines considered as obligatory for all Hindu pilgrims. These are Yamunotri, Badrinath, Gangotri and Kedarnath. While Gangotri and Badrinath are now accessible by road, Yamunotri and Kedarnath can only be reached by foot.

What sets Kedarnath apart from all other major Hindu shrines is its spectacular and rarified setting. The shrine itself is small, and sitting as it does at 3,500 metres above sea level on a spur protruding from a massif twice its height, Kedarnath blows into proportion the massive scale of the Himalayas. Here, perhaps, more than in any other temple, is brought home the ancient connection between Hinduism

and the highest mountains in the world, which are the mythological abode of many of its gods. The dramatic backdrop of snow-capped mountains includes Kedarnath, Bharathkund and Kharchkund, all above 6,500 metres in height. The building faces south as compared to most shrines, which face east.

Made of heavy, evenly cut, dark grey-blue stone, the Temple is a mix of the North Indian *nagara* and Katyuri architectural style of the hills. Its main object of worship is a 1.25 metre high conical lingam (phallic symbol associated with Shiva) in granite. Other deities present are Parvati and Ganesha, Krishna with the five Pandavas,

their wife and mother, and the figure of Vishnu installed by the Shankaracharya. Although debatable, the Shankaracharya is said to have passed his last moments here, which explains the presence of a *samadhi* dedicated to him. Behind the Temple, old timers will point to the Mahapanth trail, from where the Pandavas are said to have begun their ascent to heaven. The Temple is guarded from outside by Shiva's vehicle Nandi, the Bull. There are plenty of *pandas* (Brahmins who act as mediators between the priests and pilgrims) to facilitate the rituals of worship. It is possible to touch the lingam, and on auspicious occasions even bathe the deity with ghee and other accompaniments.

The 13 kilometre pilgrim route to Kedarnath begins at the small hamlet of Gaurikund. The latter is considered the mythical birthplace of Parvati, wife of Shiva, the God of Destruction, and the place where she performed various austerities in order to be united with her Lord. A hot sulphur spring marks the spot. Early morning is the ideal time to start walking as the crowds intensify with the day's progress. All along, the roar of the Mandakini River, the source of which is at Kedarnath, accompanies you. While there are shops selling all kinds of necessities on the walk from Gaurikund, there are a number of more removed nomadic trails to Kedarnath starting from other points in the upper Himalayas.

Bhima takes on Shiva

As they are with myriad holy places, the Pandava brothers from the epic *Mahabharata* are associated with Kedarnath. Legend has it that the five heroes longed to absolve themselves of sins incurred during the bloody battle of Kurukshetra in which they decimated members of their own clan. Even though the gods sanctioned the war, the brothers went in search of Shiva to beg for forgiveness. Shiva, however, did not reveal himself easily and having taken the disguise of a bull, mixed with a herd at Kedarnath.

Facing page bottom: A few kilometres away from the Temple is Chorabari Lake where some of the ashes of Mahatama Gandhi were scattered. Near it is the source of the Mandakini.

Bhima, the strongest of the brothers, recognised him nevertheless and grabbed the bull by the tail. The more he pulled, the deeper into the earth went the bull, until only the hump remained above the ground. Seeing their dejection, Shiva revealed himself to the Pandavas and asked them to make a temple for him there. It is said that the temple still exists, although the

eighth-century Saint Shankaracharya constructed the one that surrounds the hump of the uneven three-sided lingam. The rest of Shiva's body appeared in four other spots spread in the hills of Garhwal—Madhyamaheshwara, Tungnath, Rudranath and Kalpeswara. Together, all five are known as the Panch Kedar.

Below: Carved wooden portal of the Temple. Ganesha, the deity associated with auspiciousness and prosperity, adorns the frame.

State and capital:
Madhya Pradesh,
Bhopal (383 km)

Convenient access:
Road, air to Khajuraho,
rail to Jhansi

Accommodation:
Budget to high-end

Best season:
November to March

Also worth seeing:
Panna National Park,
26 km SE, Orchha,
170 km NW

Sublime homage to earthly desires

The Khajuraho temples celebrate erotic love

According to local legend, 84 temples were built in the 10th century near the small village of Khajuraho, located in a land with 84 lakes and 84 wells. Lying in the forested plains of the Bundelkhand region of Madhya Pradesh, Khajuraho derives its name from the many *khajur* (date) trees that grow here. It was earlier known as Kharjurvahaka or Khajirvahila (garden of dates). The temples were abandoned and forgotten for centuries, until 1838, when Captain T.S. Burt, a British army engineer, discovered them during the course of his tours. Only 25 of the original 84 temples now remain at this World Heritage Site, and most of the lakes and wells have run dry.

The temples were built under the patronage of the Chandela Rajput kings, who ruled this region for a brief period of about 100 years, leaving no real mark on political or military history. Therefore, it is remarkable that during this short historical period, a large number of such stupendous structures came up, which were to define the temple building style of North India in the ensuing centuries. The idea, developed around the cubic *garbha griha* (image chamber), grew to incorporate the *shikhara* (main tower), *mandapa* (hall), *ardh mandapa* (additional hall) and decorative elements. This evolution can be traced, in order, through the Ghantai, Javeri, Chatturbhuj and Surya Chitragupta Temples, to the climax with the Laxmana, Parsavanatha, Vishwanath and Kandariya Mahadev Temples. The Khajuraho temples rise from their

plinths in a massed crescendo of little spires embedded in relief in the soaring central *shikhara*, imitating the home of the gods in the Himalayas. Majority of the 25 temples are dedicated to Vishnu and Shiva, while six belong to the Jain patriarchs of the Digambara sect.

Profusion of sexual imagery

The temples are celebrated for the erotic sculptures adorning them. Though erotica in ancient Hindu art, literature and temple sculpture is not uncommon, nowhere is it as prolific and varied as at Khajuraho. The reason for this is uncertain, though there are many speculative theories. Some say that the Chandelas believed in Tantrism, which propounds that the gratification of earthly desires leads to spiritual awakening. Another theory is that the erotica was like a sex manual carved in stone, meant to educate the boys who resided in neighbouring hermitages for conjugal bliss. A third explanation recalls the Chandelas' professed descent from the moon. As per legend, Hemavati, the beautiful young daughter of a Brahmin priest was seduced by the Moon God and thus bore a son, Chandravarman. The unwed mother and baby hid in a dense forest, where she was both mother and *guru* to her child. One night Chandravarman, founder of the Chandela dynasty, saw his mother in a dream begging him to build temples, which would reveal both human passions, and the emptiness of human desire. Thereafter began the construction of the first of the temples, and successive kings added to them. A simple surmise attributes the decorations to the Indian craftsman's love for life in all its aspects, and another hypothesis, based on the fact that all erotic embellishment is on the exterior surfaces only, suggests that the objective may have been to ward off the evil eye.

Temples divided into groups

The western group of temples is the best known, especially the magnificent Kandariya Mahadev Temple, where the superstructure rises to 35 metres above the plinth, and exquisitely-carved celestial beings, lovers and serenading musicians are depicted in stone. The Chaunsat Yogini Temple, dedicated to Goddess Kali, is the oldest of the surviving temples, and the only one built in granite. The Chitragupta Temple has an imposing 1.5-metre-high image of the Sun God driving a chariot pulled by seven horses. An impressive three-headed image of Brahma graces the Vishwanath Temple, while the Laxmana Temple has a three-headed idol of Vishnu's incarnations—Narasimha and Varaha. The Devi Jagdambe Temple is the most erotic of all, with myriad sensuous figures engaged in *mithuna* (love-making). Of the eastern group, the outstanding Jain temples are Parsvanatha and Ghantai. Three Hindu temples, the Brahma, Vamana and Javari, also belong to this cluster. The southern group includes the Chaturbhuj Temple with a massive image of Shiva, and the Duladeo Temple.

Active worship is not carried out in the Khajuraho temples, with a few exceptions, such as the Matangeswara Temple, which has a 2.5-metre-high lingam, one of the largest in North India, made of polished yellow sandstone.

The Kandariya Mahadev Temple:
(above) an erotic panel
(below) detail of a sculpture.

Facing page: The Kandariya Mahadev Temple at Khajuraho stands on a plinth that raises it above ground level.

Sweeping greens around sleeping sultans

Lodhi Gardens are New Delhi's urban oasis

DELHI

Lodhi Gardens

State and capital:

New Delhi

Convenient access:

Road, air, rail to
New Delhi

Accommodation:

Budget to luxury

Best season:

Year round

Also worth seeing:

Safdarjung's Tomb,
0.5 km W, Delhi Zoo,
Old Fort, 3 km E

It is easy to understand why the sprawling, undulating gardens in the heart of the capital of India are acknowledged as one of the finest public spaces anywhere. Their unique appeal comes not only from the gentle undulations of evenly cut grass, random shrubbery and regal trees, but also from their non-horticultural components, which are indeed the jewel-like centrepieces of the green expanses. For the tombs of the Lodhi kings have been here for more than 500 years; the garden around them came up less than 100 years ago, thanks to the vision of Lady Willingdon, wife of the Viceroy of India during 1931-36.

In the 15th century much of the Gangetic plains were under the sway of the Delhi Sultanate. The last of the Sultanate dynasties were the Sayyids and the Lodhis. The one enduring contribution of their rule, otherwise conducted passively over a disintegrating empire, is a host of significant sepulchral monuments; about 50 of the Lodhi royals and nobles lie beneath the present city's chaotic surface. Their Sayyid predecessor Muhammad Shah's (r.1435-44) final resting place, built in the eight-cornered style, has an imposing appearance, so imparted by the size of the dome in proportion to the walls below, and subtly enhanced by the down-ward sloping outer edges of its supporting columns. An aesthetic counterbalance is provided by encircling galleries and eight cupolas placed on the shoulders of the structure. The tomb is located at the Gardens' south-western corner and is a good place to begin the two-kilometre walk, lined with varieties of seasonal flowers, that roughly swings along the park peripheries, at the end of which one realises what makes the Gardens so charming.

Wide lawns ideal for yoga sessions

The plant diversity keeps one engaged all through. One walks into alternating light and shade past stately bottle palms, slim casuarinas and silver oaks, magnificent alstonia and massive white-trunked *arjun*; through thick bamboo glades, besides masses of impenetrable

bougainvillea, under the multi-medicinal margosa, leafy *moulsri* and *kanak champa*, rock-hard *sheesham*, the odd elegantly-tentacled *kusum*, and varieties of ficus. Trees of semi-arid region like needle-fingered *kabuli kikar* (acacia) are scattered along with soaring eucalyptus, flaming silk cotton and the small but flamboyant bottle brush. Wide open, grassy spaces emerge in the central areas, the largest of which is the site for early morning yoga congregations and evening rendezvous for senior citizens—on holidays it becomes the favoured ground for family picnics and frolic amidst the scent of blooms. In the middle of this are two grand monuments. The Bara Gumbad (Big Dome) displays the second style of building prevalent during this period—the cuboid topped by a dome. Its square form is eased by use of red sandstone on the entrances and blind arches higher on the exterior. Attached to the northern end of the building are a mosque and a *sarai* (rest house)

which perhaps indicates that the Gumbad is not a tomb at all but just a grand doorway. Facing it, the Sheesh Gumbad (Mirror Dome) is so named for the peacock blue tiles clinging onto its façade.

Bridge of Eight over the lake

A rivulet that once streamed through cool jungles into the Yamuna River a few kilometres away, has been revived as a small, elongated lake with little flowering islands and a fountain, and is alive with snails, swimming insects and tadpoles that become fat croaking frogs in the monsoon. In winter, it becomes home to a few bar-headed geese and spotbills. That is another aspect of Lodhi Gardens; it is like an elementary school for bird-watchers, hosting at least 35-40 species. Grey hornbills atop silk cotton trees, the flash of yellow of a golden-backed woodpecker, the blue streak of the Indian roller, a treepie's or drongo's stray feather dangling from a branch, the

plaintive call of furtive cuckoos, the rhythmic beat of a barbet, the cry of lapwings and a spotted owlet flitting across your path at dusk are common sights and sounds.

At the head of a tucked away rose garden is a small pavilion dating to late Mughal times, and the 16th century Aathpula (Bridge of Eight), called so because its eight columns support seven arches over the watercourse, is at the Gardens' north-eastern boundary. Overlooking it from a rise is the last great Lodhi memorial, marking the crypt of Sikander (r. 1489-1517) in a style similar to his Sayyid predecessor, except that it is protected by a fortress-like wall with gateways, boasts aesthetically superior proportions, and instead of the ring of kiosks, is embellished with mini minarets.

Bottle palm lined walkways run around Muhammad Shah Sayyid's tomb, at the south-western corner of the Gardens.

MADHYA PRADESH

Bhopal

Mandu

State and capital:
Madhya Pradesh,
Bhopal (290 km)

Convenient access:
Road to Mandu, air,
rail to Indore

Accommodation:
Budget to mid-range.

Best season: July-
August, November
to March

Also worth seeing:
Temple towns of
Maheshwar,
Omkareshwar
125 km SE

City of gaiety

Its sultans dotted Mandu with playful edifices

Perched along the Vindhya Hills of Central India, 600 metres above the plains, is the city-fortress of Mandu. With its natural defences—its west face falls away into a deep ravine—Mandu was originally the fort-capital of the Hindu Paramara dynasty, which ruled over the Malwa region from the ninth to the 14th century. Archaeological evidence suggests that it was first fortified around the sixth century, when it was known as Mandapa-Durga (Durga's Hall of Worship), but the site became strategically important 400 years later when the powerful Paramaras established Dhar, 33 kilometres from Mandu, as their capital city.

Malwa first came under Muslim rule in 1305 when the Sultans of Delhi annexed it. Later, when the Mongols invaded North India in 1398, many of the nobles who had become powerful under the Tughlaq Sultans of Delhi fled and set up their own sultanates in outlying provinces. One of them was Dilawar Khan Ghori,

Governor of Dhar, who declared himself Sultan of Malwa in 1401, and augmented the fortifications of Mandu. His son, Hoshang Shah, made Mandu the capital, and it was given the name Shadiabad (City of Joy). The pervading spirit of Mandu was one of gaiety: playful palaces, as well as ornamental canals, baths and pavilions were built.

A 'swinging' palace

Hoshang Shah began work on many new buildings, including his own tomb—India's first marble-faced edifice—and the grand Jami Masjid (1431–54). Later, in the 17th century, the Mughal Emperor Shah Jahan was to send four of his architects to study the design of the Tomb, amongst whom was Ustad Hamid, associated with the construction of Taj Mahal. The Mosque's only elaborate artistry is the fine *jaali* (fretted screen) that filters sunlight falling into the mausoleum. Inspired by the great mosque of Damascus, the Jami Masjid was built of red sandstone and embellished with turquoise-blue and yellow tiles, a few of which are still visible at the entrance pavilion. Raised in about 1425, probably as a durbar hall, was the Hindola Mahal (Swinging Palace), thus called, as it seems to sway because of the sloping angle of its massive walls.

Mahmud Khan Khilji completed Hoshang Shah's tomb and the Jami Masjid. He also built the two-storeyed Jahaz Mahal (Ship Palace), between two artificial lakes, Munj Talao and Kapur Talao. Meant for his queens, the Palace had three halls with a bathing courtyard, spacious terraces, fountain courts, pavilions, kiosks and cupolas. With balconies extending over the lake, Jahaz Mahal is inspired by the design of a royal pleasure boat.

To the west of Hindola Mahal are three stepwells: the elaborate Champa Baoli, connected with underground vaulted rooms kept cool by flowing water, and with arrangements for hot water; the Ujali (Bright) Baoli; and the Andheri (Dark) Baoli. Another fascinating monument is the Nahar Jharokha, from where the royal family could watch tigers in the wild.

Roopmati, the Beautiful One

The romantic Rewa Kund palaces celebrate the love of the poet-prince Baz Bahadur for his consort, Rani Roopmati. Baz Bahadur, the last Sultan of Malwa, retreated to Mandu to study music after being defeated in battle. He fell in love with the singer Roopmati and built a palace for her on a hilltop from where she could look upon her

father's house on the plains, 300 metres below in the Narmada River valley. Rewa Kund, a reservoir with an aqueduct, was added to provide the palace with water. Hearing of Roopmati's beauty, Emperor Akbar dispatched an army to capture her and the fort in the early 1560s. Baz Bahadur fled, but Roopmati poisoned herself rather than fall into the clutches of the attackers.

In 1732, Malhar Rao Holkar defeated the Mughal Governor of Malwa, and Mandu became a Maratha holding. By the 17th century, the city had been abandoned.

Above: The underground chambers of the Champa Baoli (stepwell) were a favoured retreat during the summer months.
Left: Mandu was encircled by 45 kilometres of walls punctuated by several gates. Rani Roopmati watched over the vast plains below from a pavilion especially created for her.
Facing page top: The 120-metres-long Jahaz Mahal.
Facing page bottom: View of the mihrab of the Jami Masjid. The courtyard of the large yet simple mosque is surrounded by colonnades of arches, pillars and bays covered with domes.

State and capital:
Tamil Nadu, Chennai
(447 km)
Convenient access:
Road, air, rail to
Madurai
Accommodation:
Budget to high-end
Best season:
November to March
Also worth seeing:
Kodaikanal

Temple of splendid towers

The Meenakshi Temple reveres Parvati, yet reverberates with many other divinities

From ancient historical records it is ascertained that the city of Madurai, in Tamil Nadu, has existed at least since the fourth century BC. It was ruled successively by a series of dynasties like the Pandyas, Vijayanagara Kings and the Nayaks, and each of them were responsible for adding lavishly to its architectural and sculptural wealth, which peaked in the 17th century with the grand Meenakshi Temple, constructed under the aegis of Tirumala Nayak. There is, of course, the inevitable legend behind the Temple, which relates to Parvati, Shiva's wife, who is supposed to have been born here with three breasts. The prophecy that the third breast would fall off when she met her husband came true, and together they ruled over Madurai until it was time for their son to take over. Known also as Meenakshi or the Fish-eyed One (a symbol of extreme beauty), Parvati is revered in Madurai as the Benevolent Mother.

Built on the site of an earlier temple, Meenakshi's shrine grew in proportion and detail and is still as much the focal point of the city as it was then. One walks through one towering *gopuram* (tiered tower at the entrance of South Indian temples) to the other, passing by four consecutive enclosures to enter the main temple, from within which the fragrance of flowers and incense smoke emanates from dancing shadows cast by oil lamps. Non-Hindus are not allowed into the inner sanctum but can explore the rest of the precincts. Although the eastern gateway is the most ancient, it is the southern 52 metre-high *gopuram*, which bears a fascinating array of over 1,500 celestial beings, magical animals, gods and goddesses. Two *vyalis* (combination of an elephant and a lion) stand on either end of the tower—each of their eye's 75 centimetre diameter speaks of the massive proportions.

Hundreds of pillars and images lit by oil lamps

The main Meenakshi image is in green stone while Shiva's presence is depicted by a lingam. During festivals, however, other movable representations in bronze are used for processions that are taken out through the streets with a fanfare of cymbals and drums. Within the temple are many corridors with clusters of pillars, each unique in its own way. There are, for instance, five musical pillars, each carved further into 22 slim columns out of a single block of granite. On being struck, a different sound emerges from each one. One hall contains as many as 960 pillars, each of which is intricately carved with figures of *apsaras* (celestial maidens), mythical animals, celestial dancers and musicians. A huge figure of Nataraja is present at the end of the hall along with a smaller one of Parvati. In another part of the temple stands a tall *thiruvatchi* (frame of lamps) with a provision for 1,008 lamps, which when lit looks breathtakingly beautiful. By dusk, lamps all around the temple, including its darkest corridors are lit, bringing to life the many sculptures. Ancient paintings depict tales from the *Puranas* (sacred Hindu texts) and the wedding of Meenakshi and Sundareswara (Shiva). Also present are carvings of the *navagraha* (nine planets), 63 Nayanars (devotee-saints of Shiva), 10 incarnations of Vishnu, 3.5-metre-tall *dwarapalikas* (guards) and a host of other shrines dedicated to Saraswati, Durga, Laxmi and Ganesh—the last is a huge 2.5-metre-high monolith.

Temple water tank

An interesting story is associated with the temple's *Potramaraikulam* (Golden Lotus) Tank. During the 16th century, when Madurai was a vibrant centre for Tamil culture, language and literary conferences, it is said that manuscripts were thrown into the tank and given merit based on whether they remained afloat or sank beneath the water. Today, the tank is used for ablutions before entering the sanctum sanctorum.

Above & facing page:
Pyramidal gateways,
a characteristic of
Dravidian temple
architecture, grew
in physical stature
through the medieval
period until they
often surpassed the
main shrine in size
and magnificence.
Indeed, the
Meenakshi Temple's
gopurams are the
defining landmarks
of the city. The many
thousands of deities
and figures fashioned
on them in stucco are
repaired, painted and
reconsecrated every
12 years.

The forbidding Fort

The Rathores of Jodhpur amassed a treasury of war spoils behind Mehrangarh's walls

RAJASTHAN

Jodhpur   Jaipur

State and capital:
Rajasthan, Jaipur
(317 km)

Convenient access:
Road, air, rail to
Jodhpur

Accommodation:
Budget to luxury

Best season:
November to March

Also worth seeing:
Umaid Bhawan Palace,
Jaswant Thada
cenotaph

Rudyard Kipling called it the '.....work of giants'. Indeed, it is not just the colossal proportions, but the sheer manner in which they rise out of the rocky hill that give it the most forbidding and impregnable appearance amongst all of Rajasthan's myriad forts. Not that Mehrangarh hasn't had its share of problems. In choosing the site for its military and strategic advantages, as well as its proximity to a natural drinking water source, Rao Jodha of the powerful Rathore clan of Rajputs succeeded in earning the wrath of a Hindu saint named Chirianath, who lived near the spring. Resenting the intrusion, Chirianath cursed Rao Jodha and prophesised that droughts would wrack Jodhpur every three years. His grim prophecy comes true to this day.

In the early 15th century, Rao Jodha shifted his capital from Mandor to the city of Jodhpur, which he founded in the heart of the Thar Desert. In times to come Marwar was to become one of the largest and most powerful of the Rajput states, ruled by the Rathores from their stronghold at Jodhpur up to the 20th century. Seven gates, each named in honour of a victory punctuate Jodhpur's fort. The main entrance, Jaipol, was built by Maharaja Man Singh to commemorate his vanquishing of Maharaja Jagat Singh of Jaipur in 1808. Its massive door was brought as war booty all the way from Ahmedabad. From Loha Pol (Iron Gate), the original entrance of the Fort, Rajput princesses left as widows to immolate themselves on their husband's funeral pyres. And as they left their secure home for the last time, they dipped their hands in red henna dye, leaving their prints on the walls.

Cannons and cradles

Along the ramparts, in a rare display of its kind, are lined cannons from the fort's warring past, some engraved with exquisite Persian motifs, some in the shape of animals, and others mounted on unique wooden carriages. Within,

protected by the rugged walls, 17 generations of kings added temples, palaces, halls and courtyards. Today, there is a museum housing one of the largest collections of palanquins, elephant howdahs, cradles, miniature paintings, folk music instruments, turbans and weapons collected as spoils of war, or given to the Rathores as a mark of honour.

With its delicate colours, gold sheen, ornate ceiling and stained glass windows and screens, Phool Mahal (Palace of Flowers) is undoubtedly the grandest period room in Mehrangarh. Built in the 18th century as a hall of private audience, it has a ceiling in gold filigree and mirror work, and painted walls depicting various moods of Indian classical *ragas* (musical modes), royal portraits and incarnations of Vishnu and Durga. Especially notable in the heavily decorated Takhat Vilas are the lacquer paintings on the wooden

ceiling. In this bedchamber of Maharaja Takhat Singh (1843-73), the last of Jodhpur's kings to reside in Mehrangarh, even the floor is painted. The Palace of Glimpses has a gallery displaying a rare collection of royal cradles, including a mechanised one made for Maharaja Hanwant Singh (1947-52) by the Jodhpur Public Works Department. Visible through a series of exquisitely carved sandstone lattice windows are two courtyards, the Shringar (Coronation) Chowk, and the Daulat Khana Chowk, which hosted festivals and ceremonies. One of the oldest period rooms, built in the 16th century by Sawai Raja Sur Singh as a hall of public audience, is the Moti Mahal (Pearl Palace). Its walls are polished with lustrous lime plaster and decorated with niches in which lamps once flickered.

On the western side of the ramparts, stands the temple of Chamunda Devi. For 500 years,

princes and commoners alike have prayed here for the fort, city and its people. It is a prayer that seems to have always been granted, for right to the end, the burnished red-sandstone battlements of the mighty citadel stood unconquered. Stunned with Rathore resistance, Sher Shah Suri, the great Pathan emperor is said to have exclaimed, 'I almost lost the empire of Hindustan for a hand full of millet'.

From its 150-metre-high perch, the battle-scarred Mehrangarh fort glowers protectively over Jodhpur. The earlier practice of using indigo blue on city houses to guard against white ants was later adopted in a general way. The striking white temple-like building in the foreground is Jaswant Thada, a memorial to Jaswant Singh II, built in 1899 by his son.

The *gompas* of Ladakh

Remote and spectacular, Buddhist monasteries are the repositories of Ladakhi culture

State and capital:
Jammu & Kashmir,
Srinagar (434 km
to Leh)

Convenient access:
Road to some
gompas, others
accessible by trekking,
air to Leh

Accommodation:
Budget to high-end
at Leh

Best season: July
to September

Also worth seeing:
Zanskar *gompas*,
Nubra Valley

*Top: One of the
largest of the Ladakh
gompas, Thikse
belongs to monks of
the Gelugpa order.*

Predominantly Buddhist and Muslim, Ladakh is a trans-Himalayan high-altitude desert region in the far north of India. The finest of Ladakh's Buddhist art, and much of its historic and material wealth, lies in its *gompas* (monasteries), most tracing their present form to the 15th century. This consists of murals, images of the Buddha and Buddhist masters, *thangkas*, ritual and decorative objects, *chortens*, musical instruments, animal trophies, masks, prayer wheels, lamps, stupas, weapons, and stacks of antique religious literature. Gold, silver and turquoise are the commonly used embellishments. It is impossible to enumerate, much less describe, even a few of these unique artefacts, yet the massive Padmasambhava *thangka* at Hemis, Chemde's 29 old manuscripts lettered in gold and silver, and images of 23 manifestations of Tara at Spituk are worth special mention.

Tantric deities in dark chambers

The highly complex nature of the Tibetan Vajrayayana Buddhism practised in Ladakh is evident from colourful wall murals of the *gompas*. Unfathomably fantastic and seemingly haphazardly arranged to the unfamiliar, this picturisation is, however, interrelated and symbolic. For example, Lords of the Four Quarters protect the entrances. The *Samsara Chakra* or Wheel of Life depicts the perennial cycle of life and death. Feminine energies, injected from Hindu Tantric philosophy, are vivid as the Green and White Taras. In contrast, the fearsome Dharmapalas, absorbed from Bon, the pre-Buddhist Tibetan faith, function as guardian deities. Images and frescoes of Sakyamuni (Gautama Buddha), and the more expanded system of Buddhas in time and space are in abundance. In addition are the Bodhisattvas, most commonly prevalent as Avalokiteshwara (the compassionate),

Manjusri (the wise), Maitreya (of the future) and the saints Padmasambhava, Atisa and Tsonkapa. Present, as much of it is, in minimally lit chambers, this rich tapestry often needs additional light sources to be appreciated, and, indeed, even noticed. Though the style of murals in almost every *gompa* is the same, some renditions are more remarkable than others. However, distinct from others, the murals at the celebrated 1,000-year-old Alchi, bear more affinity to Indian Buddhist iconography than the later Tibetan form of the Second Spreading. Also, they cover more square inches of wall space than any other.

The word *gompa* means 'solitary place'—an apt term, isolated as the monasteries are over barren moonscapes, on ridges and in remote corners. Externally, they are identifiable by their fortress-like locations as well as architecture. Tapering, impregnable looking walls, spotted with windows, rise in piles of several storeys, out of which open out breathtaking views of the surrounding country. Thikse, south east of Leh, is particularly eye catching for its tiered structure, reminding of Lhasa's Potala Palace. But for sheer extremeness of its setting, Phugtal, in Zanskar is incomparable. Tucked into a cave in a sheer cliff above the river, it is serviced by monks living in dwellings squeezed somehow onto rocky projections below, connected by a dizzying system of ladders. An exception to the norm is Alchi, spread out as a cluster of five low-rise buildings on easily accessible ground.

Inside is often a bewildering labyrinth of dark and open spaces. Living quarters, courtyards, prayer halls, temples, alcoves, terraces and balconies on several levels are connected with passages, doorways, stairways or ladders. The main places for worship and prayer are the *gonkhang* (temple of guardian deities), and the *dukhang* (main temple). Apart from the intricate palette of the murals, bright pleasing colours are the order for shutters and frames, awnings, prayer wheel niches, and walls.

Gompas are controlled by different sects defined by the teachings of individual masters. Of these, monks of the Gelugpa order can be identified by their yellow hats, whereas the Nyingmapa, Saskyapa, Drigungpa and Drugpa wear red headgear. A sound administrative structure, with the *kushok* (reincarnate head of the *gompa*) at the top, keeps the day to day work ticking; the power pyramid, in fact, extends beyond the walls of the institution, connecting apex authorities like the Dalai Lama to the lowermost echelons of the humble lama. The quid pro quo relationship shared by monasteries with their neighbouring villages involves providing religious services at all kinds of occasions in return for support in terms of agricultural produce, labour and money.

Annual festivals of so-called 'devil dances'

Symbolic of the battle of good and evil within oneself, 'devil-dances' are energetic choreographies, wherein monks don elaborate costumes, put on the terrifying face masks of guardian deities and launch into bizarre and explosive movements. As an enthralled local crowd watches, an orchestra of long ceremonial trumpets, drums and cymbals provides robust accompanying music. Over the years, the festival of Hemis, which is the richest, largest and best turned out of the *gompas*, has become especially popular.

Above: The beautiful Buddha at Alchi monastery, established by the Great Translator Ringchen Zangpo. The style of imagery at Alchi owes itself to craftsmen and painters from Kashmir, who created its iconography.

Below: Ritual ceremonies at gompas *involve chanting and playing of cymbals, horns and drums. Many village families send one or more young member into monkhood, whereupon he is instructed and trained by a* lobon *(wise old lama).*

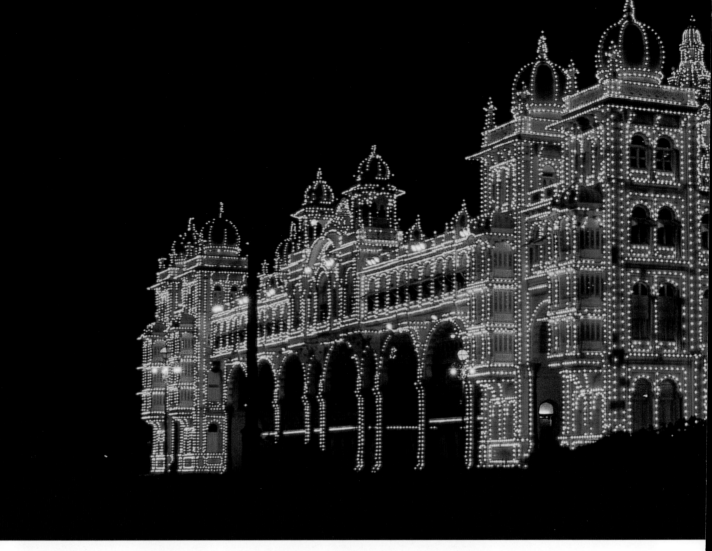

The most lavishly ornamented royal home

Mysore's fairytale Palace was rebuilt after a fire

State and capital:
Karnataka, Bengaluru
(138 km)

Convenient access:
Road, rail to Mysore,
air to Bengaluru

Accommodation:
Budget to high-end

Best season:
September to February

Also worth seeing:
Jagmohan Palace Art
Gallery, Chamundi
Temple

As part of the South Indian Vijayanagara kingdom the region of southern Karnataka was governed by the Wodeyars from their capital at Mysore. Among India's fairytale palaces, the most ornate is perhaps the Maharaja's Palace. Located in the midst of landscaped gardens in the city centre, the Palace, also known as Amba Vilas, has been the residence of the Wodeyars from the 15th century till India became independent—except for a short period of 38 years in the 18th century when it was captured by Haider Ali and his son Tipu Sultan.

When a fire destroyed the original wooden palace in 1897, the Maharaja built a new one on the same site, on a much grander scale, with the expertise of the British architect, Henry Irwin, who also built the Viceregal Lodge in Shimla. Irwin designed the new palace in the Indo-Saracenic style, combining English neo-classical forms with eastern ornamentation.

A central domed tower tops the three-storeyed building, 75 metres long and 48 metres high. Seven lofty arches dominate its imposing façade with a vast courtyard in the front, and a series of towers at cardinal points. The entire front is embellished with a profusion of arches, canopies and parapets derived from the Rajput, Mughal and South Indian sources. The surface decoration of scrolls, niches and carvings are characteristic of South Indian temple art. Though

the Mysore Palace is not one of the largest in India, it is certainly the most lavish in terms of materials and ornamentation.

Liberal use of gold and silver in ornate halls

Entry to the Palace is through the Dolls Pavilion, a gallery of Indian and European sculptures and ceremonial antiques. The main entrance is the Elephant Gate, where one can see the ceremonial howdah that was wired with red and green lights for the Maharaja to use as traffic signals for the mahout. The howdah is reportedly gilded with 84 kilograms of pure gold.

Inside the palace is the spectacular kalyana mandapa (marriage hall). Its gabled ceiling is covered

with stained glass, elegant wrought-iron pillars, and cut-glass Czech chandeliers that illuminate a peacock design on the floor and ceiling, thus according it the name 'Peacock Pavilion'. Oil paintings, depicting royal Dussehra celebrations hang on the walls.

The balcony of the Diwan-i-Aam (Hall of Public Audience) with interiors of gilded columns and an ornate ceiling inlaid with semi-precious stones affords a view of the Chamundi Hills. In here was kept the solid gold throne whose lineage goes back to the early 14th century Vijayanagara kings. Weighing 280 kilograms, it is still brought out and used by the present members of the Wodeyar family on ceremonial occasions. Frescoes depicting the Goddess Shakti and scenes from Indian epics are displayed on the walls. Of special interest is the painting by the celebrated 19th-century Indian artist Raja Ravi Verma. At the entrance of the smaller Diwan-i-Khaas (Hall of

Private Audience) is a pair of carved silver doors that were salvaged from the old palace. Gold leaf designs on the inner surfaces add to the effect of the stained-glass ceiling, in art nouveau style.

The Mysore Palace has always been the focal point of the city's life. Every year, people flock here to witness the Dussehra festivities.

Below: The Maharaja partakes in ceremony on the fabulous gold and silver throne, originally crafted in fig wood and ivory.

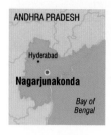

ANDHRA PRADESH

Hyderabad

Nagarjunakonda

Bay of Bengal

State and capital:
Andhra Pradesh,
Hyderabad (160 km)

Convenient access:
Road to Nagarjunsagar,
air to Hyderabad, rail
to Macherla, thereafter
boat from
Nagarjunasagar to
Nagarjunakonda Island

Accommodation:
Budget to mid-range in
Nagarjunakonda

Best season: October
to February

Also worth seeing:
Anupu excavations,
Rajiv Gandhi Wildlife
sanctuary, S

*A path winds its way
through the island
with sites on either
side. These include a
megalith (burial site)
from the second
century BC, yagya
(ritual sacrifice) sites,
including an Ikshvaku
Ashvamedha (Horse)
Yagya site, stupas
and a monastery. The
latter was inhabited
by Ceylonese monks.
It has rows of small
rooms as well as a
central hall. At the
entrance is a giant
statue of the Buddha
and facing it is an
Auddesika stupa.
Further on is the
Mahastupa or
Mahachaitya, referred
to in numerous
inscriptions of the
time. The stupa
contained a bone
relic said to be of the
Buddha, encased in
a clay container.*

Treasures of Nagarjunakonda

Second century Buddhist and Hindu artefacts are preserved on an island

Nagarjunasagar Dam on the Krishna River, south of Hyderabad, was completed in 1966, submerging the 380 square-kilometre Nagarjunakonda Valley known for the buried cultural riches of civilisations leading back to the Stone Age. The salvaged ruins of some of the structures can now be seen on an island in the flooded Valley, while another set of remains lies at Anupu, on the eastern bank of the reservoir.

King Ikshvaku built Nagarjuna's centre of learning

The Valley was named for Nagarjuna, a brilliant expounder of the Mahayana stream of Buddhism, which originated in this part of India. From the second century BC until the third century AD, Buddhism was one of the most important religions in the region. Interestingly, though the Ikshvaku kings, who ruled this area in the third century AD remained steadfastly brahmanical, their women converted to Buddhism. Nagarjuna began a centre of learning near Vijayapuri, the kingdom's capital, which comprised of a retreat, a university, libraries, hospital and monasteries. It was from here (and Amravati, a few kilometres downstream) that Buddhism spread to China, Japan and Sri Lanka. Along with the palace complex and adjoining royal buildings, Nagarjunakonda boasted numerous wells and paved cisterns, well laid out roads and colonies, temples, an amphitheatre with seating for about 1,000 spectators, wayside rest-houses and public baths with advanced drainage and plumbing facilities. Excavations have also unearthed Roman, Ikshvaku, Satvahana and Mughal coins.

The ferry to the island chugs up till the right bank of the Krishna River, close to a deeply ridged cliff covered in soil and vegetation, which is actually the remains of a hill fort built by a Reddy king long after the fall of the Ikshvaku kingdom. As the ferry approaches

the long, flat and densely green island, ancient structures are visible, some partially submerged in the reservoir waters which have been rising steadily over the past few years.

The museum

The main museum at Nagarjunakonda, patterned on a Buddhist *vihara* (monastery), is located amidst the remains of a medieval fortification. It houses a range of artefacts dating from the Stone Age till the Ikshvaku reign. Most pieces belong to the Buddhist period and are exquisite examples of Ikshvaku art: ayaka (votive) slabs, cross beams, drum and dome slabs, cornice beams, blocks and columns with inscriptions and detailed representations. The popular themes are episodes from the Buddha's life such as tales of his different births, departure, meditation, enlightenment, preaching and miracles. The few brahmanical sculptures of the period depict Karthikeya (the six-faced God of War), Shiva, Sati, figures of Vidhadharas (flying celestials), and pillars showing secular themes like children at play, war and elephants. Most of the inscriptions are in ornate Brahmi and some in Sanskrit. A large model of the valley, as it must have been during Nagarjuna's time, shows locations of villages, the university, stupas and other buildings on the basis of over 120 sites excavated before submergence. The visual panorama gives an idea of the scale and majesty of the civilisation. Close to the museum is a reconstructed bathing ghat. The stepped ghats, built with attention to even the minutest details, evoke an image of chanting monks in orange robes slowly descending down to the waters for prayer and meditation.

The ancient university of Nalanda

Its library contained nine million manuscripts

State and capital:
Bihar, Patna (90 km)

Convenient access:
Road to Nalanda, air,
rail to Patna

Accommodation:
None in Nalanda.
Budget to high-end in
Patna

Best season:
November to March

Also worth seeing:
Rajgir, 10 km SW,
Barabar rock-cut caves

Chinese travellers of the seventh century have left detailed accounts of the magnificence of Nalanda. Hieun T'sang the scholar-monk, spent 12 years there and wrote admiringly of its 'soaring domes and pinnacles, pearl-red pillars carved and ornamented, and richly adorned balustrades and roofs covered with tiles that reflect the sun in a thousand ways'. Established in mid fifth century, Nalanda was a monastery of the Mahayana Buddhist order. As one of the world's oldest residential universities, it attracted students and scholars from all parts of Asia.

A water clock marked time

As per belief, it is built on a site, which has been visited and blessed by the Buddha. Nalanda is situated near modern Patna. The monastery flourished under the benevolent patronage of the Pala kings and at its apogee boasted a library of nine million manuscripts. Today green grass whispers softly over the temple mounds and orderly brick ruins of the residential halls, but seven centuries ago the pillared halls echoed the sounds of scores of footsteps and the murmur of a dozen different languages. Nalanda's famous water clock marked the hours of the working day for scholars, sages and saffron-clad monks, and the careful cadence of Buddhist chants mingled with the everyday chatter of a bustling university.

A row of nine monasteries faced four temples along a long north-south avenue. The imposing remains of the largest structure reveal a stupa over 31 metres high. Approached by a broad flight of stairs, the main central stupa is surrounded by four small stupas at the four corners. This *panchratna* (five-towered) style of design became the standard for subsequent Buddhist architecture in South East Asia. Horizontal friezes on the outer walls, divided into niches, contained stucco images of the Buddha, Boddhisattvas and related figures. The three other temples were smaller in scale, though similar in style, to the large stupa. The remains of a carved *torana* (gateway) stand before one, while another stupa has a brick-making furnace on its north.

Monastery and a centre of arts

Located side by side in military precision, the *viharas* (monasteries) were several storeys high. Each upper floor was stepped back from the previous one to create an open-air terrace on every floor. This particular style of receding storeys can be seen many centuries later in the Panch Mahal at Fatehpur Sikri, built by the Mughal Emperor Akbar.

Right: View of the ruins of the main stupa and smaller stupas.

Facing page top: The multi-storeyed monks' quarters followed a uniform plan of rows of rooms around a central courtyard. Being halls of residence and learning, the lower rooms, built in brick, probably contained the refectory, areas of instruction and communal worship, while the upper floors built in timber had rooms for resident students.

In the days of Pala munificence, Nalanda was a centre of the arts in eastern India, producing stone, metal and terracotta images in its workshops. The basement structure of what are the remains of a seventh-century temple, features elaborately carved dado relief, with over 200 panels set between decorated pilasters. Ram, Sita and a host of divinities, as well as maidens, dancers, amorous couples, birds, lions and mythical beasts are interspersed with foliate patterns and motifs.

With the increasing authority of Muslim rule in North India, Nalanda declined, as did other centres of Buddhist learning and prayer during the 11th and 12th centuries. A Tibetan pilgrim in 1,235 records just a single teacher and a class of 70 students at Nalanda, existing on the support of a local Brahmin.

Orchha's sophisticated Indo-Islamic skyline

Gift of dynamic Bundela kings

MADHYA PRADESH

Orchha

Bhopal

State and capital:
Madhya Pradesh,
Bhopal (397 km)

Convenient access:
Road to Orchha, air to
Gwalior, Khajuraho, rail
to Jhansi

Accommodation:
Budget to high-end

Best season:
November to March

Also worth seeing:
Forts at Jhansi and
Talbehat

One of the most striking sights of Orchha is the silhouette of cenotaphs visible from across the Betwa River. These graceful structures, one of the tallest of their kind in India, are memorials to the 14 stalwarts of the Bundela dynasty of Orchha, now a large and busy, yet quaint village. The Bundelas, after whom this Central Indian region is named, trace their beginnings to a Rajput prince who offered himself as sacrifice to the Mountain Goddess Vrindavasini, who in turn, stopped him and named him Bundela (One

Who Offers Blood). When the Tughlaq Sultans of Delhi overran their capital of Garhkundar, the rulers moved their base to Orchha. Thereafter, notwithstanding setbacks due to the odd incompetent ruler, the kingdom's fortunes spiralled upwards—as did its glorious skyline—driven mainly by the Krishna-worshipping Madhukar Shah and the swashbuckling Bir Singh Deo. And eventually, by 1783, when the capital shifted to Tikamgarh, the saga of the House of Orchha played out, what remained was a unique Indo-Islamic

legacy, set in stone and plaster, hidden from the general view by woods of *dhak* (flame-of-forest). One and a half centuries later, Sir Edwin Lutyens was to incorporate some of the elements of these edifices in the Indo-Saracenic design style of New Delhi.

For a settlement of its size, Orchha has a remarkable repertoire of monuments. The first battlement of note was raised in the 16th century by the chieftain, Raja Rudra Pratap. From it evolved a golden-walled island-fortress, backed on one flank by the right

palace, Orchha became the only place in India where He came to be revered as King more than God, and out of respect for his royal incarnation, the deity is allowed three hours more 'sleep' every morning than other temple deities. During the daily *aarti* (ritual prayer) sessions at the temple, uniformed policemen stomp to attention, rifles grounded, in their figurative roles as bodyguards to His Highness.

The Mughal influence

The Chatturbhuj Temple, where the Rama idol was to be originally placed, is probably Orchha's most imposing building. With a dizzyingly high ceiling, its interior imparts a cathedral-like feel, and the soaring spires on the cruciform plan add a counterpoint to the domed kiosks of Bir Singh Deo's palace, the airy Jahangir Mahal, ensconced in the fort. The five-storeyed palace, with myriad windows and graceful *chhatris*, was built to welcome the Mughal Emperor Jahangir on his visit to Orchha. The east-facing façade is encrusted with turquoise tiles, and two stone elephants flank the stairway, holding bells in their trunks to announce the arrival of the Emperor. A fountain once spouted inside the palace courtyard and candlelight reflecting off it and the crushed-shell plastered walls created a dreamy setting for the evening's entertainment. The Sheesh Mahal (Palace of Mirrors), part of the fort complex, was built

during the early 18th century, and has been now converted into a hotel. Another of Orchha's palaces, the 17th century Rai Praveen Mahal, built for the ruler's poetess-musician lover, is landscaped with *chaarbaghs* (typical Mughal gardens).

Tucked away in the heart of town, nestles the shrine of Orchha's third great hero, Dhiman Hardaul, who gave his life to protect the queen's honour, and ballads of whose exploits are still sung across this rugged land. Outside, the bazaar brims with wares including wooden toys, kitchen implements, earthenware, fruits and vegetables, sweetmeats and the paraphernalia of religious ritual. A short trudge through the dusty lanes brings you to the town's peripheries where, streaked liberally with murals, the fortress-temple of Laxmi Narayan perches on a hillock, aloof and magnificent.

Bottom: While the sun sets behind the cenotaphs of the Bundela kings, life on the eastern bank of the Betwa carries on.
Facing page: *Residential apartments and pavilions, connected by overhanging balconies, are ranged around the fountain of the quadrangular court inside the Jahangir Mahal. Conceived at the zenith of Orchha's power, it is a superb example of a Central Indian fort-palace.*

bank of the looping Betwa. Across it lies the quaint hamlet, which the fort protected, weaving around temples and memorials, before petering off into the undulations of the Bundelkhand countryside. The Raj Mahal Palace, distinguishable from outside the fort walls by its cupola-lined parapets, was begun by Rudra Pratap, and finished during the reign of Madhukar Shah. Its inside walls have vivid frescoes depicting fantastic religious themes. During Shah's rule the Ram Raja Mandir was also erected. Actually meant as a palace for the queen, the building was surrendered to an image of the God Rama, which, as the story goes, refused to budge from its temporary abode in the palace when it was being relocated to a new temple, built especially for it. With Rama staying on in the

The wooden Palace of Padmanabhapuram

Low in scale but high in grandeur

State: Kerala, Thiruvananthapuram (55 km)

Convenient access: Road to Padmanabhapuram, air, rail to Thiruvananthapuram

Accommodation: Budget to high-end (in Thiruvananthapuram)

Best season: October to March.

Also worth seeing: Indian School of Martial Arts, Thiruvananthapuram; Kanyakumari, at the tip of the Indian peninsula

Once protected by a mud fort and a moat believed to have been infested with crocodiles, the 17th century royal residence of the old state of Travancore is now guarded by an unimpressive outer wall. But beyond this perimeter lies a sumptuous world of stone, tiles, teak and jackfruit timber, delicately carved and ingeniously designed to forbear the hot and humid climate of Kerala. It is a world that unfolds as a maze of corridors, and dark, cool rooms offset by bright courtyards, following no logical plan, except that the public areas shield the most private ones—the living quarters of the rulers.

Acres of banana plantations lead to Padmanabhapuram near Kanyakumari, the southernmost

tip of the Indian subcontinent. During its heyday, between 1590 and 1790, after which the capital of Travancore shifted back to Thiruvananthapuram, Padmanabhapuram was the centre of trade, culture and the arts in Kerala and southern Tamil Nadu. Constructed by King Iravi Varma Kulasekhara Perumal (1592-1609), this superb example of the traditional wooden architecture of the Malabar state was added on to by several successive rulers of the dynasty. The warrior King Marthand Varma (1706-1758), known as the 'founder of modern Travancore' built up the small principality of Venad into a state to reckon with, by defeating the Dutch and conquering their allying kingdoms. His supremacy

established, he proclaimed himself ruler, as the 'servant of Padmanabha', the patron deity of the royal family, and renamed the capital Padmanabhapuram.

Fine floor polish of traditional ingredients

Unlike conventional majestic royal homes, India's largest wooden palace is low in scale but makes up with the grandeur of masterful craftsmanship, evident in both its structural and decorative elements. The complex of four major units, reduced from the original 35 hectares to 2.5 hectares (approximately) has 127 rooms. From the imposing, carved, gable-roofed wooden gateway, visitors enter a *poomugham* (large entrance hall) where visiting dignitaries were

entertained. A brass lamp in the shape of a horse and rider is suspended in such a manner that its position remains perpetually horizontal, preventing the oil from spilling. Above it, the ceiling is a grid of wooden rafters, with a rosette at every intersection, altogether representing 90 different flowers in bloom. Other fascinating objects here include a carved Chinese chair, a bed made of seven pieces of granite, and a wooden reclining Vishnu. Further, on a higher level, is the *mantrahala* (council chamber), whose black, shining floor is the quintessential example of the traditional polishing techniques of the region: an admixture of burnt coconut shells, egg whites, coconut water, lime, laterite, sand and jaggery, and juices of various herbs were mixed to produce a polish so glossy that it reflected the elaborately carved ceiling and sloping walls. The *natakshala* (performance hall), with granite pillars, was built by a ruler who was a composer of Carnatic music.

Also, part of the complex comprises of bathing tanks, two large dining halls where free meals were served to the priestly class, bathhouses, stables, a weapons store, offices and a guardroom. And as it chimed the hours, the 300-year-old clock in the clock tower could once be heard from a distance of three kilometres.

In the heart of the palace stands the oldest structure, the *Thai Kottaram* (Mother Palace), built in 1550. Intricately chiselled pillars fashioned from jackfruit tree trunks rise from a glossy floor polished red with the juice of the hibiscus tree. The *upparika mallika* (king's quarters), on the other side of a large courtyard is the only four storeyed building on the ground floor of which was the treasury. In the courtyard, as the king watched from above, hopeful recruits would have to lift a 38 kilogram stone, 100 times from the top of one of the pillars, if they wished to qualify for the Royal Army. The centrepiece of the king's building, said to have

been a gift from the Dutch East India Company, is a four-poster bed made of 67 pieces of medicinal wood. Filled with exceptionally old and invaluable murals, the *puja* (prayer) room has been closed to the public to ensure protection of its painted treasures.

Above: Polish, made of natural ingredients, applied painstakingly, imparts a long lasting gleam to the floor.
Left: Stone pillars of the Navratri Mandapam are carved with divine female figures.
Facing page top & right: Views of the Palace courtyard.
Facing page bottom left: Timber beams in pyramidal formation hold up the Palace's gabled roof.

RAJASTHAN

Delhi

Jaisalmer Jaipur

Udaipur

Access: Journey starts
and ends at Delhi
Accommodation:
Luxury
Only season: Train
runs from September
to March
Schedule: Departure
every Wednesday
from Delhi Safdarjang

*Top: The train speeds
through the arid
ruggedness of
Rajasthan.*

Palace on Wheels

Travel on a luxury train like the maharajas of yore

Trains are the most widely used mode of transport in India but the journey on the fabulous Palace on Wheels is an experience like no other. During the six days and seven nights that you spend on it, the romance of the grandeur of Rajasthan comes alive as much inside the lavish and impeccably serviced interiors of the train as at the glittering historical towns and nature reserves that lie on its journey.

Coaches embellished with exquisite art

The train is made up of 14 passenger coaches which were originally the personal railway carriages of the rulers of the erstwhile princely states of Rajputana and Gujarat, and of the Nizam of Hyderabad and the Viceroy of British India. Each coach has four cabins with occupancies ranging from one to three, and a lounge area. The interiors have been refurbished with modern amenities but retain the charm and class of yesteryears.

Rajasthan's bountiful legacy of culture, art and craftsmanship is flaunted in the rich décor of paintings, carved period furniture and elegant handicrafts. Each cream-coloured coach is named after a medieval Rajasthani state, and bearing its emblem and coat of arms on the exteriors represents the unique cultural stamp and splendid heritage of that kingdom. Thus, the namesake coach of Alwar, a state with jungles popular for kingly sport, has a ceiling painted with a hunting scene. Rajasthani miniature art, a mixture of Rajput and Mughal styles, evolved with characteristics unique to different regions. Dhola-Maru, the lovers on camel back, is a legacy of Bikaner, and an oil replica of it adorns the coach's red and gold lounge, inspired by the flaming colour scheme of Junagarh Fort's coronation halls. Bundi's Raagmala paintings are displayed in its bogie, along with a water colour of its fort-palace. One of the most famous of Rajput paintings, Bani Thani—a beautiful woman with

accentuatedly elegant features, her head and shoulders covered by a filmy drape—is from Kishangarh, and a rendition of it is prominent in its coach. Though the big states of Jaipur and Udaipur had their own schools of art too, they had much else besides. The striking blue and gold frescoes from Jaipur's opulent palaces within the Amber Fort find expression on the coach's ceilings. Phad paintings, which were scroll canvases of folk heroes done in vegetable dyes, are used here to show the vibrant Gangaur and Teej Festivals. In the Udaipur coach, the Peacock Court from its magnificent City Palace has been the artistic inspiration for creating the lounge décor in relief and oxidised white metal. Jaisalmer's latticed mansions, Dungargarh's tribal art, Bharatpur's birds and Sirohi's coloured glass-work are tastefully featured in their signature coaches.

Necklace of the best Rajasthani destinations

As vistas of the stark Rajasthan country pass by, elaborately

costumed *khidmatgars* (traditional attendants) look after you. The Maharajah and Maharani restaurant saloons not only specialise in Rajasthani cuisine, but also offer continental and Indian fare. There is a well-stocked bar-lounge, and separate lounges at the end of each coach for passengers to relax when they wish to move out of their bedrooms. Since most of the railway track in Rajasthan is not welded, it is easy to be lulled to sleep by the clickety-clack of the wheels. The itinerary binds Rajasthan's finest destinations and is arranged such that the train arrives at times ideal to enjoy the sights at the stations of call. Though most meals are served on board, a few are set up at city restaurants. Most nights are spent travelling.

The royal journey begins at Delhi in the evening and the train arrives the next morning at Jaipur, capital of Rajasthan. Post a traditional Indian welcome with garlands, folk music and elephants, the day is spent at the sprawling Amber Fort, Hawa Mahal, and shopping for handicrafts. Travelling extreme west the next day towards the sand dunes of the Thar Desert, one spends the day at Jaisalmer. The fourth day brings you to Jodhpur, where lunch is organised at a palace hotel. Eastwards now, the destination is the famed Ranthambhore National Park for a possible early morning rendezvous with the tiger, and later in the day, a halt at Chittorgarh Fort. The next day is spent at Udaipur, city of palaces, and the morning of the day after, birdwatching at Bharatpur. The climax of the trip is the dazzling Taj Mahal at Agra, the only destination not in Rajasthan, but who would want to argue with that?

Top: A khidmatgar *looks out for guests from on board the Palace on Wheels.*
Middle: *Seating in the restaurant coaches is in groups of two and four.*
Right: *Lounge service.*

Museum of fine antiquities

Exhibits at the Chhatrapati Shivaji Maharaj Vastu Sangrahalaya span several millennia

The grand Chhatrapati Shivaji Maharaj Vastu Sangrahalaya (CSMVS) building also houses the Museum Society of Bombay, a voluntary organisation engaged in promoting art awareness and knowledge of India's heritage. Founded in 1963, it is the oldest museum society in the country.

The Chhatrapati Shivaji Maharaj Vastu Sangrahalaya (formerly Prince of Wales Museum), a masterpiece of Indo-Saracenic architecture, evokes the beauty of Islamic architecture as it was expressed in a refreshing and charming new idiom in India during the British rule. The imposing structure seamlessly incorporates an impressive dome, brackets and cupolas, projecting balconies and fretted screens as well as surface decoration with the use of different stones.

In designing CSMVS at a spacious crescent-shaped site in the heart of South Mumbai, George Wittet took inspiration from Bijapur's (the capital of the medieval South Indian sultanate) array of fine Islamic monuments. The Prince of Wales laid the building's foundation stone during his first visit to Mumbai in 1905. Though construction was completed in 1914, the outbreak of World War I momentarily halted its functioning as a museum; during this period the building served as a military hospital, finally opening to the public in 1922. A new wing was added on the ground floor in 1936

Gupta period terracottas and illustrated manuscripts

The collections span several millennia and cultures. Relics of the Indus Valley Civilisation (2500-1750 BC) include its signature toy cart and a bird on wheels. The archaeological collections owe their beginnings to pioneering archaeologists like Sir Henry Cousens and Sir John Marshall. Gupta period terracottas, Buddhist images from Gandhara and ceiling panels from a temple at Aihole are a few of the Museum's more valuable ancient Indian sculptures. The natural history display has a variety of Indian birds, mammals, fish and reptiles, some of which are shown in dioramas in their natural habitat.

Two hundred miniature paintings, representative of renowned art centres from all over the country, are arranged by theme. Illustrated manuscripts include the *Laur Chanda* of the mid 16th century, the *Anwar-i Suhayli*, created in the atelier of Mughal Emperor Akbar, and a few folios from the *Mewar Ramayana*, dated to 1649. The decorative arts section has some fine pieces of Indian craftsmanship in lavishly worked wood, jade, ivory and metal. Amongst the Nepalese and Tibetan treasures are the 13th-century Maitreya image and a 16th-century depiction of Songtsen Gampo, the seventh-century Tibetan ruler who introduced Buddhism in Tibet. There is also an interesting display of old beadwork from Gujarat.

Allauddin Khilji's dagger

Along with European oil paintings, the same section features some works from the initial phase of the Bombay School. A particularly noteworthy piece of Far Eastern art is Japanese craftsman Muni Yoshi's iron snake. Ruler of the Delhi Sultanate Allauddin Khilji's (r. 1296-1315) dagger and Emperor Akbar's cuirass and shield, dated to 1593, stand out at the arms and armour display.

MAHARASHTRA

• Mumbai

Arabian Sea

State and city:
Maharashtra, Mumbai
Convenient access:
Road to Museum, air, rail to Mumbai
Accommodation:
Budget to luxury
Best season:
November to March
Also worth seeing:
Fort area, Bhau Daji Lal Museum

to house the natural history section. The Museum, one of the finest in the country, houses several collections in distinct sections, some of which were gifted by private collectors, including pioneering Indian industrialists Sir Ratan Tata and Sir Dorab Tata, and art historian Karl Khandalawala.

Leading to an airy high-ceilinged lobby with a pond under the dome, the central entrance divides the building into two wings. Representative items of the wider selections inside are displayed here in glass cabinets. The main gallery on the ground floor houses treasures of Indian sculpture. At the eastern end is the natural history section beyond which is the library, while at the western end, the Coomaraswamy Hall holds exhibitions of Indian crafts and talks by scholars. Low marble steps lead to galleries on the first and second floors. The first floor has collections of miniature paintings, decorative art, artefacts from Nepal and Tibet, a maritime history section, and the modern, climate-controlled Premchand Roychand Gallery for hosting exhibitions. The second floor displays European paintings, Far Eastern art, and arms and armour.

DELHI

Qutb Minar

Delhi's towering identity

The stupendous Qutb Minar and Quwwatul Islam Mosque are synonymous with the establishment of Muslim rule in India

State and city:
New Delhi (13 km
from city centre)

Convenient access:
Road to Qutb complex,
air, rail to New Delhi

Accommodation:
Budget to luxury

Best season:
November to March

Also worth seeing:
Jamali Kamali's
mosque and tomb,
Adham Khan's tomb,
stepwells, Dargah
Qutb Sahib, all in
Mehrauli village

*Above: Detail of the
fluted façade; the
calligraphy includes
inscriptions in
Persian and
Devanagari.*
*Bottom: The pillars of
the mosque were
taken from Hindu
temples.*
*Facing page:
Whereas the lowest
storey of the Minar
alternates angular
and circular flutings,
the second and third
storeys display only
circular and angular
flutings, respectively.
The upper storeys
are liberally endowed
with marble. A
cupola which
crowned the top
originally fell
down during an
earthquake. Though
it was replaced by a
new one in the 19th
century by a British
officer, it wasn't
found to be
aesthetically
congruous and
was subsequently
removed.*

They say if you can encircle your arms around the ageless iron pillar standing in the courtyard of the Quwwatul Islam Mosque, whatever one wishes will be granted. Dedicated to God Vishnu, it is a remarkable pillar of uncertain origin, its metal virtually rust free 16 centuries after being installed. However, some 100 yards from it stands another pillar whose astounding proportions and demeanour reduces the Preserver's standard to a non-entity. The Qutb Minar is over 14 metres wide at its base, and even at its full height of 73 metres, its tapered width of 2.7 metres is about three times thicker than that of the iron pillar's base. Ibn Batuta, the 14th century Arab traveller declared it as 'one of the wonders of the world which has no parallel in the lands of Islam'. Today, despite Delhi's magnificent and varied heritage, it identifies with the city like no other monument.

The 'shadow of God' falls over the dusty plains

The Qutb rose in the closing years of the 12th century, when the dust in the wake of the clash for North India between the Afghan invader Muhammad Ghori and the incumbent ruler Prithviraj Chauhan had settled. The battle was to be one of the biggest turning points in Indian history for with the defeat of Chauhan, Muslim rule was established for the next 600 years. Though the victorious Ghori

returned to Afghanistan, he left his able and trusted commander Qutbuddin Aibak to govern the territory. Aibak declared himself Sultan—the first ruler of the Delhi Sultanate—and sourcing material from existing temples, lost no time in commissioning a congregational mosque deemed vital for sending the message that the new religious and political force was here to stay. The Mosque, fittingly called Quwwatul Islam (Might of Islam), bears the seal of the new order in its design of colonnaded cloisters enclosing a large rectangular courtyard, and an arched screen embellished with calligraphy and floral forms in front of the prayer chamber. The screen, handiwork of local craftsmen, is a manifestation of both their tentative attempts at grasping the new concept of the arch as well as their mastery of stonework, a long established tradition in the country.

If the Mosque set the footprint of Islam, then the Minar (tower), following soon thereafter, cast the 'shadow of God'. Apart from symbolising the 'pole and axis and thus the pivot of Justice, Sovereignty and of the Faith', it was a minaret for the Mosque from where the call to prayer was sounded, and a watchtower which provided a view stretching for kilometres over the dusty plains. Aibak began its construction but was only able to complete the first storey graced with alternating semi-circular and angular flutings. His successor, Shamsuddin Iltutmish, added three more storeys, continuing the inward incline of the base. The Qutb's length is punctuated with projecting balconies lavished with lace-like carving of supporting brackets, fine calligraphy and honeycombed niches. Within, 379 steps slowly spiral to the summit.

Alauddin's additions

Reflective of increasing Muslim following, Iltutmish enlarged the Mosque. For his own tomb built in 1235 in the Qutb complex, new building material was quarried. Its rich interiors of stonewall panels elaborately hewn with Quranic

verses belie the plain exteriors. The latter was a new theme, which was to steadily become more prevalent, especially with the Mughals, ultimately, the concept and imagery of eternal paradise as a reward for the true believer in the Day of Judgment was to find its most dazzling expression in the Taj Mahal.

The 'true arch' materialises in Indian Islamic construction on Sultan Balban's (1266-86) tomb near the Qutb and confidently graces succeeding monuments. Sultan Alauddin Khalji, who ascended the throne in 1296, doubled the area of the Mosque and commissioned additional edifices at some distance from the complex. Among his buildings is the beautiful Alai Darwaza, built in 1311. A gateway to the Quwwatul Islam Mosque, its pleasing proportions display a contrasting play of white marble bands on red sandstone, fine fretted screens fitted in the windows, and arches edged with tiny carved lotus-buds. In his desire to leave a legacy more emphatic than any preceding Sultan, the ambitious Alauddin laid the foundations of the Alai Minar, north of the Qutb. He died before the building got beyond the first storey and with him died his dream of a tower that was planned to be twice as tall as the Qutb.

The residence of the President

Rashtrapati Bhawan is the centrepiece of Lutyens' Delhi

DELHI

Rashtrapati Bhawan

State and capital:
New Delhi

Convenient access:
Road, air, rail to Delhi

Accommodation:
Budget to luxury

Best season:
November to March
(interior closed to
public, Mughal
Gardens open
February to March)

Also worth seeing:
India Gate, Jantar
Mantar, Purana Qila
(Old Fort)

*Above left: Ashoka
Hall, built as the state
ballroom, has a
ceiling painted in
Persian style.*

*Above right: Portraits
of past Presidents
line the walls of the
Banquet Hall.*

*Facing page:
Rashtrapati Bhawan
has 340 rooms. The
dome is more than
double the height of
the building. Rising
from the centre of
the forecourt is the
Jaipur Column,
crowned with a glass
star over a bronze
lotus.*

At the height of its power, the British Empire extended over a quarter of the earth's land surface and India was its most prestigious possession, the Jewel in the Crown. It was in India that Victoria was proclaimed Queen-Empress in 1877, and the idea of imperialism was epitomised in the British Raj. It was in this context that palatial homes were built for the Viceroy and the governors of various provinces. Primarily an expression of political supremacy in terms of size and grandeur, these mansions were also to serve the function of family homes. No doubt, the grandest of them all was to be the Viceroy's House built in New Delhi, the new capital of the British Indian Empire.

The capital moves to Delhi

Lord Hardinge, the recently appointed Viceroy, supervised the grandiose Coronation Durbar held in 1911 in Delhi to honour King George V and Queen Mary, the first British monarchs visiting India. Here, King George announced the decision to transfer the seat of government from Calcutta to 'the ancient capital of Delhi'. Hardinge actively supported the move as he saw Delhi as a 'physical symbol of Indian nationalism ... inspired by Western ideals'. In reality, he was the founder of the new capital, though today, the term Lutyens' Delhi bestows this honour to the English architect who designed the Viceroy's House (or Government House) and planned the new city around it. Edwin Landseer Lutyens was partnered by Herbert Baker, acclaimed for his work in the South African capital of Pretoria. Both

architects were, at heart, 'men representing the colonial view of the world'. Of the principal buildings of the capital, the Viceroy's House (later called Rashtrapati Bhawan, or President's House, after the swearing in of the first Indian President in 1950) was the work of Lutyens, while Baker designed the Secretariat buildings (North and South Block), and Parliament House.

Described as an arrogant, cultural chauvinist, Lutyens was highly critical of the indigenous architecture he saw. He ignored his brief, which was to create a building that would harmoniously link both western and Indian traditions, and designed his magnum opus as distinctly imperialistic, with concessional traces of Indian motifs. Rashtrapati Bhawan stands atop Raisina Hill, aloof and domineering, the official home since Indian independence to, ironically, the head of the world's largest democracy. The two major Secretariat blocks and Parliament House, all designed by Baker, look almost subserviently up a steep gradient that flattens out before the ornate iron gates leading to the building.

The Indo-Saracenic style

The massive dome dominates all, a gesture borrowed from the Sanchi stupa, though Lutyens never really acknowledged this. It is known as 'the lord sahib's dome' and highlights the central Durbar Hall it covers, witness to several historically significant events. The wide central façade below is a colonnade of Tuscan pillars, its central section approached by a sweeping flight of steps from a ceremonial forecourt.

Lutyens incorporated several Indian decorative elements in the design of the red and cream stone building: inverted bells, the lotus bud, *chhajjas* (deep cornices) and *chhattris* (umbrella-like small pavilions), the *jaali* (grill), and elephants and snakes. This mix, conceived by him as the Delhi Order, is also referred to as the Indo-Saracenic style. Walls adorned with rare paintings, exquisite carpets, frescoed ceilings, glittering chandeliers, sweeping staircases, furniture and other accessories, designed by Lutyens himself, and a retinue of red-and-gold-liveried attendants-in-waiting for state guests, complete the picture of the original viceregal palace, likened variously to the Acropolis and the Parthenon, and larger than Buckingham Palace. Eleven Indian Presidents have lived in it, their diverse personalities and attributes adding to the rich history of Rashtrapati Bhawan. Its Mughal Garden, lavishly planted with exotic flowers, is thrown open to the public once a year.

The legend of Lutyens lives on through the identification of the central part of New Delhi as Lutyens Bungalow Zone. In fact, of the several old colonial mansions meant as residences for the *burra* sahibs (higher officers of government), that exist on sprawling plots in this part of the city. Only four were designed by Lutyens, which are within the President's Estate. The rest were the work of other prominent English architects, including Herbert Baker.

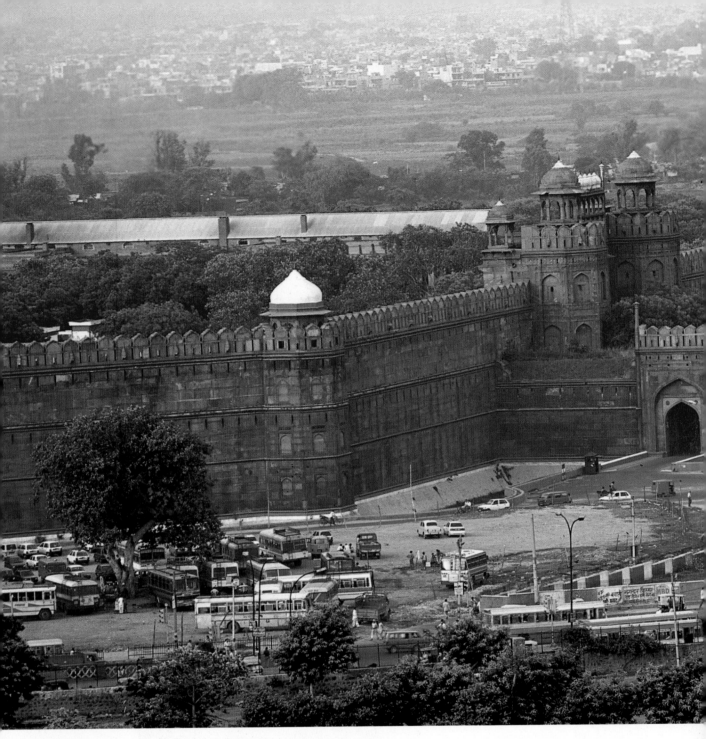

The blushing fort of opulence

The Red Fort was the seat of Mughal authority over India

DELHI

Red Fort

State and city: Delhi

Convenient access:
Road, air, rail to Delhi

Accommodation:
Budget to luxury

Best season:
November to March

Also worth seeing:
Jama Masjid, Chandni
Chowk

In design it resembled a palace fortress, like the Alhambra in Spain, but in style and ornamentation, it perhaps matched the Palace of Versailles in France. Shah Jahan named his fort Qila-i-Mubarak (The Auspicious Citadel). Together with the adjoining Salim-garh Fort, it occupied an area of 48 hectares on the banks of the Yamuna River that once flowed past its walls. Over time, it came to be known as the Red Fort because of its surrounding red sandstone walls.

Delhi's Red Fort was built in 1648 and served as a stage for what was, at the time, one of the richest and most sophisticated courts in the world. At the head of, and part thereof, the larger city of Shahjahanabad, the fortress, with its palaces, royal meeting halls, bazaars and gardens was a city by itself. Unlike the earlier Mughal capital at Agra, it was a planned city, conceptualised by Emperor Shah Jahan, fifth in the dynasty of the great Mughals, who took a personal interest in its construction.

The Fort has two main gates. The Emperor and his retinue used the Lahore Gate, and soldiers and the imperial staff used the Delhi Gate. Within it are many buildings that speak of the Fort's former glory, even though successive invaders ransacked them after the decline of the Mughal Empire. The Chatta Chowk or Meena Bazaar, which now accommodates a souvenir market, housed the palace bazaar. The Naqqar Khana (Drum House) announced the passage of time five times a day and musicians played from the gallery above during state

The Khas Mahal housed the Emperor's private apartments, with a special robe room. It is noted for its marble-latticed screens and wall carvings, one of which depicts the scales of justice. Adjoining this is a tower balcony from where the Emperor appeared daily before his subjects to prove that he was alive and well. The marble-floored *hamaams* (royal baths) had three enclosures, one each for hot, cold and scented rose water.

The Peacock Throne

The Diwan-i-Khaas (Hall of Private Audience), most fabulous of all the pavilions, was where the Emperor received special guests and conferred with his ministers. This pillared hall, in white marble, was heavily ornamented with pietra dura work, much of which still remains. On the empty marble dais in the centre stood the legendary Peacock Throne, with its pillars and crown in the shape of two peacocks crafted in pure gold, and studded with sapphires, rubies, pearls, diamonds and emeralds. This exquisite work of art, which took seven years to make, was dismantled by the Persian invader Nadir Shah in 1739 and carried away as booty. Emperor Aurangzeb added the Moti Masjid (Pearl Mosque) to the Fort's many buildings in 1659. But though its arches and domes are built in the Mughal style, it lacks the architectural refinement of the Jama Masjid nearby. Yet, it displays fine carvings and a floor inlaid with a prayer mat design.

The Red Fort is a World Heritage Site and a national monument—from the ramparts above the Lahore Gate, the Prime Minister of India addresses the nation on Independence Day.

Bottom: The original silver ceiling of the Diwan-i-Khaas, embedded with precious stones, was looted by the Marathas in 1760. Only the inscription above the dais stands witness to the pavilion's splendour: 'If there be a paradise on earth, it is this, it is this, it is this.' **Left:** The Red Fort is a World Heritage Site and a National Monument—from the ramparts above the Lahore Gate the Prime Minister of India addresses the nation on Independence Day.

functions and festivals. Now it houses a martial museum, noted for its collection of firearms. The Diwan-i-Aam (Hall of Public Audience) is a 60-pillared sandstone hall where the Emperor heard petitions from his subjects and dispensed justice. In the centre is the throne balcony, built in white marble with pietra dura inlay decorations. Beneath it sat the Emperor, with his Chief Minister sitting on a lower white marble bench to receive petitions. The wall behind has panels painted with floral and bird motifs.

The main palaces are the Mumtaz Mahal, Rang Mahal and Khas Mahal. The Mumtaz Mahal now contains a museum while the Rang Mahal offers a glimpse of former luxury in its marble wall carvings, traces of gilding on the ceiling, and a carved marble pool with a fountain shaped like a lotus.

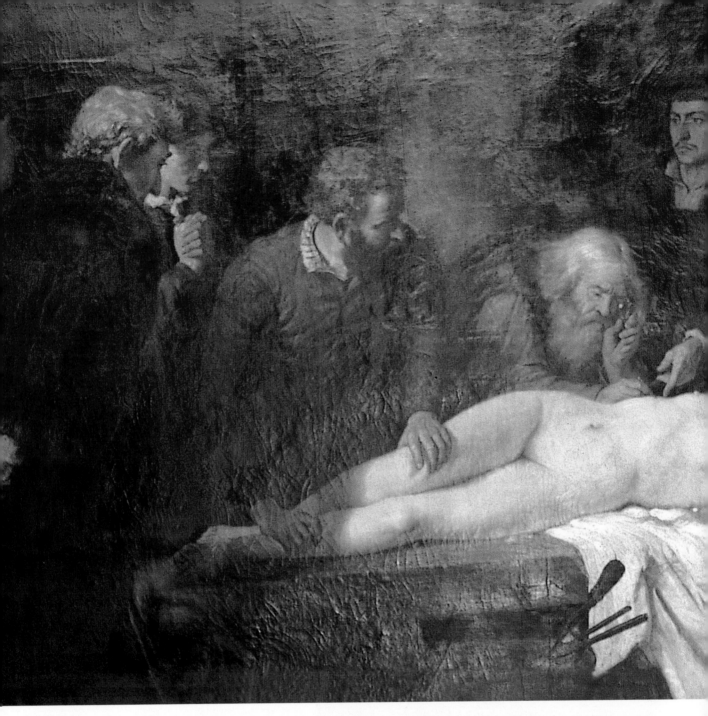

A mammoth art collection

Hyderabad's Salar Jung Museum showcases the passion of three generations

Hyderabad

Bay of
Bengal

State and capital:
Andhra Pradesh,
Hyderabad

Convenient access:
Road, air, rail to
Hyderabad

Accommodation:
Budget to luxury

Best season:
November to March

Also worth seeing:
Charminar, Churi
Bazaar, Jama Masjid

One of the largest one-man art collections in the world was the culmination of the personal interest and enterprise of three generations of art aficionados, the last being Abdul Kasim Mir Yusuf Ali Khan, more popularly known as Salar Jung III. His collection of over 35,000 items, including numerous priceless pieces and a separate library, is housed in a museum in Hyderabad, Andhra Pradesh.

Mir Yusuf Ali Khan, born in 1889 in Pune, was the last descendant of an immensely powerful Hyderabad family, the Salar Jungs. By the nineteenth century they had assumed such importance that five of the family's members served as Prime Ministers to successive Nizams of Hyderabad. Mir Yusuf Ali Khan passionately loved and collected art and anti-ques. This passion started young as he grew up amongst the many priceless pieces acquired by his father, Nawab Mir Laiq Ali Khan Salar Jung II and his grandfather, Nawab Mir Turab Ali Khan, Sir Salar Jung I. Their acquisitions laid the foundation for his collection.

Mir Laiq Ali Khan, Prime Minister from 1884 to 1887, died young at 26 years of age, leaving behind his infant son Mir Yusuf Ali Khan. Like his father, Mir Yusuf Ali Khan became Prime Minister in 1912, but relinquished the post in 1914 following a difference of opinion with the Nizam. Thereafter, he devoted his life to his collection. Art dealers constantly thronged his palace, his agents monitored the availability of treasures worldwide, and he personally toured Europe and West Asia in search of fine artefacts. In love with his collec-

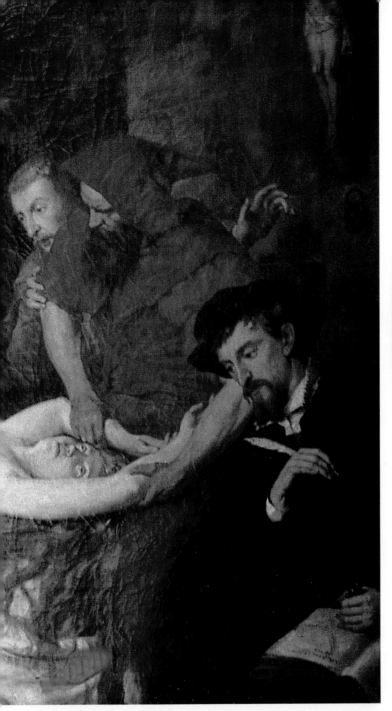

school, Italian landscapes and works by Munich painters. With the *Veiled Rebecca*—purchased by Mir Turab Ali Khan in Rome, in 1876—as the centrepiece, statues from Italy, France and England form a sizable bulk of the collection. *Mephistopheles and Margaretta*, a figure carved from a single wooden log, is outstanding. Larger than life, it gives life to Goethe's *Faust*, depicting a man and a woman on the two faces of the carving, one good, and the other evil. The *Mother and Child*, *Bacchus* and *Daphne* are other invaluable pieces. The glass section is dominated by vases of Serves porcelain. Perfume bottles, sugar bowls, decanters and wine glasses represent English glass and Bohemian crystal. Mirrors, furniture, arms of various kinds, heavily embroidered cloth, jewellery are also part of the general exhibits.

The Library houses over 8000 manuscripts and 14,000 books in the Arabic, Persian and Turkish and over 30,000 in English. This collection, although begun in 1665, was mainly developed by Mir Turab Ali Khan and continued by his son and grandson.

Ideally, at least three days are required to enjoy the museum at leisure, but a quick visit is vastly informative as well.

Above: Amongst the Museum's priceless displays are Mughal Emperor Aurangzeb's sword, daggers belonging to Queen Noor Jahan, Emperor Jahangir and Shah Jahan. The toy collection includes pieces from European and Asian countries. Especially interesting is the Clock Room which houses some 300 antique clocks.
Left: Stigmata Diabolicum *by the Dutch painter Van der Haeghen.* The Museum houses an extensive collection of European oils and water colours from the 19th century.

tions, Mir Yusuf Ali Khan died a bachelor in 1949. The palace received his last purchase, a set of ivory chairs said to have belonged to Tipu Sultan of Mysore, after his death. In the absence of direct descendants, his treasured accumulations were eventually housed in the Salar Jung Museum, which was specially established for this purpose in 1951 at Diwan Deodhi, Salar Jung III's residential palace. In 1968, the Museum and Library were transferred to the present building in central Hyderabad.

The *Veiled Rebecca* is the centrepiece amongst European statues

The Museum's repertoire is divided into four main sections, Indian, Middle-Eastern, Far Eastern and European Art, with a separate Children's section, and one devoted to the Salar Jung family. Each is spilt according to type. The Indian hoard includes stone sculptures, bronzes, textiles, carvings, paintings, metal ware, and arms and armour. The Far Eastern aggregation boasts Sino-Japanese and Chinese artefacts that include porcelain, bronze, enamel and lacquer ware, embroidery, paintings, wood and inlay work. Jars from the Ming Dynasty and Buddha figures from the 17th and 18th centuries are highlights of this display. The European collection, considered amongst the best in the country, comprises oil and water colours, ivory and glass objects, wood carvings, enamel ware, clocks and sundry other items. The paintings constitute mainly 19th century British, the traditional French

Sanchi's crowning glory

The Great Stupa represents an upturned alms bowl of Buddhist monks

MADHYA PRADESH

Bhopal • Sanchi

State and capital:
Madhya Pradesh,
Bhopal (46 km)

Convenient access:
Road to Sanchi, air,
rail to Bhopal

Accommodation:
Budget to mid-range
at Sanchi, luxury in
Bhopal

Best season:
November to March

Also worth seeing:
Bhimbetka caves,
Udaygiri, Udayapur

*Below: The carvings
on the* toranas,
*venerating the
Buddha, depicted
recognisable images
from the ordinary life
of the worshipper's
world, making it easy
to comprehend the
message they
carried.*

The Great Stupa of Sanchi, in Madhya Pradesh, dating to the third-second century BC, is India's finest monument personifying the philosophy of Buddhism—its simplicity and withdrawal, yet connectivity with daily life. The sacred spot where the stupa stands atop a hill actually contains several other stupas, temples and monasteries that continued to be built up to the seventh century. None is, however, as well preserved as the Great Stupa, the most magnificent of them all, whose hemispherical dome, 37 metres in diameter, is symbolically likened to the upturned alms bowl used by Buddhist monks. At its core is the original small brick stupa, built by Emperor Ashoka who, after his conversion to Buddhism, enshrined surviving Buddhist relics in these burial mounds in principal towns of his empire. Vidisha, home of Ashoka's wife, is located nearby. The subsequent building and embellishment of Sanchi owes much to the patronage of wealthy merchants from Vidisha.

The stupa saw its transformation under the Sunga rulers when there was a great revival of the arts, and their successors, the Satavahanas, in the middle of the first century BC. The present stone monument covers the original mound and, rising to a height of 16 metres, is almost double its size. Two of the smaller ones contain the relics of the Master's two favourite disciples, who later became teachers. As Buddhism declined in India, so did Sanchi, until an English army officer discovered the stupa in 1818. Subsequently ravaged by treasure seekers, it was extensively restored by the Archaeological Survey of India only in 1912.

Carvings of Buddha and other beings

Sited in peaceful undulating country surrounded by green fields, Sanchi's crowning glory are the four huge, carved stone *toranas* (gateways) located at the cardinal points of the Great Stupa. These ornamental entrances, each of which had its own donor, served more than one purpose. They led to the two circumambulatory paths around the stupa, past statues of meditating Buddhas looking outwards. In their magnificence the entranceways also humbled the worshipper into acknowledging the greatness of the founder and his faith.

Rising to a height of 8.5 metres, the four gateways consist of three separate, horizontal cross beams, carved as if scrolled at the ends, and supported on square pillars crowned by lions, elephants and fat dwarfs. All four are a sculptural feast for the eyes, but the most glorious and best preserved is the one facing north. Various episodes from the *Jataka* tales, animals and mythological figures, horse riders and celestial beings are shown in relief on the *toranas*. The Buddha is

shown symbolically through iconic motifs when events from his historical life are depicted. In stories of his earlier incarnations, he is shown in human form. A particularly sensuous carving entitled *Salabhanjika* depicts a voluptuous tree nymph, upholding an architrave of the east gateway, as she languidly reclines under a mango tree.

A balustrade encloses both the ambulatories. A double stairway leads up to the higher pathway, which forms a narrow terrace around the dome. Elaborate vegetal and faunal motifs, as also the names of donors, decorate the posts and railings of the balustrade. What is remarkable about its construction is its perfect replication in stone or wooden form and technique.

The ruins of monasteries, temples and smaller stupas surround the Great Stupa. Perhaps the temple ruin on the eastern side is that of the earliest extant stone temple in India. The broken shaft of an Ashokan pillar, with a four-headed lion capital, lies near the southern gateway, with an inscription warning Buddhist monks and nuns not to create schisms among followers of the faith.

There is an archaeological museum in the complex of this World Heritage Site, displaying sculptural pieces broken off from the original structures. Nothing, however, can evoke the beauty of the Great Stupa itself, as it slowly comes into view when you drive in to Sanchi, its vast dome crowned with a triple umbrella in the centre of a square railing enclosure, a symbol of royalty.

Above: *Once covered in white lime plaster, the Great Stupa's nomenclature does not derive from its size, which is modest compared to similar structures in Asia, but by its significance to Buddhists. The inner circumambulatory balustrade is remarkable for its replication in stone of wooden form and technique.*

Colours of tradition and change

The painted homes of Shekhawati were a measure of their owners' wealth

RAJASTHAN

Shekhawati •
• Jaipur

State and capital:
Rajasthan, Jaipur (185
km from Jhunjhunu)

Convenient access:
Road to Shekhawati,
air to Jaipur, rail to
Jaipur and other
Shekhawati towns

Accommodation:
Budget to high-end in
main towns

Best season:
November to March

Also worth seeing:
Nawalgarh, Dunlodh,
Mukungarh and
Mandawa Forts

Lying between Jaipur and Bikaner, the arid Shekhawati region is dotted with hundreds of *havelis* (mansions) of the enterprising Marwari community of Rajasthan. Made in the 18th, 19th and early 20th centuries, many of these are now uncared for, unlived in and left under lock and key in the hands of caretakers. But described on them, nevertheless, is a legacy that has led the entire region to be acclaimed as an art gallery.

Merchants outdo each other

Spanning some 30,000 square kilometres, Shekhawati derives its name from the Rajput Kachhwaha chieftain Rao Shekha, whose descendants were vassals of Jaipur. At that time, land trade routes across India connecting to the seaports of Gujarat were losing their importance to the newly established British ports of Calcutta (Kolkata) and Bombay (Mumbai). Astute and instinctive businessmen

as they were, the Marwari traders, lost no time in migrating to the newly emerging commercial centres of India, where they amassed huge fortunes. Despite having moved on from nondescript Shekhawati, they channelled back some of this wealth to their hometowns. Whereas a part of it went into philanthropic causes like educational institutions, temples, wells and hospitals, much went into building lavish personal mansions which publicly announced their dizzying financial ascendancy. Though architecturally, too, the structures are worth beholding, they are undoubtedly most remarkable for the fabulously intricate frescoes that adorn their walls.

New elements are introduced

The frescoes, painted by craftsmen called *chiteras*, are predominantly in shades derived from natural pigments: *kaajal* (lamp soot) for

black, *safeda* (lime) for white, *harabhata* (terra verte) for green, *neel* (indigo) for blue, *geru* (red stone powder) for red and maroon, *kesar* (saffron) for orange and *pevri* (yellow clay) for yellow ochre. These colours, mixed in lime water and subsequently beaten into plaster, remained true and vivid for long. Mythological and religious themes, local legends, flora and fauna, sports like hunting and wrestling, portraits of the owners and scenes of every-day life prevail in the earlier paintings (1830-1900 AD). Later, new elements and motifs crept in with the influence of British rule and of changes brought forth by industrial and technological advancement. Accordingly there was the inclusion of English men and women, cars, trains, balloons, telephones and ladies with gramophones, and of leaders of the Indian national movement like Jawaharlal Nehru. The end result was a charmingly hybrid content. The process of execution also became easier. Earlier, natural dyes had demanded a technique whereby only a part of the wall at a time was plastered and the design drawn and painted on the yet damp last layer, which consisted of fine and filtered lime dust. Now, synthetic dyes from Germany and England, designed to be painted on dry plaster, meant that the *chitera* did not need to paint hurriedly before the plaster dried up.

Elephants vie with trains

Beautiful examples of Indian themes can be seen in the Krishna paintings at Nawalgarh's exquisite Murarka Haveli; Indra riding an elephant and Shiva on his Bull at the Hanuman Prasad Goenka

Haveli in Mandawa; Krishna with his milkmaids at Mohanlal Ishwardas Haveli, and the predominantly blue Islamic floral motifs at the Narudin Farooqi Haveli, both in Jhunjhunu. The mixed depictions are all over. One fresco in a home near Nawalgarh Fort features elephants, horses and camels, another has a steam locomotive. The fact that the latter is a constantly recurring subject is evidence of how strongly trains had caught the imagination of Indians: the Khedwal Bhawan has a woman on a swing celebrating the Teej festival while a train crosses a bridge; Mandawa's Murmuria Haveli has a train at a crowded level crossing with a crow flying overhead; and the Tibrewal Haveli in Jhunjhunu shows a goods train laden with livestock cross a passenger train. Amongst everyday scenes is the moustache-stroking Maharaja at the Saraf home in

Mandawa and the grandmother having her hair groomed at the Shyamji Sharaf Haveli, in the small village of Parasrampuria, where some of the preserved paintings are ensconced. Eye-catching European scenes show British men holding guns at Fatehpur's Singhania Haveli, and an Englishwoman in polished boots holding a parasol and a frieze of Europeans in a car at the Sharaf Haveli. Foreign subjects even pervaded Dunlodh's Satyanarayan Temple built by the Goenka family. A big fresco on its walls portrays British men and women on bicycles and cars and the inevitable long train passing by telegraph wires. These are accompanied by portrayals of a slower, more graceful aristocratic life: a nobleman smells flowers or reads, a turbaned man holds a bird and a woman admires herself in the mirror.

Top: *A painting from the Bansidhar Newatia Haveli in Mandawa reflects the new influences and technology that had begun to pervade upper class Indian society in the early 20th century.*
Above: *Arched entrance façade of a haveli typically leads to an open courtyard around which are rooms and storeys in a four-sided plan. Elaborately decorated elephants were commonly painted on the outer walls.*
Facing page: *Fresco from the Chaudhari Haveli in Fatehpur of wrestling and other manly sports.*

Shrine on the shore

The granite temples of Mamallapuram marked the zenith
of Pallava art

State and capital:
Tamil Nadu, Chennai
(58 km)

Convenient access:
Road to
Mamallapuram, air,
rail to Chennai

Accommodation:
Budget to mid-range
at beach resorts

Best season:
December to February

Also worth seeing:
Dakshina Chitra Folk
Museum, 50 km from
Chennai, Temple town
of Tiruvannamalai,
Pondicherry

*Top: A bas relief
panel shows the
Goddess Durga
shooting down a
buffalo demon.*
*Facing page: The
Shore Temple has
two spires: the long
one over the main
shrine devoted to
Shiva and the
short one over
the subsidiary
Vishnu shrine.*

Mamallapuram (formerly
known as Mahabali-
puram) in Tamil Nadu
was once the main seaport of the
Pallava kings, who ruled the region
from the sixth to the ninth centuries
AD. King Rajasimhavarman built
the complex of rock-cut caves
and pavilions, bas-relief sculptures,
and pagoda-style temples, on the
edge of the sea in the seventh
century. Of the original series of
pagodas, which have since been
eroded by the sea, only the present
Shore Temple remains intact. In
2004, when a tsunami struck
Tamil Nadu, the ruins of the other
temples were dramatically revealed
from the sea. The prototype for
South Indian temple architecture,
Mamallapuram's style also influenced the temple art of
Cambodia and Indonesia. It is now
a UNESCO World Heritage Site.

The Shore Temple was the first
Pallava temple to be built from
blocks of granite (as opposed to the
earlier structures cut from rock),
giving its sculptors greater freedom
in design and ornamentation.
Another innovative feature is the
form of the *shikhara* (spire) over the
shrine, here a tiered, elongated
structure rather than a rounded
form. The Temple's unusual plan
has it poised on the rocky shoreline
extending on to the sea. To catch
the first rays of the sun at dawn, the
Shiva shrine faces east, but the
gateway, courtyard and the main
hall are located behind the sanctum.
Interconnected cisterns around
the building allowed sea water to
enter the complex and magically
transform it into a water shrine.
Being a seafaring people, the
Pallavas regularly conducted rituals

of water worship. The Vishnu
temple faces inland.

The world's largest bas-relief
Carved on the face of two massive
rocks, *Arjuna's Penance* also referred
to as the *Descent of the Ganga* depicts
the ascetic Bhagirath, beseeching
the Ganga River to descend to
earth. Measuring 27 metres by nine
metres, it is the world's largest bas-
relief. To portray the flowing river
holes were drilled into a natural cleft
in the rocks, through which water
spouted. A series of mythological
scenes as well as those from everyday life are also displayed. The most
famous of the figures is that of the
warrior Arjuna, standing on one leg
in penance, and praying to Shiva
for a divine weapon to defeat his
enemies. Scattered around the area
are various religious sites, a cave
with three empty shrines, the Isvara
Temple, standing like a lighthouse
on the highest point, and the *rathas*
and ten *mandapas* (pillared halls),
carved out from the exterior,
inwards. The pillars are decorated
with sculptures of gods, goddesses
and mythological figures.

The *rathas* are eight monolithic,
rock-cut temples, faithful reproduc-
tions of original prototypes of
wooden chariots, right down to
the grain of the wood on stone.
Dharmaraja Ratha, the largest has
a square hall topped by a vaulted
roof. Five of the southern *rathas*
have been excavated from top to
bottom, and are named after the
Pandava brothers—Nakula and
Sahadeva have the same shrine—
and their wife Draupadi, from the
epic *Mahabharata*. The Draupadi
Ratha is the smallest, resembling a
thatched hut balanced on the back
of lions and elephants. It was
probably a replica of a movable
village shrine.

Monolith of a Jain saint

The Gomateswara statue is carved out of a single granite slab

In the small town of Sravanabelagola (Monk of the White Pond) stands a massive image in stone of the Jain ascetic Gomateswara, an object of reverence and homage to millions who follow the faith. Gomateswara was said to be the son of King Vrishabhadeva, the first Jain *tirthankara*, also known as Adinatha. (The Jain religion has a pantheon of 24 saints known as *tirthankaras*, literally meaning ford-makers). When his father abdicated the throne, the young prince, known as Bahubali, fought tooth and nail against his brother to acquire the kingdom. But once victorious, he had a vision of the meaninglessness behind the war, and following the footsteps of his father, renounced everything, spending his remaining days in deep meditation.

The making of Bahubali

Changragupta Maurya, one of India's greatest emperors, visited Sravanabelagola in the third century BC. Influenced by the teachings of his guru Bhadrabahu Swami, Jainism spread through South India, finding staunch followers in the next ruling dynasty as well. It was during the reign of the Ganga ruler Rachamalla II that the magnificent statue of Gomateswara was commissioned, and the order carried out by the sculptor Aristenemi, who completed it in 981 AD. It was called Gommata or the Handsome One.

The gigantic figure soars from the summit of the Indragiri Hill. A climb of 614 steps leads from the top of the acclivity to the toes of the 17 metre-high Gomateswara. Said to be one of the largest freestanding rock sculpture carved out of a single slab of granite in the world, it can be seen from 25 kilometres away. His face is passive and serene, while on the legs are depicted the creepers that entwined themselves around him as he stayed immersed in contemplation in the yogic pose.

Rituals of worship

Once every 12 years is the occasion for the Mahamastakabhisheka, an 11 day-long festival during which an estimated three quarters of the Jain population of the world is said to visit and participate in the ceremonies. According to legend, Chamundaraya, the Commander-in-Chief of the Ganga Dynasty, first initiated the consecration of Gomateswara. However, as he performed the ceremony with an air of vanity, no matter what the quantity of liquids poured from the top, they would not pass the navel. It was only after a celestial nymph disguised as an old woman performed the task successfully, that Chamundaraya realised his mistake, and with devotion and humility was able to perform the ritual. Starting at the bottom, worshippers stand respectfully, each carrying his or her personal offering of water or coconut water. Inching up to the top of the statue on makeshift scaffolding takes hours, and once there, the devotee pours the contents from his urn, thereby anointing the figure himself. The air is charged with chanting, which reaches a crescendo as the time of the final anointing approaches. After that, the priests pour out large quantities of water, coconut water, yoghurt, ghee, sugarcane juice, sandalwood, milk, liquid saffron, precious stones and red vermillion from huge urns and bowls on top of the statue, all to the accompaniment of drums and the frenzied cheering of the gathered masses below, who by now are as drenched and colourful as Bahubali himself. The final anointing is done with flowers and all those present are allowed to pick them from where they lie scattered next to Gomateswara's feet. Considered holy, these are supposed to bring luck and protection. The next Mahamastakabhisheka will take place in 2017.

State and capital:
Karnataka, Bengaluru (158 km)

Convenient access:
Road to Sravanabelagola, air to Bengaluru, rail to Hassan

Accommodation:
Budget

Best season:
November to February

Also worth seeing:
Temples of Belur and Halebid, 85 km NW

Top: Devotees praying at the foot of the Gomateswara statue.

Facing page: Jain masters are typically depicted in a nude state. Standing meditation is also a unique Jain practice.

The stepwells of Gujarat are more than just water reservoirs

Elaborate architecture and impeccable engineering made them perfect community areas

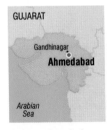

GUJARAT

Gandhinagar

Ahmedabad

Arabian Sea

State and capital:
Gujarat, Gandhinagar

Convenient access:
Road, air, rail to
Ahmedabad (Dada
Harir Vav), then road
to Adalaj, and Patan
(Rani ni Vav)

Accommodation:
Budget to high-end (in
Ahmedabad)

Best season:
November to March

Also worth seeing:
Sabarmati Ashram,
Siddi Saiyad Mosque,
Ambarpur Vav, Sarkhej

The *vavs* (stepwells) of western Indian are a fantastic example of subterranean architecture and engineering skills. Nowhere except in arid Gujarat and Rajasthan, where water was available only at great depths, did these unusual building types take shape. Though the original patrons were Hindus, the Muslims later developed the art form. Apart from serving an essential purpose stepwells fulfilled the social needs of the community in a gloriously artistic environment, serving as shrines, sanctuaries and community spaces. Often they were named after the deity who was enshrined within, or after the place or patron who built them. The cool ambience created in their cavernous interiors was ideal for formal ceremonies and informal gatherings.

In the dry heat of Gujarat, building these wells was considered an act of charity. Most villages had one, however small, but of these just a handful survive. The earliest

examples date to before the sixth century AD but most of the extant and most elaborate belong to a later period, around the 11th century.

Typically, the wells have three parts: the entrance pavilion at the ground level, the steps, and the tank at the bottom. The variety of both sculptural and architectural treatment often equalled that of temple art, with an abundance of columns, brackets, beams and wall niches encrusted with ornamentation. Though the wells themselves may no longer be in use, they still provide welcome cool and shade, particularly for the women in nearby settlements, as they create a haven of peace and spiritual solace from the routine of everyday life. As soft light filters down to the depths, it illuminates the figures of deities, birds, plants and flowers in the pavilions that break the descent to the water, at the well shaft and tank level itself.

Two wells owe their existence to aristocratic ladies

Seventeen kilometres north of Ahmedabad is one of the most impressive of Gujarat's stepwells. Located at Adalaj, after which it is named, its entrance is marked by two pyramidical roofed structures. Pillared galleries surround the wide flight of steps descending to the well opening at a depth of 30 metres, and are connected all around at each of the five levels by narrow passageways supported by beams and columns. Rudabai, wife of a local Hindu chieftain, who was killed by the Muslim Sultan Mahmud Beghara, built the well. According to legend, the Sultan then asked Rudabai to marry him but to stall him she begged for time to complete the well. He pursued her for 20 years and though the canopy was still to be completed, she plunged to her death in the well to save her honour, and also to appease the water deity so that it may continue replenishing the

water in the well. At Adalaj there is an intermediate tank close to the main well, with an octagonal well shaft.

Rivalling Adalaj, a larger stepwell, the 11th-century Rani ni Vav at Patan, is located 140 kilometres from Ahmedabad. Rani Udayamati, after whom it is named, was the queen of one of the most powerful kings of the Chalukya dynasty. Sumptuous stone carving fills the interior with almost 800 sculptural elements going down to a depth of 87 metres. Even the inside of the circular well is ornamented with corbelled brackets. Images of the Hindu God Vishnu intersperse with female figures suggestive of fertility or with erotic connotations, such as them being disrobed by monkeys or by themselves as scorpions climb up their thighs. Martial and other rites of passage are also depicted.

The east facing Rani ni Vav has a stepped corridor with regularly interspersed compartments and four multi-storeyed pavilions with pillars marking the descent. There are almost 400 niches in the walls sculpted with images of gods, mythological figures and decorative elements.

The Cathedral of Kolkata

St Paul's is renowned for its paintings, plaques and stained glass windows

Kolkata (earlier Calcutta) was the capital of the British Empire until it lost this distinction to Delhi, in the early 20th century. Renowned for its 18th and 19th century colonial architecture, its southern section boasted of St Paul's Cathedral along with the Victoria Memorial. St Paul's has the distinction of being Kolkata's first Anglican and the first Episcopal cathedral built in the East. Situated in the southeast corner of the Maidan (ground), it is noted for its Indo-Gothic architecture and superb stained-glass windows.

The foundation of the Cathedral was laid in 1839, largely through the efforts of Bishop Wilson, who raised most of the funds for its construction. It was designed by Major W.N. Forbes of the Bengal Engineers and consecrated in 1847. This imposing structure is 75 metres long, 25 metres wide, and ranks among the finest cathedrals in the world.

The interiors of the church offer a feast for the eyes in terms of architecture, art and historic plaques commemorating the British soldiers who gave their lives in the

the vestry, which houses a statue of Bishop Heber, one of the most eminent Bishops in the diocese of Kolkata. The statue is the work of the well-known English sculptor Chantry and once occupied place of pride at the St Paul's Cathedral in London.

The main cathedral is noted for its iron-trussed ceiling decorated with Gothic carvings. In its time it had one of the widest spans in existence. There is no typical nave and side aisle, possibly because of the weak subsoil below. The wall behind the altar is adorned with scenes from the life of St Paul, portrayed in alabaster and coloured mosaic. Above the altar are three stained-glass windows interspersed by two Florentine frescoes. The altar is decorated with paintings announcing the birth of Christ, a gift from the Bengal Chamber of Commerce. The church also possesses a silver communion service, which was a gift from Queen Victoria. To the right of the bishop's throne are two memorial windows dedicated to former bishops, including Bishop Cotton, who founded several schools in India. Below the altar is the sanctuary, where a vault contains the remains of Bishop Wilson.

Situated in the choir loft opposite the main altar is a magnificent, old-fashioned pipe organ that was built by Willis and Sons of London. The candlelit carol service on Christmas Eve at St Paul's Cathedral is a popular event in Kolkata's festive calendar, attracting visitors from all faiths. Easter service at sunrise is also an unforgettable experience as the sun's rays illuminate the stained glass, east-facing windows above the altar in a dazzling play of colour and light.

WEST BENGAL

Kolkata

Bay of Bengal

State and capital:
West Bengal, Kolkata

Convenient access:
Road, air, rail to Kolkata

Accommodation:
Budget to luxury

Best season:
November to March

Also worth seeing:
Victoria Memorial, Raj Bhawan, Indian Museum, Rajendra Mullick's Marble Palace

service of the Empire. On entering the church from the western porch, one is greeted by an elegant white marble, baptismal fort. Memorial tablets dedicated to the officers of the Bengal Lancers and Sir Henry Lawrence, who perished in the Mutiny of 1857 line the walls. On the right is a commemorative bust of the architect, Major Forbes. A staircase leads to the antiquarian library donated by Bishop Wilson, which is also noted for its magnificent stained-glass window designed by the well-known English artist, Edward Burne-Jones. The Government of India presented this in 1880 to honour Lord Mayo,

Governor-General and Viceroy, who was assassinated in 1872 in the Andaman Islands.

Memorials of soldiers and bishops

Below the bell tower are two chapels—the Jesus Chapel, decorated with paintings depicting the life of Christ, and the Chapel of Remembrance, lined with memorial tablets commemorating the heroes of World War I. A light is kept constantly burning in the latter in their memory. The commemorative plaques around the church offer interesting insights on the history of British India. Opposite the chapel is

Chariot of the Sun God

The Konark Temple is 'driven' by seven horses

ORISSA

Bhubaneshwar •
Konark

Bay of
Bengal

State and capital:

Orissa, Bhubaneshwar
(65 km)

Convenient access:

Road, air, rail to
Bhubaneshwar

Accommodation:

Budget to mid-range
in Puri

Best season:

November to March

Also worth seeing:

Puri, 60 km NE,
Bhubaneshwar,
65 km NW

Like any monument of stature, the Sun Temple of Konark comes wrapped in legends. The story goes that Samba, Krishna's son, extremely proud of his beauty, once laughed at the plain-looking Sage Narada. The quick-tempered Narada took his revenge by luring Samba to the pool where his stepmothers were bathing, and made sure that Krishna heard of this impropriety. Krishna was furious and cursed his son with leprosy. Later, when he realised that Samba had been the cunning Narada's victim, Krishna was unable to revoke his curse, and advised Samba to worship the Sun God, Surya, healer of all diseases. Samba underwent 12 years of

penance, and at last, at Surya's bidding, he bathed in the sea—some say a pond—at Konark and was cured. Delighted and grateful, Samba erected a Surya temple on the Konark beach. Now every year, on the seventh day (*saptami*) of the bright half of the Hindu month of Magha (January/February), thousands of pilgrims visit Konark for the Chandrabhaga or Magha Saptami Fair. They take a dip in the 'curative' waters of the pool near the beach, and upon sunrise participate in the ritual ceremony.

Twelve pairs of wheels

Konark derives its name from Konarka, the presiding deity of the Sun Temple. Konarka is actually a

combination of two words, *kona* (corner) and *arka* (sun). The Temple was built by King Narasimhadev I (1238-64), of the Ganga dynasty, nicknamed Langulia, or 'One with a Tail'. It is conjecturised that Narasimhadev may have had a spinal swelling and raised the shrine as a petition to Surya to relieve him of it. Whatever may have been the origins, Konark was one of the earliest centres of sun worship in India. Conceived by the architect, Sibei Samantaray, as a massive chariot, and positioned on an east-west axis following the path of the sun, the building took 16 years to complete, with the efforts of 1,200 artisans and 12,000 labourers. The Temple consists of the *deula*

Above: Four carved wheels on each side convey the idea of a chariot.

(sanctuary) and the *jagamohana* (audience hall), next to each other, and also a *natamandapa* (hall for female devotees to dance in praise of the God). Twenty-four wheels (12 pairs representing the months in a year) are carved around the base of the edifice. Eight spokes of each wheel serve as sundials; the shadows thrown by them give the precise time and divide the day into three-hour sections. Seven galloping horses representing the seven days of the week and the seven sages who govern the constellations pull the chariot carrying Surya across the sky. Three images of the Sun God are positioned to catch the rays of the sun at dawn, noon and sunset, and two sculpted lions guard the entrance. The courtyard around the temple was enclosed by walls—now disintegrated by the salinity of the environment or swallowed up by dunes—whose sides measured 264

metres by 165 metres, giving an idea of the immensity of the complex. Over the centuries, though, the sea receded, and the temple is now over three kilometres inland.

Like the temples at Khajuraho, the Konark Temple is covered with erotic sculptures. But its thousands of images, including those on the terraces between each of the three tiers of the roof, also depict deities, heavenly beauties, musicians, dancers and scenes from courtly life. A large stone slab in the northeast is carved with divinities representing the nine planets.

Black Pagoda

Konark was once a bustling port of Kalinga (Orissa) and had maritime trade relations with Southeast Asian countries. Since its spire was visible from far out at sea, sailors, who used it as a navigational aid, named the Temple the 'Black Pagoda'.

Another explanation attached to this nomenclature is that the Temple had a powerful lodestone on its apex, whose magnetic effect made compass needles go haywire, either luring ships shoreward to their destruction, or guiding them away on a safe passage. Konark fell into disuse in the early 17th century after an envoy of the Mughal Emperor Jahangir desecrated it. Declared a World Heritage Site by UNESCO, today it sits in solitary splendour, surrounded by lawns and casuarina trees, and further, by drifting sands.

Above: Harnessed and elaborately caparisoned steeds are portrayed in a powerful exertion to heave the great mass of the chariot over the dancing hall and fly it into the sky.
Facing page: Only the audience hall of the Temple is still intact though, sealed with rubble and sand to prevent its collapse, it cannot be entered.

The marvel in marble

The Taj Mahal embodies a Mughal emperor's love for his queen in dazzling perfection

Between the bobbing heads of visitors walking through the dark portal of the grand western gateway appears what has been described as one of the most ingeniously conceived and famous views in the world. The gateway, bearing 26 marble *chhattris* and inlaid with Quranic verses invites the faithful to Paradise, and truly, the first faraway glimpse at one of the wonders of the world is the proverbial light at the end of a tunnel. Stepping through it, the monument suddenly comes into full view, stunning the visitor with its architectural and aesthetic perfection.

Emperor Shah Jahan commissioned the Taj Mahal in memory of his beloved wife, Arjumand Bano Begum, who died giving birth to their 14th child. The name Taj Mahal (Crown of Palaces) derives from its original reference, *Taj Bibi ka Rauza* (Mausoleum of the Queen). Construction continued through 1631-49 by over 20,000 men under the Emperor's personal supervision. There is a lack of unanimity over its architects; some attribute it to Makramat Khan and Mir Abdul Karim, others to the Persian master builder Ustad Isa Khan, who left the detailing to his pupil Ustad Ahmed. The name of an Italian, Geronimo Verroneo, also figures in some accounts.

Cenotaphs enclosed by fine-fretted marble screens

Designed in the tradition of domed Islamic sepulchral buildings, the Taj

UTTAR PRADESH

Agra • Lucknow

State and capital:
Uttar Pradesh,
Lucknow (376 km)
Convenient access:
Road, air, rail to Agra
Accommodation:
Budget to luxury
Best season:
November to March
Also worth seeing:
Agra Fort, tomb of
Itmad-ud-daullah,
Akbar's tomb at
Sikandra, Fatehpur
Sikri, 35 km SW

stands on the banks of the Yamuna River at Agra. Unlike the customary plan of Mughal mausoleum complexes wherein the main edifice stood in the centre of a *chaarbagh* (quartered formal garden divided by water channels, fountains and pathways into a geometrical grid of smaller squares) the Taj's location at the head of the symbolic Garden of Paradise, gives the beholder an accentuated sense of depth and perspective.

The tomb stands elevated on a 5.5-metre-high plinth, in a spatial frame of four slender kiosk-crowned minarets, which rise at each corner of the platform. Not easily discernible to the unaware eye, the minarets are oriented slightly outwards as insurance against a calamitous toppling onto the mausoleum. Entry to the octagonal central chamber is through a high-arched portal flanked by recessed arched spaces and chamfered corners. Within lie the cenotaphs of the Emperor and his wife, enclosed by fine fretted screens carved in lacy patterns out of single slabs of marble (the original screen of jewelled gold was replaced by Shah Jahan's son, Aurangzeb). The actual graves are in a crypt below.

The Taj's awe-inspiring effect comes from its symmetrical exactness, the choice of building material and its ornamentation. The massive scale—built on a 95 metre wide platform, the Taj's

height is more than a 20 storeyed modern building—is played down by the white marble and begins to impose itself only as one walks closer to it. A red sandstone mosque on the west and a similar structure, a guesthouse, on the east, complete the balanced symmetry of the complex. However, inside the burial hall is the one symmetrical imperfection of the composition: Shah Jahan's grave, placed next to the centrally aligned cenotaph of his wife is so because it was never intended to be here. The emperor had planned his final resting place in an identical monument made of black stone across the river, which failed to materialise before he died.

Light is naturally absorbed and reflected off the texture and colour of the marble, producing different tonal effects with the changing angles and brightness of the sun, even in mist and darkness. Mined from Makrana in Rajasthan, the brilliant stone dazzles in the heat of the day, blushes softly at sunrise and sunset, and glows ethereally in the moonlight.

Pietra dura in precious and semi-precious stones

Unquestionably, it is the wealth of pietra dura work that is the Taj's most remarkable decorative element. Forty-three different precious and semi-precious gemstones, used to inlay curvaceous motifs of flowering plants, were sourced from various

parts of Asia: nephrite jade was brought from Chinese Turkestan, lapis lazuli from Afghanistan, yellow amber from Upper Burma, turquoise from Tibet, chrysolite from Egypt, amethyst from Persia, agates from Yemen, malachite from Russia, and carnelian, jasper, heliotrope, green beryl, diamonds and mother of pearl from different parts of India. The aim to achieve minute effects is evident from the composition of a particular single leaf wherein 35 pieces of carnelian, each subtly varying in hue, have been employed.

Above: A peep at the Taj through the main gateway. The archways and style of decoration is much the same as that on the mausoleum.
Below: A feature of the intensive calligraphy around the recessed external arches of the tomb structure is the larger size of the lettering higher up on the walls compared to the lower levels. To the viewer looking up, the clever treatment creates an illusion of uniformly sized writing from bottom to top.

Size and sculpture surrounds the reclining Vishnu

Sri Ranganathaswamy Temple lies within seven walled enclosures

The South Indian state of Tamil Nadu has some of the most outstanding specimens of Hindu religious architecture and it is not always easy to claim the supremacy of one over the other in terms of spiritual importance, form and style, art and iconography. Nevertheless, the temple of Sri Ranganathaswamy located at Tiruchirapalli, also known as Trichy, is considered second in importance after Tirupati in Andhra Pradesh for worshippers of Vishnu. However, as the largest temple complex in the country with the highest *gopuram* (gateway), it is second to none in architectural grandeur.

Spread over 62 hectares on the island of Srirangam, the temple lies within seven walled enclosures punctuated by 21 *gopurams* of differing sizes. While the outermost, a mammoth 13-storeyed, 70 metre-high structure was constructed as recently as 1987, the remaining *gopurams* date to between the 14th and 17th centuries. Non-Hindus are allowed to enter the first six enclosures but not the one with the main deity. In the innermost sanctum, Lord Ranganatha or Vishnu reclines on the coils of the five-hooded serpent Sheshnaga, with his consorts Bhu Devi (Earth Goddess) and Sri Devi (Goddess of Wealth) at his feet. The *utsava murti* or the figure taken out during processions is also present in the same sanctum. Above the main altar is the gold-plated *vimana* (tower) with four aspects of Vishnu on each corner.

Sculpture of a shepherd, yogi and damsel

Although it were the Nayaks of Madurai who were largely responsible for the present temple, subsequent contributions made by the Pallavas, Pandyas, Cholas and the Vijayanagara Kings—some of the most dynamic dynasties of southern India—are significant. The date of original construction is not definite but estimates place it between the 10th and the 13th centuries. The Ranganathaswamy

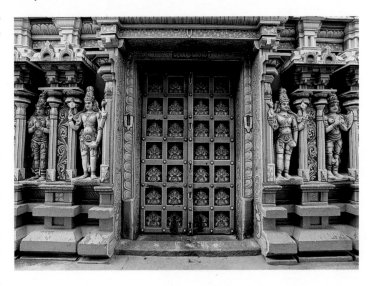

Temple was a favourite of the Alvar saints who helped revive Hinduism with the Tamil Bhakti movement between the seventh and 10th centuries, and thus many of the shrines have been dedicated to their memory. Songs and hymns written by the Alvars are sung to this day in the temple precincts. In the 12th century, the revered philosopher-saint Ramanuja established himself here and laid the rules for the worship conducted in the temple. His samadhi is situated in the fourth enclosure.

Within the first six enclosures, other than the bazaars and residences of the priests, there are innumerable shrines of various gods and goddesses. Some of the notable ones are the Vamana Temple of Vishnu (in his Dwarf aspect), Jagannatha Temple, Venugopal Temple, with some beautiful paintings of Krishna and the *gopis* (cowherdesses the God flirted with) on its ceiling, and the Chakrathalwar Temple, where the object of worship is Vishnu's Sudarshan Chakra (discus).

Graceful sculptures exist from the first enclosure onwards. As they are not always placed prominently, it is only on studying the pillars amidst the shadows that some of the most inconspicuous but artistically-interesting subjects—a shepherd carved out in straight lines, a yogi sitting in contemplation, a young damsel spilling woes to a pet parrot—are revealed. True to the

style of Tamil architecture, there are several *mandapas* (halls) with many clusters of pillars. While the Hall of the Thousand Pillars has 953 five-and-a-half-metre-tall, sculpted pillars, it is the Garuda Mandapa, with 12 rows of 16 pillars each and two centre rows of 10 pillars, which are regarded as the most stunning. In various corners are the many customary temple tanks each with its own legend.

The Rock Fort Temple

Seen from a distance, Trichy's other main site appears perched on a rocky outcrop, the geological date of which is more than a billion years. Built by the Nayaks, the Rock Fort Temple (probably named so by the British due to the general nature of the site) actually has two main temples, the Sri Thayumana Swamy Temple dedicated to Shiva, and the Ganesh Temple at the summit of the hill. Though non-Hindus are not allowed into the main sanctum of the temples, the steep climb of 430 steps is well worth the effort for sprawling views of the surrounding country-side.

State and capital:
Tamil Nadu, Chennai (325 km)

Convenient access:
Road, air, rail to Tiruchirapalli

Accommodation:
Budget to high-end

Best season:
November to March

Also worth seeing:
Jambukeshwara Temple, Thanjavur, 56 km E

Above: Decorated in stucco, Pavanapadavasal or Gate of Salvation leads to the sanctum. It is opened on ekadishi (December-January).

Facing page:
The piers of the Sheshagirirayar Mandapa are made as handsome, life-sized rearing horses, with sharply defined bridles and ornamentation and accompanying warriors, including the disproportionately small riders.

Pleasure retreat on a lake

The Lake Palace at Udaipur was a special abode of the Sisodia kings

State and capital:
Rajasthan, Jaipur (347 km from Udaipur)

Convenient access:
Road, air, rail to Udaipur

Accommodation:
Budget to luxury

Best season:
November to March

As the capital of the 1500-year-old Mewar dynasty for 400 years, Udaipur is home to some of the most stupendous palaces of India, of which the City Palace is the largest palace complex in Rajasthan. The origins of this lofty, sprawling abode of the Sisodia kings, rising majestically over the scenic shoreline of Lake Pichola, are traced to a small shrine built by Maharana Udai Singh II in the late 1500s. Over the ensuing centuries, successive rulers commissioned new palaces and initiated changes to earlier structures, causing the Palace walls to stretch almost a mile along the waterfront. Within is a vast complex of inner courtyards, apartments and exquisite halls lavished with frescoes, miniature paintings, and stone and glass inlay. Much of the City Palace is open to the public and a visit to the complex and its Museum displaying prized artefacts, unfolds the history of the erstwhile kingdom of Mewar.

Chequered history

Seemingly afloat on the heart of the same lake, edged on the far side by the Aravallis, the oldest fold mountains in the world, is the delectable white form of the Lake Palace. The story goes that it was suggested by his father to Maharana Jagat Singh II, the 62nd successor of the House of Mewar, that he cease his moonlit picnics with the ladies of his *zenana* in Jag Mandir, a neighbouring island palace, and build his own pleasure abode. (Jag Mandir itself has an interesting history, being a refuge to the Mughal Prince Khurram, later known as Emperor Shah Jahan, when he revolted against his father Emperor Jahangir in 1623). Jagat Singh II took it upon himself to implement his father's suggestion, and supplied with labour and

coveted by Udaipur's rulers. Apartments and enclosures decorated in contemporary style or according to personal fancy were added by successive Maharanas. The rooms, offering views of the lake and hills, were embellished by miniature paintings and portraits, carved and inlaid furniture, chandeliers and knotted carpets. Over two centuries, Jag Niwas, cooled by the lake breeze and set away from mainstream life, fulfilled its role as a respite from the heat of Rajasthan and the hurly burly of politics and governance, and as luxurious lodgings for guests of the royal family.

In 1963 Maharana Bhagat Singh thought it wise to convert Jag Niwas into a hotel to preserve its heritage and romance. In 1971, a big hotel chain took over the management of the property following an agreement with Maharana Bhagwat Singh and introduced several changes to suit the royal lifestyle experience it wanted to offer its guests. Built on an island meant that space was defined and dating back to 1746 meant that its structure had to be handled carefully as well as preserved in sync with the heritage laws. After a thorough research in local history, architecture and crafts, the interiors were refurbished with traditional decorative techniques and rooms and amenities added, while keeping the original façade untouched.

Bottom: Each room of the Palace is an amalgam of restored glass, mirror and pietra dura inlay, frescoes, sculpted stone and decorative gilt moulding, artefacts, lamps and other fine furnishings.
Facing page: The resplendent Jag Niwas, better known as the Lake Palace, casts a shimmering reflection on Lake Pichola.

materials ferried from the shore by boat, construction of a marble and granite retreat soon commenced on a 1.5 hecatres rocky island. Three years later, in February 1746, the building was inaugurated with royal ceremony, pomp, feasting and merriment stretching over several days, attended by a large gathering of royals and nobles. It was named Jag Niwas after the Maharana who gifted elephants, horses, jewellery and attire on the occasion.

In the years that followed, the island palace with its delicate cusped arches, painted lintels, frescoed ceilings, sculpted panels and pillars, curved roofs, intimate nooks and open courtyards, sunlit corridors and breezy pavilions, ponds and patios, gardens and fountains, and a shrine, was much

The holiest Hindu city

The ghats of Varanasi are the gateway to nirvana

There are estimated to be almost 100 bathing ghats on the Ganga at Varanasi. Named after people or places, some are fairly quiet, while others reverberate with activity. At the top of the steps stand temples, shrines and ashrams, built in different periods by ruler patrons.

As ancient as Athens and Jerusalem, it is one of the world's oldest continuously inhabited cities. The name Varanasi is derived from two rivulets, the *Varuna* in the north, and *Assi* in the south. Significantly, however, the city lies on the northern bend of the sacred Ganga River, as it continues its journey westward into the Indian heartland. Also known as Banaras, a corruption of its original name, it is called Kashi or City of Light by the devout, a name that expresses the ancient pedigree of the nearly 3,000-year-old centre of temples and ashrams, where those seeking the understanding of the enigma of existence come to find answers. The sweeping ghats framing the riverfront are for many the final destination of mortal life. Here, the drama of life and death is enacted each day, as the devout bathe in the holy waters of the river, praying for a better afterlife; as priests, sadhus and residents perform the endless cycle of daily rituals; and as the dead are brought for their final rites, in the traditional belief that they

Queen Ahilya Bai built the present structure in 1777, and its roof was plated with 750 kilograms of gold provided by Maharaja Ranjit Singh, in 1835. The Gyan Vapi Mosque of Aurangzeb bears evidence in its foundations and rear columns of the original temple. Alamgir Mosque, further north, is the smaller of Aurangzeb's mosques, built over the original Vishnu temple of the Marathas.

Dasashwamedha Ghat (Place of the 10 Horse Sacrifice) is centrally located and is Varanasi's holiest spot. This is where Lord Brahma, (the Creator of Hinduism's Holy Trinity) is said to have asked for a sacrifice to be performed by the king of Kashi, appointed by him to rid the world of chaos. At the Narad and Chauki Ghats, the Buddha is said to have meditated. Two ghats, Harishchandra and Manikarna, are dedicated to cremating the dead. The fort behind Shivala Ghat contains the old palace of the ex-Maharaja and he privately owns the ghat. The ruler's family now lives in the Ramnagar Fort further upstream. Tulsi Ghat is named after the saint-poet Tulsidas, who translated the *Ramayana* into Hindi from Sanskrit, while Anandamayi Ghat and the ashram behind, are named after the 20th century Bengali saint Anandamayi Ma.

Varanasi is also the main centre of Sanskrit learning in North India. From ancient times, saints and sages have resided here, teaching the *Vedas* and the deeper meanings of yogic practice. The Bhakti saints, Kabir and Ramananda, both lived here. Scholars come to the Banaras Hindu University, one of the country's oldest and most renowned institutions of learning, to study its collection of old manuscripts. Behind the ghats, Varanasi's dense streets and alleys are vibrant with the buzz of daily life-cycle rickshaws snake their way past shops selling, betel nut, street food, famous Banarsi silk saris, marigold flowers and garlands and various other accessories of worship and the cacophony of human voices, temple bells, car horns and loudspeakers blaring devotional hymns, mix with each other.

UTTAR PRADESH

State and capital:
Uttar Pradesh,
Lucknow (286 km)
Convenient access:
Road, air, rail to
Varanasi
Accommodation:
Budget to high-end
Best season:
November to March
Also worth seeing:
Sarnath, 12 km NE

will then be liberated from the continuous cycle of rebirth and attain *nirvana*.

Life along the waterfront
The ghats lie more than six kilometres along the western bank of the river, stretching in a semi-circle from the southernmost Assi Ghat to the Adi Keshava Ghat before Malaviya Bridge. Varanasi is regarded as the dwelling place of Lord Shiva on earth, whose all pervading presence is manifested through his emblem, the lingam or phallus symbol, in the innumerable small shrines along the ghats, and more magnificently, in the Vishwanath Temple, the main Shiva shrine. Built more than 1,000 years ago, the Temple was first destroyed in the 12th century when much of the city was ravaged, and mosques replaced temples. Rebuilt in the 16th century, it was torn down again by the zealous Mughal Emperor Aurangzeb, but the sacred lingam was saved by being thrown into the neighbouring Gyan Vapi (Well of Knowledge). Indore's

Indian Renaissance style at its flamboyant best

The former Viceregal Lodge was the British Government's summer seat of power

Spacious galleries and verandahs run around the grand building, either leading into the gardens from the lower levels or affording views of the mountains from the upper floors. After its conversion into the Indian Institute of Advanced Studies, the state drawing room, ballroom, and dining room were adapted for a library.

During its heydays, 700 people were employed on the staff of the palace of the Viceroy of India. An army of gardeners looked after the substantial 132 hectares, and the only sole duty of a dozen men was to shoo away monkeys, which continue to remain a nuisance in present day Shimla, the erstwhile summer capital of British India.

Set in the bracing climate of the mid-Himalayan ranges, the older part of Shimla follows a wide curve over a series of interconnected hills. All around are woods of oak, flowering rhododendron, pine and cedar. And of the many grand structures dotted on the dips and rises, none is as magnificent as the earlier Viceregal Lodge—the building of the Indian Institute of

Advanced Studies. From here, once, for the better part of every year, one-fifth of the human race was governed for well over five decades.

Shades of a Scottish castle

The site atop Observatory Hill—a watershed figuratively standing astride India, as the trickle from one side eventually finds its way down to the Bay of Bengal, and from the

grimaces, depending on the point of view—was formed. It was the first building with electric lighting in Shimla.

Amusing anecdotes

Several momentous meetings and conferences that mark India's march to Independence took place at the Viceregal Lodge. In 1945 the historic Shimla Conference for deciding a significant reconstitution of the government was held here. Amongst other leaders, it was attended by Muhammad Ali Jinnah, the moving spirit behind the founding of Pakistan. In 1947, many of the discussions that led to the Partition of India took place within the building's prodigious walls. Apart from it being the venue of consequential proceedings, the Lodge's past is replete with lighter anecdotes. The story is told of Lady Dufferin, who, during its construction, found the workpeople on the site 'amusing' and declared the women at work as, 'most picturesque masons'. Amusement came in other forms, especially where the more than colourful princes of India were involved: there was one who tried to bribe his way to a dinner with Viceroy Lord Wavell and another who disliked dogs and could not bear to touch the leather upholstery.

After Independence in 1947, the Viceregal Lodge building became the property of the President of India and was renamed Rashtrapati Niwas. At the instance of the President of India, Professor S. Radhakrishnan, the Indian Institute of Advanced Study was formally inaugurated at Shimla and housed in the Lodge, where it continues to function from.

State and capital:
Himachal Pradesh, Shimla

Convenient access:
Road, rail, air to Shimla

Accommodation:
Budget to luxury

Best season:
September to June (can snow during December to February)

Also worth seeing:
Gorton Castle, Railway Board Building, Secretariat at Ellerslie, Barnes Court, Naldehra, 22 km NE

other, to the Arabian Sea—was selected by Viceroy Lord Lytton (1876-80); while the overall plan was Viceroy Lord Dufferin's (1884-88), the execution under his supervision, was the architect Henry Irvine's. Work on what was to result in one of the most flamboyant buildings of the British Empire began with the levelling of the top of Observatory Hill into a wide plateau. Concrete was liberally used as remedy for the crushed shale, 'fissured and cracked in every direction', which lay under the thin top-soil. Later a massive shipment of teak was summoned from Burma to create the ornately panelled interior. The structure of light blue-grey stone masonry with tiled

pitch roofing that finally rose from the ground had a style of architecture loosely termed as English Renaissance and drew inspiration from the forms of the Elizabethan era, though elements of Scottish castles are quite overwhelming. Embellished with wrought stonework, the main block has three storeys and the kitchen wing has five. A tower, whose height was increased during Lord Curzon's tenure (1899-1905), strikes above the rest of the building, and a public entry building was added during the time of Lord Irwin (1926-31). By this date the character of the Lodge as seen in the present day, with all the strength of its limbs, fine features—or distorted architectural

The Taj Mahal of the British Raj

Kolkata's Victoria Memorial is one of the Empire's lasting symbols

The Victoria Memorial is the distinguished symbol of Kolkata (earlier Calcutta). Set in 26 hectares of landscaped gardens in the Maidan, the city's main promenade, the edifice was built to commemorate Queen Victoria's 25-year rule as the Empress of India. After her death in 1901, Lord Curzon, the Viceroy of India, proposed a monument to be erected in her memory that would glorify her and celebrate British rule in its largest and most coveted colony.

The foundation stone was laid by the Prince of Wales (later King George V) on a royal visit to Calcutta on 4 January, 1906. It took nearly 20 years to build at a cost of 10 million rupees, raised entirely through public subscriptions from Indian princes and prominent members of India's business community. Inaugurated by another Prince of Wales (later King Edward VIII) on 28 December, 1921, the

spacious gardens laid out by Lord Redesdale and Sir David Prain, created an overall impression of grandeur.

World's largest collection of paintings by the Daniells

The monument houses many interesting relics from the Raj. These include 3,000 exhibits in 25 galleries. The main focus is Sir George Frampton's bronze statue of Queen Victoria, seated at the entrance, wearing her royal insignia, the Star of India. Another statue of the Empress in the central hall depicts her at a much younger age. The entrance dome over the rotunda is engraved with the text of her proclamation speech. Displayed inside and outside the building are statues of notable Englishmen and Governor-Generals, including Robert Clive and Warren Hastings.

The memorial has a large collection of art by European painters such as Charles D'Oyly, Johann Zoffany, Balthazar Solvyns, and Emily Eden, to name a few. It also houses the world's largest collection of paintings by Thomas and William Daniell, who visited India in 1791. In the Royal Gallery paintings illustrate episodes from Queen Victoria's long and eventful life. Some of her personal possessions, including her writing desk and chair, and scrapbooks of her letters, are also displayed here.

Among other artefacts is a collection of weapons—the dagger of Tipu Sultan and cannons from the Battle of Plassey—rare books and manuscripts like Abul Fazl's *Ain-i-Akbari*, as well as postage stamps and coins. After Independence, a National Leaders' Gallery was added with portraits and relics of Indian freedom fighters. Among the eminent Indians featured here are Keshab Chandra Sen, Michael Madhusudan Dutt, Rabindranath Tagore and his grandfather Dwarkanath Tagore.

Long after the sun has set on the British Empire, Victoria Memorial continues to enjoy a place of pride amongst India's grand architectural wonders. Illuminated in the evenings, it has a musical fountain, and is Kolkata's most popular meeting spot for walkers, lovers, tourists and young people.

State and capital:
West Bengal, Kolkata
Convenient access:
Road, air, rail to Kolkata
Accommodation:
Budget to luxury
Best season:
November to March
Also worth seeing:
St Paul's Cathedral, Writers Building, Raj Bhawan

Victoria Memorial was designed by Sir William Emerson, President of the British Institute of Architects, and supervised by Vincent J. Esch, who contributed many decorative details that made it one of the finest examples of British architecture in India. Built in white marble in the Indo-Saracenic style, it combines elements of classical Western architecture with Indian forms that offer striking similarities with the Taj Mahal in Agra. This can be seen in the great dome flanked by four octagonal, domed *chattris* (cupolas), high entrance portals, the surrounding marble terrace and domed corner towers. Like the Taj, this monument was also dedicated to an empress and the marble was acquired from Makrana in Rajasthan, as it was for the Taj.

Emerson's design was enhanced by Vincent Esch's details such as the allegorical sculptures for Motherhood, Prudence and Learning over the entrances, and around the dome, statues symbolising Art, Architecture, Justice and Charity. All this, including the elegant bridge on the north side, and the decorative gates, together with the

The impressive building, covering an area of 7,210 square metres rises to a height of 56 metres at the dome, which is topped by a figure of Victory, another five metres high. This astonishing bronze statue of an angel is designed to rotate in the wind.

From shed to stupendous railway station

Chhatrapati Shivaji Terminus mirrors Mumbai's mayhem

Chhatrapati Shivaji Terminus is remarkable for its staggering functionality: about 2.5 million people, 1,050 suburban, and 68 long distance trains arrive and depart through it everyday, and 1,000 people provide the manpower for its numerous operations.

Getting off a train at Chhatrapati Shivaji Terminus (CST), the traveller is engulfed by a magnificent matrix of arches, galleries, turrets, gables, rose windows, projecting gargoyles, profusely carved surfaces, crocheting and decorative finials. CST, the first functional administrative building to be put on the UNESCO World Heritage Site list, serves as the headquarters, terminus and western-most end point for the Central Railways, as well as the terminus for the Central and Harbour lines of the Mumbai Suburban Railway. Regarded as one of the most impressive stations in the world, it was, as old photographs and picture postcards testify, one of India's liberally photographed monuments of the late 19th and early 20th centuries.

Originally named Victoria Terminus on Jubilee Day, 1887, in honour of Queen Victoria, CST was built over 10 years (1878-88). It was from this site that India's first railway venture took off on

In sharp contrast to the small original shed of Bori Bunder, the Frederick William Stevens-designed terminus is one of the largest and most significant buildings of the European idiom in India. The main office block has two wings that stand at right angles to it at either end, with a striking central dome surmounted by the statue of Progress, grand corridors and a wealth of carved friezes. Decorative elements featuring animals are fascinating: gargoyles, peacocks with fanned tails, a cat with a mouse in its mouth, a leaping griffin, a cobra and a mongoose, owls and monkeys. Medallion portraits of the Directors of the GIPR, responsible for its success and development, bedeck the walls, and cartouches carry the GIPR coat of arms. The three prominent gables bear sculptures representing Engineering, Commerce and Agriculture, and flanking the gate to the office block, a seated lion and tiger, represent Britain and India, respectively.

Within the main block a cantilevered staircase winds up the levels, taking one closer to the dome filled in with beautiful, long, stained-glass windows. Besides providing aesthetical value, the panels of coloured glass reduce the sun's glare yet allow enough light to promote a feeling of spaciousness. The interior dressing includes carved capitals, ornamental railings and grills, and woodwork.

A hundred and twenty years after its raising, CST remains synonymous with the ethos of modern Mumbai, conveying an indelible feeling of optimism, exuberance and energy.

MAHARASHTRA

• Mumbai

Arabian Sea

State and capital:
Maharashtra, Mumbai
Convenient access:
Road, rail to CST, air to Mumbai
Accommodation:
Budget to luxury
Best season:
November to March
Also worth seeing:
Fort precincts, Kala Ghoda precincts, Gateway of India, Chhatrapati Shivaji Maharaj Vastu Sangrahalaya, Afghan Church, Mani Bhavan

16 April, 1853. On that historic birthday of the Great Indian Peninsular Railway, 21 guns boomed a royal salute, the Governor's band played and the huge *Sahib*, *Sindh* and *Sultan* engines heaved their carriages, puffing off, from Bori Bunder to Thane, 34 kilometres away. While 'the beauty, rank and fashion of Bombay' filled the modest awning and shed of Bori Bunder and cheered the train, 'the natives *salaamed*' the creature that slithered on rails. They believed the creation, moving without assistance of any animals was a miracle, and offered it flowers and coconuts.

The initiation of railways in India ushered in a revolution in communications and transport. It meant speedy movement of men and cargo, improved access to raw materials and a boost in trade, developments that would precipitate British political control of India. Three decades later, keeping in line with the tradition of architecture encouraged in Mumbai, the stunning Neo-Gothic terminus was raised. Not only did it impress the onlooker with its form, it also emphatically underlined the message of British presence and authority in India.

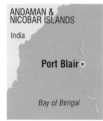

Capital: Port Blair on South Andaman Island (1,225 km from Kolkata)

Convenient access: Air, sea to Port Blair. Local boats between islands

Accommodation: Budget to high-end

Best season: November to March

Archipelago of tropical forests and prehistoric people

Andaman and Nicobar Islands were once infamous as penal settlements

The three emblems of the Union Territory of the Andaman and Nicobar Islands are the Andaman padauk, a tall deciduous tree with highly prized timber; the Andaman wood pigeon; and the Dugong or sea cow, a herbivorous marine mammal. That all are either endemic, rare or endangered, or all three, is an indication of the peculiar and vulnerable ecological wealth of this archipelago of 572 islands, islets and rocks located in the south-east Bay of Bengal, spread along a north-south oriented arc over 800 kilometres. Only 36 islands are inhabited.

Over 100 sanctuaries and national parks

The hilly terrain of the island—Saddle Peak (732 metres), the highest point in the North Andaman Islands, is followed by Mt. Thullier (642 metres) on Great Nicobar—is almost totally covered in evergreen tropical rainforests and mangrove lined creeks, and most of it is reserved and protected in over an astounding 100 different sanctuaries and national parks. Marine life and corals thrive in the ocean around the islands; the Mahatma Gandhi Marine National Park is one such protected area filled with shells, corals, varieties of

coloured fish, sea turtles and other species. More than 271 varieties of birds, including the Nicobarese megapode, with over 39 endemics, 50 kinds of forest mammals and 225 species of butterflies and moths live on the island chain.

The name Andaman is said to be a variant of Hanuman, the Hindu monkey god, who was known as Handuman on the Islands. It finds mention in the accounts of the second-century Greek geographer Ptolemy, Chinese travellers Fa Hien and I T'sing in the sixth and seventh centuries, and Marco Polo in the 13th century, who is believed to be the first

Westerner to set foot on the Islands. Though Great Britain was the ruling colonial power for almost 80 years (1869 to 1947), two other European countries, Austria and Denmark, held the territories for brief spells in the 18th and 19th centuries. While the first British settlement was established in 1789, only to be abandoned seven years later, the second, set up after the First War of Independence mainly had a penal purpose: today one of the Islands' tourist curiosity, Port Blair's infamous Cellular Jail was completed in 1910 to lodge political prisoners in 698 decidedly unspacious cells, each 12 square metres small, with a single, tiny window, three metres above the floor. One of its famous inmates was Vinayak Damodar Savarkar, the 20th century espouser of Hindu nationalism. Now in ruins, the more sinister Viper Chain Gang Jail on Viper Island was reserved for hardened criminals who were imprisoned there in shackles. It was also a hanging site; during India's independence movement it became

a convenient place to intern prominent members of the struggle. Here, on 30 December, 1943, during the Japanese occupation of the Andamans, the militant Indian revolutionary Subhas Chandra Bose hoisted the flag of Indian independence.

Aborigines on the verge of vanishing

Besides flora and fauna, the archipelago's other big treasure is its amazing anthropology. Nicobar fell on the sea route from South India and Sri Lanka to South East Asia, and voyagers referred to it as the 'Land of the Naked', or Nakkavar. In China, the islands were known as Lo-Jan Kuo (Land of the Naked People). The names owed themselves to the now tiny populations of six local aboriginal tribes, true inhabitants of this removed outpost of humanity. Of these, the Nicobarese and Shompens are of Mongoloid ancestry, and while the former have entered the mainstream, the latter, numbering not more than 250-300, remain

removed. The Great Andamanese, Onges, Jarawas, and Sentinelese are of Negrito origin. Reduced to a near extinct 40 individuals, the Great Andamanese are a very ancient pygmy people of a palaeolithic hunting-gathering way. The Onges and Jarawas together number not more than a few hundred, and residents of North Sentinel Island, the Sentinelese are probably the world's only surviving palaeolithic people without contact with any other group or community. Their numbers are estimated at anywhere between 50 and 500.

Above: Havelock Island has some of the best beaches, waters and coral reefs for snorkelling and scuba diving.
Top: The ruined gallows of Viper Island.
Facing page: Geologically, the Islands were once a mountain range extending from Myanmar to Indonesia, a fact evident by the mix of Indian, Myanmarese and Malaysian strains found in its various flora and fauna.

Tigers reign over Bandhavgarh's wilderness

Chances of spotting the beautiful cat are high at this National Park

MADHYA PRADESH

Bandhavgarh
Bhopal

State and capital:
Madhya Pradesh,
Bhopal (458 km)

Convenient access:
Road to the Park, air to
Jabalpur, rail to Umaria

Accommodation:
Budget to high-end

Best season:
November to March

Also worth seeing:
Caves in Park with
inscriptions from first
century BC, Baghel
Museum, Kanha
National Park, 240 km

*Above: Bandhavgarh
is one of the most
densely populated
tiger reserves of
India, and this
translates into high
sighting odds: a
bemused tiger
emerges out of the
bush.*

It was for some reason considered auspicious for successive heads of the erstwhile Rewa State, whose private hunting preserve encompassed the forests that now form a part of Bandhavgarh National Park, to shoot down 109 tigers. Each determined maharaja tried to reach the magic figure until, in 1914, Maharaja Venkat Raman Singh finally hit and surpassed the target with a tally of 111. Another interesting bit of Bandhavgarh history took place in 1951 when the Rewa forests produced a unique specimen of the big cat. This was Mohun, a white (albino) tiger cub captured by Maharaja Martand Singh. Today, all white tigers in the zoos of the world trace their genetic lineage to Mohun.

Jungle in the fort

In 1968 the royal jungles were handed over to the government and declared a national park. As the tiger population showed signs of growing, additional area was taken into the ambit to encompass a total of 448 square kilometres. Out of the few thousand tigers remaining in the world's wildernesses, two-thirds exist on the Indian subcontinent, and some of the best sightings of the magnificent animal can be had today at Bandhavgarh. Actually, Bandhavgarh's history goes much farther back than the Rewa line. Beginning from the 12th century, first the Chandellas, and then the Baghels held sway over this rugged region, and both ruled from the massive Bandhavgarh Fort, the origins of which fade back into the mists of myth. The Fort is part of the Park and indeed one of its big attractions. Its natural fortifications of rocky hillside, painted with the droppings of nesting raptors, soar a sheer 300 metres above ground level before terminating on a huge plateau. A fascinating overgrown mess, the hilltop flatland is scattered with sculptures, crumbling monuments, desolate temples, broken walls and ancient water tanks, which emerge out of the foliage as one tries to pick one's way over winding, barely discernible paths. Signs of big cats—droppings, pug marks, maybe a half-eaten kill—are not uncommon, and a glimpse, if rare, is not impossible. The more remarkable and visible sculptures in and on the peripheries of the Fort area are of various manifestations of the Hindu God Vishnu. Starting with a reclining figure at the foot of the climb, from whence emanates one of the park's perennial streams, the one-hour trudge up to the only functioning temple of the Fort brings up the Preserver's Tortoise, Boar, Narasimha (half-man half-beast) and Fish incarnates hewn in granite. The view from the top is stupendous; pimpled with 32 hills, a wild jigsaw of grasslands, forests of sal, stands of bamboo and numerous small lakes stretch as far as the eyes can see. And though the entire park is veined with dirt roads, the area around the citadel is where most of the wildlife-viewing action occurs.

Four-horned deer

Like many other parks, the two modes of seeking wildlife at Bandhavgarh are by four-wheel drive or on elephant back. However, here elephants are used more precisely to try and maximise the chances for tiger-hungry tourists. Early morning, mahouts set off with their steeds into the jungle in an effort to locate the big cat. If successful, they come back and take visitors to where the animal is lying up or moving about, so that one is sure of a sighting. Besides the tiger, Bandhavgarh's mammals range across 22 species, which include leopards, wild boars, spotted deer, sambar, barking deer and the diminutive *chousingha* (four-horned deer). Standing just about half a metre above the ground, this is the smallest antelope in Asia and the only antelope in the world with two pairs of horns. The gazelle family is represented by the shy, biscuit-brown chinkara.

Bandhavgarh's vegetation varies from sal forests, meadows and swamps created by its streams and constantly trickling springs. The different habitats attract approximately 250 species of birds, amongst which are elegant sarus cranes and white ibis, predatory steppe eagles and white-eyed buzzards, whistling teals and little grebe, and the paradise fly-catcher, fairy-like with its wispy, trailing tail.

Below: Claw markings are a way of defining territory.
Facing page bottom: *The Fort overlooks the forest.*

CHHATTISGARH

Raipur

Bastar

Bay of Bengal

State and capital:
Chhattisgarh, Raipur
(297 km to Jagdalpur,
district headquarters)

Convenient access:
Road, rail to Bastar, air
to Raipur

Accommodation:
Budget to mid-range

Best season:
November to March

Also worth seeing:
(from Jagdalpur)
Chitrakote waterfalls,
38 km NW, Kanger
Valley National Park,
35 km S

A tribal culture vigorously alive

Bastar's aboriginal people still have an indigenous lifestyle

Geographically, the district of Bastar lies on a 600-metre-high plateau, on the western fringes of the Eastern Ghats. Its main river, the Indravati, flows for about 400 kilometres through the region to finally con-fluence with the Godavari, which empties into the Bay of Bengal. Seventy-five per cent of Bastar is covered by broadleaved forest, and almost three quarters of its population is tribal. What makes the area interesting is that minimal interaction with the world outside has kept much of Bastar's tribal tradition vigorously alive and untarnished. Indigenous people still lead an aboriginal lifestyle with their own unique customs and rituals. A barter economy, sub-sistence farming, shifting agri-culture, dependency on forest produce and hunting are still a reality for many of them.

Bastar's history is hazy up to the 15th century, when it emerges as the kingdom of a branch of the Kakatiya rulers of Warangal, from the neighbouring state of Andhra

Pradesh. In the 19th century, the British assumed administrative control over it through their local feudatories. On Independence Bastar became a part of the Central Indian state of Madhya Pradesh, and in the year 2000, when the state was split into two, it was incorporated into the new state of Chhattisgarh.

Bastar's tribal groups consist of Gonds—spread across a few other states, they are the largest tribal group in India—and non-Gonds. Gond sub groups include the Marias, Murias, Abhujmarias, Dhurwas and Dorlas, while the non-Gonds are the Bhatras and Halbas. Besides Hindi and Telugu, they speak a variety of indigenous languages and local dialects. As the nature of terrain and thick vegetation has often restricted interaction between settlements in relative proximity of each other, it is not uncommon that two villages, in different valleys separated by a few kilometres, speak different dialects. Another differentiating feature between tribes is the headgear, such as the deer-horn mask worn by the

Muria, or the bison-horn mask of the Maria.

The *ghotul* system

Although Bastar tribals in general have been the subjects of extensive research, one group, the Murias, have attracted particular attention for their *ghotul* system of community interaction amongst the young generation. This can be best described as a primitive youth club or dormitory system regarded as training ground for learning customary tribal laws and norms, with the mandatory song, dance, eating and drinking. A key activity during the *ghotul* days is uninhibited courtship between unmarried tribal boys and girls. Verrier Elwin (1902-64), the British Oxford cleric turned anthropologist, who came to India to work with Gandhi was so fascinated by the aboriginal way of life that he settled and got married amongst the Bastar tribals. Apart from his celebrated autobiography *The Tribal World of Verrier Elwin*, he also wrote a book on the *ghotul* custom.

Travelling through Bastar one

commonly sees rows of tribal women in their simple but colourful attire, sporting metal jewellery and beads, carrying vessels on their heads. Totem poles with paintings of plants and animals are planted near roads in memory of the departed. The animistic faith of the tribals is centred on worshipping various animals like cows, tigers, scorpions, and spirits of the forests. Each village has its own deity, but overall, Danteshwari is the supreme Goddess amongst most groups. Dussehra is the biggest festival in Bastar. Curiously, however, unlike as in other parts of the country, the focus here is not on Rama and his victory over Ravana, but on Danteshwari, with deities from all over the region assembling at the Goddess' temple in Jagdalpur.

Distinct tradition of crafts

Bell metal, terracotta, wood and bamboo are the materials used by tribal craftsmen for myriad creations. Immediately identifiable with Bastar are the animal, plant and human figurines manufactured with wrought iron, characterised by accentuated long, thin body parts imparting a very primeval feel. Apart from natural themes, drummers, dancing girls and caparisoned elephants are popular subjects for potters and metal workers. A delightful artefact is the 'singing stick', a bamboo stem crafted so in its hollow that waving it produces mellow, lilting sounds most conducive for musical compositions. Artisans can be watched first-hand at work at *shilpagrams* (craftsmen villages) of Nagarnar, Belvapadar and Lanjora.

Facing page: Abhuj Maria tribals dressed for a festival. The man with stilts is set to perform the Parab dance whereas the woman is attired for the Gedia. The Abhuj Marias are hill dwelling people, who were once one of the fiercest of the Bastar tribals. There is no private ownership of land in their community and they do not plough the earth as they believe it will cause her injury. Instead, pointed wooden pieces are used to till the soil.
Left: Totem poles are painted with natural and human motifs.
Bottom: Elaborately decorated terracotta elephants are fashioned at the tribal crafts village of Kondagaon.

Three mass nesting sites along the beaches

Arguably, Bhitarkanika's most famous animal is the Olive Ridley, approximately a million of which nest here annually. Homing in from as far as the southern Pacific Ocean, they lay almost 84 million eggs, making these beaches the world's largest rookery for this long-distance swimmer. Such nesting occurs in only three other locations in the world—two beaches along the Costa Rica coast, and one in Mexico. Conservation began in this area only after the discovery of the Gahirmatha rookery in 1974. In 1981, a second mass nesting at the Devi River mouth was discovered, and in 1994, a third at the mouth of the Rushikulya River, both south of Gahirmatha. As a result, Bhitarkanika was designated a Ramsar Wetland of international importance. However, despite it being a protected area, the turtles continue to be under threat from predating animals, poachers and the nets of fishing trawlers plying illegally during the breeding season. Habitat depletion and the pressures exerted by increasing local human population and economic development are other contributing factors.

Over 200 species of birds, including eight varieties of kingfishers, are found in this wetland. With more than 20,000 birds ranging across 11 species, it happens to be one of the country's largest heronries. Bar-headed geese, grey pelicans, ruddy shelducks and whistling teal are regular visitors. Open-billed storks, egrets, white ibis and the white-bellied sea eagle can also be spotted. Two of the best birding locations are Bagaghan Island, near Suajore Creek, and Palmyra Point, on the southern tip of the Parsula River. Bhitarkanika is also the east coast's major nursery for brackish water and estuarine fish fauna. It is home to several mammal species, the striped hyena, fishing cat, jungle cat, smooth Indian otter, civet cat, Indian porcupine, wild boar, spotted deer and sambar. The most common of five varieties of marine dolphins found in these waters is the Indo-Pacific humpbacked.

ORISSA

Bhitarkanika

Bhubaneshwar

Bay of Bengal

State and capital:
Orissa, Bhubaneshwar (120 km)

Convenient access:
Road to Bhitarkanika, rail to Bhadrak, air to Bhubaneshwar. Boat into sanctuary

Accommodation:
Budget

Best season: March to July, September to November

Also worth seeing:
Kendrapara, Cuttack, Konark

Above: Boats take you through the creeks and rivers that meander through the Park.

Facing page: An Olive Ridley turtle crawls out of the sea on Gahirmatha beach to lay eggs. Such mass nesting occurs in only three other locations in the world: two beaches along the Costa Rica coast, and one in Mexico. The turtle is a globally endangered species.

Where a million turtles nest

Bhitarkanika is the world's largest rookery for the Olive Ridley turtle

In Oriya *bhitar* means 'interior', and *kanika* is that which is 'extraordinarily beautiful'. The description holds for this wildlife sanctuary located on the coast of the Bay of Bengal, between Paradip and Chandipur, at the estuarine confluence of the Brahmini, Baitarani and Dhamara Rivers, in the state of Orissa. Bhitarkanika and its adjoining 35-kilometre-long Gahirmatha Beach are a unique habitat to some of the rare and endangered wild creatures of the world.

Bhitarkanika extends over an area of about 800 square kilometres, 380 kilometres of which is forest while the rest consists of mud flats, mangroves, islands and marshes. Bhitarkanika National Park, declared in 1998, has an area of about 140 square kilometres. It was created from the core of the Bhitarkanika Wildlife Sanctuary, designated in 1975 over 672 square kilometres. The Gahirmatha Marine Wildlife Sanctuary, which binds Bhitarkanika Wildlife Sanctuary to the east, was created in September 1997 and encompasses Gahirmatha Beach and an adjacent portion of the Bay of Bengal.

Bhitarkanika is one of the largest contiguous patches of mangrove forest in the country, representing the Indo-Malayan mangrove community. Though home to 55 of India's 58 known mangrove species, two species, *kanika sundari* and *bana lembu* (local names), both exclusive to Bhitarkanika, are predominant. Other species include *kalban* or *bada bani*, *baniya*, *kala bani*, *hental* and *rai*. Numerous kinds of grasses and herbs are also found here, and a variety of wild rice found on the tidal mud flats have been used to develop several saline and flood resistant varieties of rice.

Bhitarkanika Wildlife Sanctuary harbours nearly 700 saltwater crocodiles making it one of India's largest single population of the reptile. A large ongoing breeding and conservation programme for these amphibious animals ensures that the population is growing. Additionally, five species of amphibians, nine kinds of lizards, 18 species of snakes and seven types of turtles, including the Olive Ridley, hawksbill, leather-backs and Bibron's soft-shelled turtle are part of the Bhitarkanika repertoire.

Son of Brahma, the Creator

The Brahmaputra is India's only 'male' river

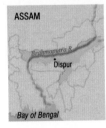
State and capital:
Arunachal Pradesh,
Itanagar; Assam,
Dispur

Convenient access:
Road to Tuting,
Pasighat (AP), Tezpur,
Guwahati, Dibrugarh
and other towns
(Assam), air to Itanagar
(AP), Tezpur, Guwahati,
Dibrugarh (Assam), rail
to Dibrugarh, Guwahati

Accommodation:
Budget in AP; mid-
range in Dibrugarh,
high-end in Guwahati

Best season:
November to March

A river that tracks 2,880 kilometres through three countries, providing sustenance to people of three of the world's great religions—Buddhism, Hinduism and Islam—apart from ancient animistic faiths, has to have a plural identity. Thus, the glacial trickle of the Brahmaputra's source, near the legendary Mt. Kailash, in the Tibetan mountains, christened Tamchok Khambab or the Celestial Horse's Mouth becomes the Tsang Po (Great River) in eastern Tibet. Descending off the plateau, it storms into Arunachal Pradesh, in India's extreme north-east, as the Dihang or Siang.

Up to the 1930s, Arunachal Pradesh, known as an inaccessible and inhospitable land of leech-infested rainforests and unfriendly tribals, held attraction only for intrepid ethnologists and botanists. Cutting through its green tangle, the blue-green Siang pools and drops, forming massive rapids that offer one of the world's most exhilarating white-water trips. Over these rest-less waters, the sun-moon wor-shipping Adi tribals have thrown swinging rope bridges, sometimes with large gaps between foot planks. Hillocks of logs and mangled trees, torn out of the hillsides with powerful flash floods, are often found piled along the banks. More picturesquely, the forest breaks to create occasional pristine beaches, under the rocks of which live beetles eaten raw as a delicacy by the tribals.

Majuli is the largest island of silt

Already wide and deep for a mountain stream, the River breaks into the plains at Pasighat and enters Assam. Assuming its most famous identity—Brahmaputra, Son of the Creator—it rapidly acquires an immensity best appreciated from an aircraft over Dibrugarh or Guwahati, the gateways to this region. Below, the heavily braided, widespread course seems like many rivers and the vast swathes of silt are unending islands rather than mere sandbanks. This scale is not always evident while on a river ferry, for often the craft noses into channels to avoid treacherous shallows. From these sub-streams, what seems to be the River's true edge is actually a big island; beyond it, there is another channel, and another sandbank, sometimes up to a dozen such fluvial features. During the monsoon, of course, all of this is consumed and the River literally becomes a mind-boggling sea, making inroads kilometres inland,

so that only a horizon of water is in sight. Because of the destruction caused, it is also referred to as the Sorrow of Assam.

Island formation reaches its zenith with Majuli, the world's largest riverine atoll. At 880 square kilometres, it is large enough to carry a population of almost 1,50,000 people spread over 155 villages, and even boasts its own capital at Garmur. Majuli is especially visited for its monasteries. Established by the poet-philosopher Sankardeva in the 15th century as a seat of Hindu Vaishnavite learning, the institution of *satra* (monastery) is alive today in 22 centres scattered across the Island. These are rich repositories of traditional classical culture, including dance, music, art, and antique handicrafts.

Flowing past sanctuaries and historic towns

India's only 'male' river nourishes a formidable ecology—56,700 square kilometres of tropical and sub-tropical moist, broad-leaved forests flourishing in its basin have been designated a distinct eco-region. Visible on misty, low hills in the distance, and often creeping right up to the banks, 12 of these tracts have been protected as sanctuaries and national parks. Beginning upstream with Dibru Saikhowa National Park—grazing ground of the feral horse—these include Pobha and Gorompani Wildlife Sanctuaries; Kaziranga and Nameri National Parks; Laokhuwa, Orang and Pobitora Wildlife Sanctuaries, and Manas National Park, a World Heritage Site.

Towns steeped in history pass by: at Tezpur is the 1,500-year-old Da Parbatia Temple, Assam's finest and oldest example of sculptural art; Guwahati is most famous for the Kamakhya shrine, an ancient tantric seat where the deity is a manifestation of Shakti. East of the city, from Saraighat Bridge, one can watch the huge mass of water ripple enchantingly in the sun's dying rays. Continuing onward to Bangladesh, the River fades away into the evening mist. And by the time its journey through the Indian plains is complete, the Son of Brahma has gained the strength of more than 100 tributaries. Streaming into Bangladesh as the Jamuna, there-after confluencing with the Ganga and becoming the Padma, the vast mass of vascularised water ultimately merges into the Bay of Bengal as the world's greatest delta.

Blue-green river amid labyrinthine ravines

The Chambal Wildlife Sanctuary was once the lair of dacoits

MADHYA PRADESH

Chambal

Bhopal

State and capital:
Uttar Pradesh
(Lucknow), Madhya
Pradesh (Bhopal),
Rajasthan (Jaipur)

Convenient access:
Road (via Agra, UP),
air, rail to Agra

Accommodation:
Budget to luxury at
Agra, mid-range at
Jarar (near Sanctuary)

Best season:
November to March

Also worth seeing:
Agra 97 km NW of
Sanctuary jetty,
Bateshwar temples
25 km N

*Top: A gharial
basking on a
sandbank.*

Bordering the meandering Chambal River, sometimes for 10 kilometres on each side, is a unique system of shallow, scrub-forested ravines created by centuries of soil erosion. These unstable formations crumble, shift, change shape and reform every year with the rise and ebb of flood waters. It is a bewildering maze, very easy to get lost in. For long, this jigsaw of mud hillocks was used by dacoits to melt away from the fumbling arm of law without a trace. The fearsome brigands are much dwindled now, leaving the beautiful River to its natural, wild denizens, and allowing it to emerge out of obscurity on to India's wildlife map.

Debouching from the Vindhya-chal Mountains of Central India, the Chambal is India's only major north-flowing stream. Its initial content, myth says, came from the blood of cows sacrificed by a king to please the gods and ask them to bestow him supremacy over his rivals. Alarmed by the ruler's ambitions, the priestly class reacted by cursing him and the crimson

effluence he had created, and it is a result of this, it is said, that no temple towns have ever come up on the banks. Peering though, into the cyan translucence (sometimes transparence) of the waters, it is hard to find traces of the king's misjudged sacrifice. For the Chambal is certainly one of Indian plains' least polluted and pristine rivers.

Aggressive crocodiles, gamboling otters

The Chambal Wildlife Sanctuary covers 400 kilometres of the Chambal River, from Kota, through its confluence with the Yamuna, extending 40 kilometres further along the Yamuna itself, up to its confluence with the Sind at Panchnada. Two big predators, the freshwater crocodile and the gharial reign over this aquamarine kingdom. In the 1970s, with the gharial population of India severely endangered, the valley's fluvial habitat was demarcated to attempt a recovery. Almost 1,500 of these reptiles and a few crocodiles were reared and released into the river.

With adequate protection, they thrived, and today, the Chambal is one of their strong bastions. Though it is easy to mistake a motionless, long, thin-snouted gharial for a piece of driftwood, both species can be spotted basking on the sandbanks. Appearing deceptively sluggish and unobservant, they speedily slither into the water on being disturbed. Some of the crocodiles are massive, and are known to make grabbing assaults on unwary humans or cattle which stray into their territory. The Chambal also hosts smooth-coated otters seen gamboling in groups, at least eight kinds of tortoises that tumble off into the water from rocks like dislodged stones as the boat passes by, and 30 varieties of fish. Besides these, a prized species of the Sanctuary is the acutely threatened Gangetic dolphin, which makes its presence felt occasionally by fleeting surface rolls on the deeper stretches.

Refuge of skimmers

However, more than for its healthy stock of reptiles and mammals, the Chambal is known for its 250 species

of resident and migratory birds. Though the biggest avian draw here is a colony of Indian skimmers, a bird whose numbers have been observed to be on the wane, cruising down on the boat one also runs into masses of cormorants, bar-headed geese, gulls, ruddy shelducks, pintails and pochards taking off, wheeling and flying low over the turquoise blue expanse of the rippling river. Flamingoes, Plovers, lapwings, sandpipers, stilts, naktas, ibises herons, storks, kingfishers, cranes and many other birds can be spotted on the banks, while raptors like Pallas's fish eagles, harriers, ospreys and buzzards sit on bare tree stumps or soar on thermals. Within the cracks of the ravines dwell francolins and quails, shrikes and orioles, larks and warblers.

On the harsh landscape of the ravines are the scattered ruins of a series of medieval forts, built to guard trade routes extending across the river. The 800-year-old Ater Fort with its exquisite pavilions is an example of the Rajput and Muslim architecture prevalent in those times. Founded by Tomar Rajputs, Ater's ramparts were manned at different periods by Mughals, Bhadoria Rajputs and the Marathas. Today, they make perfect vantage points for panoramic views that reveal the astounding network of the Chambal ravines.

Above: *Take out point of the river safari; the ravines extend outward from the far bank.*
Below: *Camels are commonly domesticated in this arid region.*
Bottom: *Indian skimmers, Chambal's prize avian species.*

A fertile junction of waters

Chilika is the largest inland lake on the subcontinent

ORISSA

Bhubaneshwar

Chilika Lake

Bay of Bengal

State and capital:

Orissa, Bhubaneshwar (100 km)

Convenient access:

Road to Lake, air to Bhubaneshwar, rail to Rambha, Balugaon

Accommodation:

Budget to mid-range

Best season:

November to March

Also worth seeing:

Puri, 50 km NE, Gopalpur on sea, 45 km SW

It is said that many hundreds of years ago the pirate king Raktabahu arrived on the eastern coast of the Indian sub-continent, close to the estuary of the Mahanadi River, to ransack the rich city of Puri. His daunting fleet of fast ships anchored just over the horizon out of sight of the coast. But the Sea washed up the ship's refuse to the shore warning the townspeople, who then fled with all their possessions. Thus when Raktabahu set foot ashore he found a deserted city. Furious at what he saw as the Sea's

betrayal, he attacked it with his entire army. The Sea initially gave way, and then surged back in anger, drowning the army and forming what is now known as Chilika Lake. Historically, Chilika has been integral to the economy and culture of coastal Orissa. A poem penned 400 years ago by the saint-poet Purshottam Das elaborates on Lord Krishna dancing on its shores with a local curd-seller girl, Maniki. Even today the village of Manikagauda (Gauda is the local cowherd caste) stands on Chilika's bank.

Biodiversity influenced by saline and fresh water

Located on coastal Orissa, Chilika is the largest inland lake on the Indian subcontinent. Sixty-four kilometres long and with an average width of 20 kilometres, the Lake was a part of the Bay of Bengal until a spit of sand grew between the sea and the open lagoon, leaving it connected to the former by a narrow mouth. This mouth is unstable, varying with time in both location and size. Often it gets completely blocked, whereupon it is dredged open, usually by local fisherfolk, whose livelihoods depend on maintaining a sea inflow into Chilika. Presently the sea is connected to the Lake by a 32-kilometres long, narrow, outer channel near the village of Motto. However, due to Chilika's huge size, the influence of the sea is restricted

to the zone closest to the open mouth. As a result of this constant movement of water, the Lake changes size in different seasons. During the monsoon, when fresh water pours in from the rivers it expands to over 1,150 square kilometres, whereas in the dry summer it shrinks to about 900 square kilometres.

Being the junction of fresh and saline water bodies, the Lake is a unique ecosystem and a biodiversity hotspot. Animal and plant life, adapted to a range of conditions, includes over 220 fish species, numerous aquatic plant species, and about 720 land based plants in the immediate surroundings. The Indian Zoological Survey recorded over 800 types of fauna from the lake region, with a number of rare and endangered species like the Barakudia limbless skink, found nowhere else in the world, estuarine turtles, numerous kinds of snakes, rodents, otters, bats, and sloth bears on the hills around Chilika. Once commonly seen following boats and playing near the Lake's mouth, the rare Irrawaddy dolphin is now sighted only occasionally. A huge migrant bird community, some from Central Asia, Russia, South East Asia and Ladakh, flies in to feed and breed in the fertile waters. A recent survey identified 205 avian species in the Chilika environs.

The continuous input of river silt has made Chilika very shallow, creating islands, many of which are inhabited by fishermen—more than 150,000 fisherfolk live in and around the lake—who scour the waters for mackerel, prawn and crab. Nalaban, a 10-square-kilometre marshy island, is one of the largest. Completely submerged during the monsoon, it is a major feeding and roosting habitat during winter for over 100 species of migratory birds and has been declared a bird sanctuary.

Jim Corbett's jungle

To many, Corbett National Park is the mecca of wildlife in India

State and capital:
Uttarakhand, Dehradun
(225 km)

Convenient access:
Road to Corbett, air to
Dehradun, New Delhi,
rail to Ramnagar

Accommodation:
Budget to high-end

Best season:
November to March
May-June for tiger
spotting; Park closed
from mid-June to mid-
November

Also worth seeing:
Corbett's house at
Kaladhungi, 40 km E

*Above: The Pallas'
Fish Eagle is seen in
the vicinity of
streams and water
bodies, and also on
the branches of dried
trees from where it
keeps its eagle eye
out for likely prey. Its
loud, raucous shrieks
can be identified
from long distances.*

*Facing page: In the
dry season the
Ramganga River is
reduced to two or
three spread-apart
channels, thus
opening up a broad
valley plain which,
apart from being a
stamping ground of
elephants, is also
favoured by grazing
and resting ungulates
as it prevents a
stalking tiger or
leopard from getting
close to them without
being seen. It is not
uncommon to see up
to three or four
separate herds of
spotted deer,
numbering 50-60
animals each, at the
same time on the
valley floor.*

It was an era in India when hunting was still a respected 'sport', and the first of the hunters-turned-conservationists were only just emerging. One of these was Edward James 'Jim' Corbett, an Englishman born and bred in India. Though he gave up shooting for pleasure, Corbett continued to employ his vast knowledge of Indian jungles to rid the Central Himalayan foothills of the scourge of man-eating tigers. Between 1907 and 1938, Corbett tracked and shot dead about 15 man-eaters, who, between them accounted for more than 1,500 humans. Many of these exciting adventures are recounted by him in bestselling books like *Man-Eaters of Kumaon*, and *The Man-Eating Leopard of Rudraprayag*, while the author's own life has been documented by a number of other writers and film makers. Corbett became a legend, not just in India, but with wildlife enthusiasts in the whole world.

Knowledgeable mahouts

Corbett National Park was conceived in 1907, at a time when the great game reserves of Africa had not even been dreamed of. In 1936, it became India's first National Park, and thereon grew in stature and size, encompassing an area of about 1,300 square kilometres. Set in its namesake's backyard, in a geographical zone known locally as bhabar, where the Shivalik Hills give way to the plains of North India, Corbett is now possibly the country's best known protected area. The thickly forested,

undulating terrain of the region has always been rich in wildlife, and continues to be the home of a large population of tigers and elephants. In 1973, with the Indian tiger teetering on the brink of obliteration (reduced to a paltry 2,000 from 40,000 at the turn of the century), Corbett became the launch pad of the ambitious Project Tiger conservation programme.

The Park's vegetation comprises mainly of the tall and stately sal, with *sheesham*, bamboo, mango, *jamun* (java plum), *haldu*, various climbers, shrubs and grasses. Dirt roads wind through the jungles providing enough opportunity for viewing game from jeeps. Much of the wildlife, especially ungulates like sambar, spotted deer and hog deer can be easily seen on wide *chaurs* (savannahs) that intersperse the forests. Where vehicles can't go, riding elephants manned by knowledgeable mahouts—some who are part of the Corbett folklore in their own right—take over. Apart from this, there are machaans (watch towers) where one can spend many hours scanning the landscape. However, there is no guarantee of spotting a tiger. While pugmarks, the alarm call of deer or langur, or the remains of a kill might provide clues to its whereabouts, at the end, luck is the determining factor, for the tiger is solitary and elusive by nature. At the same time, the big feline sometimes could emerge, all of a sudden, on a hunting charge, or simply walking on the road, just when it is least expected.

600 species of birds

In 1974, a dam on the Ramganga River, which runs through the reserve, created a 40-square-kilometre reservoir, which though submerging some of the Park area created another habitat. Besides crocodiles and fish-eating gharials lying on the banks, (also visible from vantage points upstream), the lake attracts a multitude of water birds. In fact, Corbett, with as many as 600 migratory and local species, is a birdwatchers' paradise. The avifauna includes raptors like the handsome Pallas' eagle and crested serpent eagle, plovers and cormorants, various woodpeckers, sunbirds and warblers. Huge Himalayan hornbills can at times be spied flying from one treetop to the other with an impressive swish of wings.

Next to the tiger, the leopard is the Corbett's biggest cat. As reclusive as its cousin, it is more likely seen in the higher reaches, as are mountain goats. Grunting and shuffling as it forages, the ferocious wild pig of Corbett is known to grow over 100 kilograms in weight. However, of the 50 species of mammals, elephants are the biggest. Mostly seen in groups on the *chaurs*, with babies protectively shielded by their massive mothers, they also are often heard breaking trees and crashing through the undergrowth. Sometimes a lone tusker can stubbornly block the road and even make mock charges. One of the most enduring sights of Corbett is provided by the big pachyderms as a herd crosses the Ramganga with successive ranges of misty blue hills in the background.

Home of the Nilgiri tahr

The goat-antelope is the mascot of Eravikulam National Park

KERALA

Arabian Sea — Eravikulam

Thiruvananthapuram

State and Capital:
Kerala,
Thiruvananthapuram
(314 km)

Convenient access:
Road to Park, air to
Kochi, Ernakulam, rail
to Kochi, Aluva

Accommodation:
Budget to high-end

Best season:
September-October

Also worth seeing:
Chinnar and Indira
Gandhi Wildlife
Sanctuaries, adjoining
N, Top Station for
views of Western
Ghats, SE, Thattekad
Bird Sanctuary, SW

*Below: Stocky and
handsome, the tahr
is distinguishable by
the colour of its fur,
ranging from brown
to almost black, and
the curvaceous
backward bent of
its horns.*

Though the exciting fauna of Eravikulam includes tiger, leopard, boar and wild dogs, it is the grey-brown Nilgiri tahr, an endangered species of goat-antelope not found anywhere else in the world, which is its most well-known resident and biggest draw.

In the early 19th century, British planters discovered the bracing, emerald-green uplands of Munnar in Kerala, and began clearing forests to replace them with tea, coffee and cinchona plantations. Higher areas, where the soil seemed unusable due to extreme cold, were set aside for hunting the plentiful wildlife. Tahr numbers, already under pressure from pre-British habitat depletion, began dwindling fast, and the sure-footed ungulate, sometimes tipping the scales at a 100 kilograms, would have certainly disappeared off the face of the earth had protective measures not been taken at the turn of the century. One of the places that the tahr hung on was Hamilton's Plateau, then the private hunting reserve of the Kannan Devan Hills Produce Company. Today, this breathtakingly beautiful area, 2,000 metres above sea level is the 97-square-kilometre Eravikulam National Park. But the crisis was not over. In 1997, came another sudden drop in the population, resulting in a renewed bout of intense conservation effort, and although slow to respond, the tahr again made a comeback.

A riot of blue

Essentially, Eravikulam is made up of undulating windswept grass-lands, with plateaus and knolls rolling ceaselessly into one another. Amongst the surrounding peaks is Anamudi, at 2,694 metres the highest mountain in South India. The many streams and waterfalls, which cut across, enhance the Park's natural beauty and the Byzantine clusters of dark-hued *sholas*, which are unique high-altitude montane forests of stunted trees found only in South India. *Sholas* grow in depressions and look like giant moss carpets that have taken over portions of the grassy plateau. The

upper forest canopy of leathery leaves in different colours, ranging from dark greens to purple, consists of a mixture of small tree species, which include rhododendron, mahonia, rudraksh—the rudraksh seed is used as a symbolic Hindu talisman—and holly. Below this is an understorey, followed by a lowermost layer of dense shrubbery. Navigating through the branches of these *shola* stretches is not always easy, and because of the dampness, leeches are in plenty. A spectacular event on the Eravikulam meadows is the blooming of *neelakkurinji* every 12 years (though according to botanists it can also happen once

in about six to seven years). Comprising of various species of strobilanthus, all of which have blue flowers, the mass eruption of *neelakkurinji* transforms the vast stretches of emerald greens into carpets of blue.

In many of the numerous wildlife parks of India, visitors can roam in the tourist-demarcated areas in vehicles for a restricted time, during which chances of spotting fauna and looking and exploring beyond the immediate masses of dense vegetation are limited. There are, however, a few exceptions, especially bird sanctuaries like Vedanthangal,

Keoladeo, Kumarakom, etc., where one can access the interiors on foot, making the experience unusually interesting, as well as offering an opportunity to closely study smaller beings like butterflies, insects and reptile species. Eravikulam is one such park. The tourist zone, known as Rajamala, while not allowing the panoramic views of grasslands and valleys as available in the core area, affords a sight quite lovely in itself. A motorable road leads to the gate of the Park beyond which tourists have to climb for about 20 minutes to reach the first plateau. Depending on the mist, sweeping views of the Park are visible from here, and at

times the Nilgiri tahr can be spotted, if not within, then very close to the tourist zone. For the serious visitor who wants a more intimate experience of the unique Park terrain, several treks are possible in the areas around Munnar where all the characteristic ingredients, including scattered wildlife, of the Eravikulam core zone can be found.

Above: Spread over the southern Western Ghats and their offshoot ranges, Nilgiri tahr are now estimated to number between 2,500 and 3,000. Of these, 1,000 are in Eravikulam. It is the only viable population left.

Where the Ganga is born

At Gangotri, near her glacial source, she is a raging torrent

State and capital:
Uttarakhand, Dehradun
(275 km)

Convenient access:
Road to Gangotri, air
to Dehradun, rail to
Haridwar

Accommodation:
Budget

Best season: April to
June, September-
October

Also worth seeing:
Treks to the meadows
of Tapovan and
Nandanvan, Kedartal
Lake, up the trail from
Gangotri

*Above: Over
millennia the sheer
rocky sides have
been smoothened by
the powerful flow
into glistening curves
and hollows.*
*Facing page: The
diminutive temple
of Gangotri.*

From the face of a cow (Gaumukh) drips the essence of Hinduism's most holy river. The metaphorical cow, over 30 kilometres long and up to 2.5 kilometres broad, 'lives' high up in the Himalayas. Sleek and icy, it is constantly on the move, inching its massive body down from snowfields 7,100 metres high before transforming from its glacial form, 3,000 metres lower down, to the newborn Ganga. Then begins a journey, more than 2,500 kilometres long through the plains of North India, bestowing along the way sacred stature to settlements touched and gathering the spiritual aspirations of many millions who wet themselves with its waters, before the end in the Bay of Bengal.

Actually the Ganga acquires its name further down the valley, when she meets the Alaknanda River at Devprayag. At her source she is Bhagirathi, named after King Bhagirath who, it is said, called her down to earth to wash away the sins of his ancestors so that they could go to heaven. But had this daughter of Meru landed directly, her force would have shattered the earth. So to soften the impact, Shiva agreed to receive her in his matted locks, and the place where he did so, 18 kilometres below Gaumukh, is called Gangotri. It seems that after

facilitating the smooth entry of the sin cleansing river, Shiva retreated into the background, for today he is present as a natural rock shivaling under her waters, visible only in winter when the stream recedes. Gangotri is a small temple town, encircled with snow-capped peaks and forests of cedar and pine. At the centre of it all is the River Goddess' temple, a simple whitewashed structure built by the Gorkha General Amar Singh Thapa in the 18th century, and later rebuilt by the Maharaja of Jaipur. The Goddess is not in residence the year round; in winter her idol is taken to Mukhba, 25 kilometres away, so that the freezing conditions are not allowed to cause a break in worship, most interesting of which is the evening *aarti* (ritual prayer), a cadence of chanting, bells and oil lamps. Much music and dance accompany her return in summer, an event at least 700 years old, with lesser deities from nearby villages joining the procession.

Feats and austerities of sadhus

Most palpable, however, at Gangotri is the Goddess' natural form. By now from a shallow gurgling stream near her inception, she is a racing, surging, roaring torrent, smashing, swirling and foaming through a

narrow chasm. Pilgrims, undeterred by the freezing temperature of the water, take customary dips at more mellow spots, filling bottles of holy water to take back home. Along its path, all the way up to Gaumukh is a fascinating facet of Hindu religiosity. Wandering sadhus, bearded, with long locks, their foreheads painted with the three horizontal lines signifying Shiva devotees, have set up home in huts, caves and under trees. Chief amongst their handful of possessions are a *lota* (all-purpose vessel) and a trident, and they survive on offerings of pilgrims and marijuana. Many, unaffected by the shivering cold, wear scanty clothes—the Naga sadhus are naked, their bodies smeared only with ash. A select few are known for extreme practices like consciously never moving an arm, allowing it to whither away or keeping a limb immersed in the chilling waters of the river; always remaining mute; sleeping bound or leaning against a tree instead of lying down.

Roar of the Asiatic lion

The 'pride' of Gir National Park

GUJARAT

Gandhinagar

Gir

Arabian Sea

State and capital:
Gujarat, Ahmedabad
(400 km)

Convenient access:
Road to Junagadh,
air to Ahmedabad,
Rajkot, rail to
Junagadh

Accommodation:
Budget to high-end

Best season:
November to March

Also worth seeing:
Junagadh Fort and
caves, 42 km NW, old
Portuguese town of
Diu, 110 km SW

At the foothills of the Girnar mountain stands what is possibly the world's first decree for the conservation of wildlife. It is an edict, carved in stone, dating back to the third century BC in the name of Emperor Ashoka, who on seeing the ravages of a fierce battle fought by him in present day Orissa turned to the teachings of the Buddha and came to believe that all life was sacred and worth protecting. Spreading out from these hills, which appear as blue shadows from the scrubby flatlands of the Park, the Gir jungle of south-western Saurashtra was once so thick and lush and surrounded by streams that horses had difficulty in passing through. Now, the corridors that linked the forest are lost and they exist as two smaller, separate jungles. In these jungles live the last wild lions outside the African continent.

Asiatic lions once roamed from Central India to Arabia and Persia, even as far as Greece, but coveted as a hunter's prized trophy, were nearly wiped out. The Nawabs of Junagadh, in whose domain the Gir jungles lay, organised hunts for the largest, most handsome beasts with the heaviest manes for British Viceroys and officials, and their own favoured friends. Yet, to their credit, it was the Nawab himself, on the urgings of Lord Curzon— 'The preservation of fauna and flora is more important than the preservation of any of the great monuments which after all were fashioned by man and can be recreated at a price. The present generation owes it to its successors to restore the only species of a large mammal lost in the plains of India in historical times. Failure to do so would not be forgiven by the judgment of history'—who put a ban on the hunting. By this time only a dozen or so individuals survived. But protected across the National Park area of 1,412 square kilometres, they have come back strongly and today Gir is home to about 300 lions. In fact, the point has been reached where the forest can support no more of the big beasts and the government is trying to set up another sanctuary to relocate some of the population.

Pastoral Maldharis coexist with wildlife

Apart from its lions, Gir has 300 leopards making this the largest concentration of big cats in any

Left: Spotted deer
are a favourite prey
for the lions.
Facing page & below:
Asiatic lions, a
subspecies that split
from their African
cousins perhaps
100,000 years ago,
hang on today to an
impossibly small
slice of their former
domain. The entire
Gir population,
originating from the
common gene pool
of a handful of
animals that survived
in these forests, is
highly vulnerable
to epidemics.

national park of India. On their menu are sambar and spotted deer, nilgai antelope, *chousingha* (the world's only four-horned antelope), chinkara (Indian gazelle) and wild boar. Jackal, striped hyena, jungle cat, rusty-spotted cat, langur, porcupine, and the black-naped Indian hare represent the smaller mammals. The marsh crocodile is one of the 40 species of reptiles and amphibians, and the checklist of birds numbers 250. All these can be sighted in jeeps provided by the forest department; the deciduous vegetation, interspersed with large patches of grasslands, is conducive to long pleasant drives through thick forest cover. Gir's trees are mostly broad leaved and evergreen, giving the area cool shade and moisture content. Of the six well-designated routes in the Park, the longest one is 31 kilometres.

Coexisting with the galaxy of animals, in settlements called nesses, are Hindu and Muslim pastoral people called Maldharis.

One comes across them, while driving through the Park, wearing traditional clothes, colourful turbans and earrings, and carrying huge *lathis* (sticks) to protect their buffaloes, cattle, camels, sheep and goats from wild animals. Also settled in the vicinity of Gir are the Siddis

of African origin, who first came here many years ago as mercenaries, slaves and labour, some rising to become generals and rulers in their own right. Today their villages are famous with visitors for lively dances and performances.

In Goa, all roads lead to the beach

The coastline of this former Portuguese colony is a feast of sand and local culture

The quintessential Goan beach is lively with shacks serving beer and seafood, flea markets and vendors offering everything from sarongs and scarves to alternative lifestyles, and the ubiquitous sun umbrellas.

The Konkan coast of western India, merging into the Arabian Sea, is known for its verdant beauty. From the east, the Western Ghats tumble down to the coastal plain in a rush of undulating green, giving way to coconut plantations and paddy fields, and villages seeped in the famous Goan *sussegad* culture: a laid-back life where food, feni (the local cashewnut liquor) and siestas are as important as making a livelihood. The Portuguese ruled Goa for 400 years, and left their mark on its religion, dress, cuisine and architecture. But more than anything else it is what was already there, the enchanting beaches, lying along 106 kilometres of seaface, that the little state is most famous for.

Varied line of sand

From Querim in the north to Palolem in the south are about 30 beaches of various sizes, ranging from less than two to more than 20 kilometres in length. Crowded or unfrequented and quiet; studded with big resorts, food shacks, water sport facilities or with virtually no infrastructure; those good for swimming and those just for sunbathing; each has its own character. Options for adventure

Rivers, crossing which, one heads south. Enroute, a little off the circuit, Bogmalo, packing a luxury hotel, is the favoured beach of the rich and famous—however, in India, since beaches cannot be owned privately, they are accessible to everyone, regardless of a big resort or hotel on its edge. Majorda is famous for its European-style baked breads, leavened with coconut toddy. Behind the beaches are mazes of narrow roads winding through villages, often with old churches: Colva beach's Church of Our Lady of Mercy is well known and its sands are often laid out with mackerel drying in the sun. Further south, Bernaulim is another fishing beach village with its attendant Church of St John, the Baptist, on a hill. During the time of its festival and accompanying feast, young men wearing crowns of fruits and leaves move around the area singing songs and asking for presents. The golden sands of Varca, Carvellosim and Mabor, humming with mellow activity, yet clean and lovely, are ranged near the mouth of the Sal River, and beyond them is tiny Betul, also a fishing port below a promontory of the Western Ghats. The three-kilometre long palm- and casuarina-lined Agonda, almost devoid of any facilities, and thus people, is perhaps the most beautiful and pristine of them all, and the crescent-shaped Palolem, the last bit of sand before the Konkan coast enters Karnataka, is perhaps the most appropriate place to watch a spectacular sunset over the blue Arabian Sea.

State and capital:
Goa, Panaji (72 km and 34 km from the last beaches in the S and N)

Convenient access:
Road to all the beaches, air to Dabolim, rail to Margao, Vasco da Gama

Accommodation:
Budget to luxury

Best season:
November to February

Also worth seeing:
Mangueshi Temple, Basilica of Bom Jesus, Se Cathedral, old Portuguese mansions

Below: Many beaches have their associated local fishing communities and their boats add to the pretty surroundings.

sports include canoeing, parasailing and jet skiing. Early morning sees dolphin watchers crowd the railings on small launches; beach umbrellas dot the sands through the day until sunset, when the focus shifts to night-time revelry with Goan bands playing a mix of Konkani and popular music.

With Panaji in the centre, the beaches fall either in the northern or southern part of the state. Aguada is the first beach in the north. Sinquerim, the next one is the beginning of a virtually unbroken line of sand extending 30 kilometres up the coast, where one beach merges into another. This stretch includes the one-time hippie hang-outs of Candolim, Calangute and Baga, hugely popular and more entertaining than the others. Further up at Anjuna and Vagator, things start settling down, and across the Chapora River, finally there is peace at Arambol. The Portuguese built a series of coastal forts to guard their Indian possessions and the sparkling white citadel of Terakhol, looking over the idyllic Querim beach, is one of them.

Fishing villages and village churches

Panaji is sandwiched between the mouths of the Mandovi and Zuari

Above: *The picture-perfect Sonamarg scenery.*

The Meadows of Kashmir

They nestle deep in the lap of stunning mountain vistas

One of the most arrestingly beautiful regions in India is Kashmir. Its lush and sweet smelling forests consist of oaks, pines, silver-coloured birches, maple and poplars. Orchards of apples, fields of red chillies and saffron, and acres of poppy plantations spread into the deep reaches of the valleys. The Mughals loved Kashmir and many of its monuments and exquisite gardens are their legacy. Particularly a favourite with them was Gulmarg, literally meaning the Meadow of Flowers, nestling at a height of 2,730 metres. Originally called Gaurimarg by shepherds, the cup shaped meadow was later renamed by Sultan Yusuf Shah in the 16th century. Five hundred years later its blossoms continue to thrive with abandon, especially in spring when colonies of wildflowers fan out in every direction. During this time people of all ages can be seen frolicking on the green undulating meadows. Walks are in plenty here. An 11 kilometre circular path runs along the circumference and smaller trails

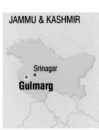

Srinagar

Gulmarg

State and capital:
Jammu & Kashmir,
Srinagar (Gulmarg
52 km E, Sonamarg 84
km NW)

Convenient access:
Road to Gulmarg,
Sonamarg, air to
Srinagar, rail to Jammu

Accommodation:
Budget to high-end

Best season:
December to March
for skiing, otherwise
all through except
July-August

Also worth seeing:
Charar-i-Sharif

*Below: The succulent
grasses of the
meadows are
favoured by
shepherds for
grazing their sheep.*

network the expanse, with occasional trout filled streams cutting across. Around the boundaries are thick forests with secluded picnic spots. An hour long popular hike leads up 600 metres to Khilanmarg, from where one gets breathtaking panoramic views of the Himalayan ranges, including the 7,000-metre plus twin peaks of Nun and Kun. A little higher than Khilanmarg is a high altitude lake, where stray chunks of floating ice can be found even in summer.

Gulmarg holds the distinction of fielding the highest golf course in the world. In winter the town becomes a premier skiing resort of the country. A venue for the National Winter Games since 1998, it has been consistently upgraded and maintained. The ski season commences by the middle of December and lasts till roughly the end of March, by when the snow turns to slush. Skiing paraphernalia and instructors are available locally.

Sonamarg or the Meadow of Gold, one of the base points for the annual pilgrimage to the Amarnath Cave, lies at 3,000 metres near the highway to Kargil and Leh. A short two-hour hike from here leads up to the Thajiwas glacier, a popular place for sled rides. Though not always open to tourists, Yusmarg or the Beautiful Meadow, at 2,700 metres, is the quietest of the three but considered by some to boast the best spring flowers in Kashmir.

Sentinel of the eastern Himalayas

Kanchenjunga remains one of the lesser-climbed 8,000-metre peaks

Above: Because of its difficult accessibility and tight restrictions on climbing expeditions, the inner sanctum of Kanchenjunga remains largely untouched and spared of the attendant litter that sometimes mars other popular Himalayan base camps.

Whether it is because the mountain is actually composed of five peaks, or because the five Buddhist treasures of gold, silver, precious stones, grain and holy scriptures believed to be concealed amongst its pinnacles or, as wildlife enthusiasts would have it, due to the presence of five exotic species of flora and fauna—rhododendron, blood pheasant, the lammergeyer vulture, Sikkim's state animal, the red panda,

and the phantasmal snow leopard—translated, Kanchenjunga, also spelled as Khangchendzonga, means 'The Five Treasures of Snows'. While Mt. Everest is well known and an imposing mountain in its own right and K2 is fierce and remote, Kanchenjunga is a beautiful peak when seen from any direction. Rising to 8,585 metres, it is the highest mountain in India, and the third highest in the world, after Everest and K2.

Rhododendrons and the red panda

It was Sir Joseph Dalton Hooker, the 19th century British botanist and explorer, who first highlighted the area's rich biodiversity to the world, estimating that on its higher altitudes, the mountainous terrain of the Kingdom of Sikkim harboured the entire alpine flora of Europe and North America combined. In 1977, India declared 1,784 square kilometres around the

mountainscapes. Just as the wildlife in the upper reaches is unique, the features of the lower forests are as fascinating: trees laden with bunches of flowering orchids, yellow-backed sunbirds on forest blooms, gurgling streams, energetic waterfalls cascading into limpid pools, swinging bridges and infuriating leeches.

Sunrise at Dzongri

Three of Kanchenjunga's peaks border the Indian state of Sikkim and the Taplejung district of Nepal, while two lie entirely in Nepal. Most visitors approach the Park from the Sikkimese town of Yuksum, the old capital. Here, on the directions of the venerated Buddhist Saint Padmasambhava, the first king of Sikkim was consecrated under a massive 400-year-old pine tree. The two to three days long trek passes through Bakhim or Tsokha, along the Rathong River in its initial stretches, with wonderful panoramas of soaring finials, glaciers and torrents. From the camping grounds at Dzongri (3,890 metres), 25 kilometres from Yuksum, one gets magical sunrise views of the mountain, as well as the peaks of Siniolchu, Pauhunri, Kabru and Rathong, framed by Buddhist prayer flags. Seasoned trekkers can venture further, to Goechala, which offers even better views. With the tree-line far below, yak herders tend to their large herds beyond the Dzongri plain, and the peaceful isolation is broken with the distant tinkle of yak bells, the occasional scream of a chough or an accentor, amidst the fragrance of

dwarf rhododendron in the clear mountain air.

After four preceding unsuccessful expeditions, Kanchenjunga was finally climbed in 1955 by the British mountaineers Joe Brown and George Band. Out of respect to the religious sentiments of the Sikkimese people, who hold the mountain sacred, the duo stopped a few metres short of the summit, without actually stepping onto it. Pierre Beghin made the first successful solo ascent without oxygen in 1983, and in 1998, Ginette Harrison became the first woman to reach the top.

SIKKIM

Kanchenjunga

Gangtok

State and capital:
Sikkim, Gangtok
(130 km)
Convenient access:
Road to Yuksum, air to Bagdogra, Gangtok, rail to New Jalpaiguri
Accommodation:
Budget to mid-range at Yuksum; forest rest-houses and camping in Park.
Best season: April to June, September to November. Largely snowbound from December to February
Also see: Barsey Rhododendron Sanctuary, S, Maenam Wildlife Sanctuary, SE, Buddhist monasteries, 20-35 km S

Below: Hikers in the sanctuary area.

peak, upwards in altitude from 1,830 metres, as a National Park, thus protecting its immense natural wealth. This is most vivid in spring with the abundant display of flowering shrubs, dwarf rhododendrons, primulas, irises and numerous other wildflowers on high-altitude meadows, slopes of juniper, pristine forests and the banks of glacial flows. In addition, the Park hosts a wide array of rare Himalayan wildlife including the retiring snow leopard. Easier but not commonly seen are the leopard, black bear, blue sheep and barking deer. The furry arboreal red panda, of course, is a bonus. Various species of thrushes, sunbirds, finches, pheasants and raptors inhabit the

Foothold to stronghold of the one-horned rhino

The big beast thrives on the wet savannah grasslands of Kaziranga National Park

E.P. Gee, the famous conservationist closely associated with Kaziranga in its early years, wrote in its visitors' book of an elephant-back foray into the jungles, 'Twice charged by rhino, and the elephants each time bolted for some distance.' Some months later, he recalls, other visitors wrote in the same book, 'Rather disap-

pointing. Charged only by the Forest Department!' This is one of the stories of Kaziranga, now a World Heritage Site, illustrating how it developed from a place of swamps, leeches and malaria, not accessible to even elephants, where its prize species, the Indian one-horned rhinoceros, would, unused to being disturbed by any other

being, respond aggressively to intruders. And then, when the sanctuary opened to public in 1938, the 'armoured' beasts soon became accustomed to outsiders, allowing themselves to be watched as they grazed or wallowed in slushy mud. Another interesting anecdote preceding this one goes back to 1904, when Lady Curzon, wife of

State and capital:
Assam, Dispur
(250 km)

Convenient access:
Road to Kaziranga,
air to Jorhat and
Guwahati, rail to
Guwahati

Accommodation:
Budget to mid-range

Best season:
November to March

Also worth seeing:
Nearby tea plantations,
Karbi and Mising tribal
villages

thing that makes them coveted by man; their horn is still in high demand in the illegal market where it is sold mainly for use in Chinese traditional medicine and ornamental accessories. The horn, between 20 and 60 centimetres long, is not strictly a horn as it consists of a mass of tightly compressed hair placed above the nose.

Home of India's only ape

Kaziranga is divided into four ranges. The eastern woodlands interspersed with grassland and waterbodies constitute the Agoratoli range, while at the centre is the Kohora range. The western Baguri range has the highest rhinoceros density and Burhapahar, the fourth range, covers the first additional area attached to the Park. Wet savannah grasslands, which cover about 70 per cent of the Park comprise tall grasses, mostly reeds, bulrushes and elephant grass. The dominant force, which shapes the Park is the monsoon, when the Brahmaputra floods low-lying grasslands for several weeks, sometimes months, causing animals to migrate to higher ground. Amongst over 52 mammalian species recorded in the area are the rare Gangetic dolphin, Chinese pangolin, hog-badger, and the tail-devoid hoolock gibbon. The latter, India's only ape, is called the musical animal. Others like the hog deer, sloth bear, jungle cats, otters, capped langurs, wild boar and jackals are more common. Thirty-nine reptiles make the list, including the gharial and the Assam roofed turtle. Both the reticulated and rock pythons occur here.

A few 100 Bengal floricans

Rich of avian fauna, the Park's different habitat zones host over 250 local and 100 migratory species. At small lakes, locally called *bheels*, are found pelicans and the increasingly rare greater adjutant storks. The grasslands are prime raptor country; the oriental honey buzzard, Pallas's fishing eagle and Himalayan griffon are usually seen. But most well known of Kaziranga's winged denizen is the Bengal florican, of which only 400 still survive.

Located in north-eastern India on the floodplain of the Brahmaputra River, the wildernesses of Kaziranga are home to the Indian 'Big Five': the elephant, wild buffalo, tiger, swamp deer and rhino, of which the Park identifies most with the latter. Rhinos are solitary animals with a lifespan of about 40 years. Often weighing considerably over two tons, approximately 1.7 metres tall at the shoulder and about 3.5 metres in length, they have no natural enemies except opportunistic tigers preying on the occasional calf.

the then British Viceroy to India, hoping to see rhinos had to be satisfied with only a few hoof prints because the animal had been so mindlessly hunted that only 'a few dozen' remained. Disappointed, she convinced her husband to have the forests declared as reserved and closed to hunting. The biggest story, however, is undoubtedly of the fierce battle that has been fought since then by several generations of Indian and British forest officers, and conservationists, to bring the Kaziranga rhino back from the edge of decimation. About 122 anti-poaching camps are now scattered throughout the 430 square-kilometres of swamps,

thickets, floodplain wetlands and forest that make up the National Park. Today, with its rhino numbers standing at about 1,700—genetically, the most viable population anywhere—the Park is considered one of the most successful conservation efforts in the world.

Whereas other parks of India are better known for the big striped cat, at Kaziranga its density, at about 17 per 100 square kilometres, is highest. Yet, Kaziranga is known best for its rhinoceros, not just because they are not found anywhere in India outside its northeastern region, but also because the park terrain allows for easy viewing. Unfortunately, rhinos have some-

Bird watchers' pilgrimage

Keoladeo Ghana National Park resounds with the call of over 400 bird species

RAJASTHAN

Bharatpur

Jaipur

State and capital:
Rajasthan, Jaipur
(179 km)

Convenient access:
Road to Keoladeo, air
to Agra, Delhi, rail to
Bharatpur

Accommodation:
Budget to high-end

Best season:
Year round

Also worth seeing:
Bharatpur fort, 5 km
NW, Deeg, 41 km NW,
Mathura, 43 km NE,
Agra, 60 km E

Above: *The black
necked stork is one
of Keoladeo's stork
species which include
the black, white,
painted and open-bill
storks.*

At the confluence of Gambhir and Banganga Rivers in the Bharatpur district of Rajasthan lies, arguably, the best wetland bird sanctuary in India. The Keoladeo Ghana National Park (also known simply as Bharatpur), a UNESCO World Heritage and Ramsar Site, is famous for its fish eating birds (heronry), cranes and thousands of other migrants, including waterfowl, waders, passerines, ducks and raptors, that visit it during winter.

For bird watchers around the world, a trip to this sanctuary is a pilgrimage of sorts. The National Park, with its shallow marshes, scrub jungle, greenwoods, and golden grassland, plays host to over 400 species of birds—about as many as in the entire United Kingdom. Many of the IUCN (International Union for the Conservation of Nature and Natural Resources) endangered species can be spotted at Bharatpur.

The origin of Bharatpur is linked with the ancient kingdom of Matsya Desh, which finds mention in the *Mahabharata*. Year after year, a natural depression spread over a considerable area, trapping rainwater and wildfowl homed in. The local maharaja identified it as a waterfowl hunting preserve, and it became the site of regular carnage committed by royals and the colonial elite. In the early part of the 20th century, more than 5,000 birds fell victim to guns during a single shoot in Lord Linglithgow's honour, a record etched on sandstone plaques near the Keoladeo Temple. Hunting was banned in 1971, thanks to the efforts of the legendary ornithologist Salim Ali.

Prime heronry of the world

One can explore the Park on foot, by bicycle or by a rickshaw; the rickshaw pullers have evolved as bird guides and are excellent sources of bird-related trivia. The birding area lies on either side of the four-kilometre-long road running straight through the park to the Keoladeo Temple.

The Mansarovar and Hansarovar marshes and swamps constitute one of the most important heronries of the world, and it was for this that Keoladeo was notified a World Heritage Site. Thirteen species of heronry (herons, storks and cormorants) nest here in thousands. Post monsoon and in early winter, the Park resounds with the cacophony of storks, cormorants, herons and their voracious chicks. Openbills, egrets, night herons, grey herons, black-headed ibis, darters and cormorants jostle for space on the kikar (a species of acacia) trees. Water levels permitting, one can hire a boat for a closer look at bird families. The raptor cast includes steppe, imperial, tawny, greater, lesser-spotted and crested serpent eagles, Eurasian hobby, shikra and kestrel, their cries echoing down as they glide the sky.

Rare visitors from North and Central Asia

Until the recent past, the most celebrated visitors to the Park have been the Siberian cranes, migrants to India for more than 30 years. Keoladeo was the only wintering site in India for this bird, which travels more than 6,000 kilometres from its summer homeland. While in 1984-85, 41 birds made it to Keoladeo, this figure had drastically fallen to two by 2001, prompting the setting up of the 'Save the Crane Project' jointly by the Governments of India and Russia, the International Crane Foundation and the Wild Bird Society of Japan. Cranes bred in captivity were released amongst the existing Siberian cranes in the hope that they would instinctively migrate. Additionally, to build up the crane population within the Park, birds were released into Keoladeo. However, except for the fact that the introduced cranes survived successfully, the project did not yield the desired results. Since then very few Siberian cranes have flown into Keoladeo over the years.

Recently, the spotlight has turned onto another winged visitor—the sociable plover. In India, Bharatpur is the only wintering ground of the rare bird, which flies in from Kazakhstan and the bordering regions of Russia. With a reported population of only 200 breeding pairs in the world, this species is on the verge of extinction. Around 22 plovers were spotted in 2004 at Bharatpur, but in 2006 sightings had plunged to not more than a dozen.

Apart from birds, Keoladeo has five and seven species of lizards and turtles, respectively. Of the 13 types of resident snakes, the most famous are the big rock pythons that can be seen soaking the winter sun at the various 'Python Points'. Neelgai antelope, sambar deer and wild boar are the big mammals, and the porcupine one of the smaller ones.

Above: A sleeping trio of barred jungle owl chicks. Other owls found in Bharatpur are barn owl, oriental scops owl, collared scops owl, Eurasian eagle owl, dusky eagle owl, brown fish owl, mottled wood owl, spotted owlet, brown hawk owl and the short-eared owl.

Right: About one third of the Park's 29-square-kilometre area is made up of shallow lakes fed by streams and rainwater—if the water is high enough, usually in the monsoon, which is the main time for breeding, boats are a good way to explore. Besides birds one can see monitor lizards, water snakes and turtles. In a single day, it is not uncommon to spot as many as 100 species of birds by boat and land.

Backwaters of Kerala

A coastline cruise enhances the experience of enjoying the state's history and ecology

It is estimated that the deltas of 44 rivers and streams and 29 major lakes, besides myriad canals and lagoons are part of the Kerala backwaters, a natural system, which forms an intermediate mass of water and islands between the coastline of south western India and the Arabian Sea. This intricate ecological network, of which over 750 square kilometres are navigable, is distinct for Keralan coastal life and history. The traditional mode of transport on these waters are houseboats called kettuvallams, a composition of wooden planks of jackfruit trees 'stitched' together using only coir, without employing even a single nail, and covered with bamboo matting. One can see these vessels being constructed at Karunagapalli, 23 kilometres from Kollam, an ancient seaport on the banks of the Ashtamudi Lake, from where one enters the labyrinthine water passages that make Monroe Island. Ashtamudi, formed in 1866 by a flood, is the second largest of the backwater lakes.

Ancient seaports and life along the coast

Several littoral towns are located on various backwater segments from each of which one can cruise to another town. Many of these belong to the 16th century, when 400 years of European occupation commenced. For example, the fort at Kochi was established by the Portuguese and subsequently taken over by the Dutch and British. Lying on the 83 kilometre-long Vembanad, the largest of the lakes,

the Fort area contains many old colonial houses. The Portuguese also built the Matancherry Palace. Saint Frances' Church, raised in 1503, was once the burial place of Vasco da Gama, the Portuguese explorer who was the first person to sail directly from Europe to India. Today Kochi continues its traditional commerce in spices like cinnamon, pepper and cloves. The Champakkulam Church at Alappuzha, said to be one of the seven established by Saint Thomas, is one of the oldest in Kerala. Near the same town at Chavara Bhavan, ancestral home of the 19th century saint Kuriakose Elias Chavara, a 250-year-old light beacon is preserved. The town of Kottayam has a mix of temples and churches. The Thirunakkara Mahadeva temple was constructed by the local Raja in the early part of the 16th century. As many as three churches of Saint Mary show both Hindu and Persian influences in their architecture.

Fishing in the backwaters is practised with traditional methods. Women wade neck deep into the water and probe for fish with their toes. When one is found, either the women dive down, scoop it up by its tail and deposit it in their floating terracotta pots, or the waiting fishermen trap it in their nets. Kerala is paddy country and, along with palm and thick foliage, fields of the green crop line the coast, at times extending even a few feet below the sea. The expanses of water are rich in bird life—Vembanad and its cluster of islands is designated as the Kumarakom

Bird Sanctuary. Both migratory and endemic species of terns, ducks, herons, kingfishers and raptors are a part of the repertoire of winged creatures. Over recent years, due to an unprecedented increase in local population, expanding tourist activity as well as the use of illegal and harmful fishing techniques, the aquatic eco-system has been undergoing alarming changes. Many species of birds have stopped coming here and a lot of the marine life is under threat of being destroyed.

The Snake Boat Race

A famous event on Lake Punnamada is the *Vallamkali* or Boat Race, held every year in August during the Onam harvest festival. Though many kinds of traditional boats are raced, the chundanvellam race is most popular. Chundanvellams, popularly known as snake boats because of their rearing three-metre high cobra like sterns, measure up to 45 metres or more in length. Their manufacture and usage is as per the instructions laid down in the *Sthap Athya Veda*, an ancient Hindu boat-building treatise. Thus, a lot of customs and rituals are associated with them: handling them is an all male domain that too in bare feet; the captain has to be of a particular caste; each member of the crew, which includes dozens of oarsmen and singers, is symbolic of some element of Hindu religion and culture.

KERALA

Arabian Sea

Backwaters

Thiruvananthapuram

State and capital:
Kerala, Thiruvananthapuram (71 km from Kollam, 150 km from Alappuzha)

Convenient access:
Road, rail to Alappuzha, Kollam, Kochi (air also), Thiruvananthapuram (air also)

Accommodation:
Budget to luxury in the towns. Option for boat stay.

Best season:
November to March

Above: Worshipped as divinities, the boats are beautified with lace, umbrellas and flags and treated with oil, eggs and coconut husk to keep them slick and speedy in water.
Below: Many kettuvallams, some over 100 years old, have been converted to tourist houseboats.
Facing page: View of a palm-fringed channel in the backwaters.

Kheechan's annual winged visitors

The small village attracts multitudes of demoiselle cranes

RAJASTHAN

Kheechan   Jaipur

State and capital:
Rajasthan, Jaipur (457 km via Jodhpur)

Convenient access:
Road to Kheechan, air, rail to Jodhpur

Accommodation:
Budget to mid-range in Phalodi

Only season:
November to March

Also worth seeing:
Jodhpur, 140 km SE, Osian temples, 25 km SE, Nagaur Fort, 120 km E

Facing page: The demoiselles' desert home.
Below: Villagers go about their business unmindful of the multitudes of cranes in their proximity.

As the surrounding sand dunes get kissed by the first rays of the morning sun, the silence of the night is shattered, heralding the arrival of thousands of wheeling, circling, soaring and calling demoiselle cranes, coming home to their annual winter migration. A small, sleepy, nondescript desert village in the Thar Desert of western Rajasthan, Kheechan has earned an international reputation and status among ornithological circles for its open-house policy towards the demoiselles. When the heat of the summer sun begins to lose its ferocity, Kheechan starts preparing for its visitors. For years, its 5,000 residents have been pooling their resources to provide food and a safe haven for the cranes.

Demoiselles are the smallest of the world's 15 species of cranes, and one of five crane varieties found in India; so far they are not necessarily threatened. Though the name demoiselle is archaic for damsel, the appearance of this bird is as sagely as is feminine. The light grey plumage ending at drooping tail feathers contributes to a stooping visage. Alert red eyes are backed with a professor-like white tuft at the base of the head, and a long black neck with feathers trailing below the chest, akin to a necktie donned for dinner, completes the venerable look that distinguishes them from all other birds. A delicate frame and dainty gait gives them an elegant appearance. That these creatures fly for thousands of kilometres every year from South-East Europe, Ukraine, Russia, Kazakhstan, Mongolia and North China, reaching altitudes of 6,000 metres to negotiate Himalayan passes, and have braved bullets and anti-aircraft fire during the Afghan war, to reach a miniscule spot in the Indian desert is incredible.

Part of local folklore

It is perhaps in recognition of this feat that the villagers welcome their beloved *kurjas*, as the birds are locally known, and have assimilated them in folklore and love songs. Cranes mate for life, making them symbols of faithfulness and love, and the song 'Kurjaen maro bhanwar mila de lo' (O cranes, please carry our messages to our beloveds and help us unite) says it all. The local people are active in the conservation of the natural surroundings, discouraging any new developments that would disturb the birds; in the past they have successfully warded off enthusiastic hotel ventures that were to come up close to Kheechan.

A *chugga ghar* (feeding enclosure) has been built within the village, and the birds, sure of their welcome, congregate here in numbers between 9,000 and 12,000. Five hundred kilograms of sorghum is scattered twice daily for the morning and evening feed. This translates to over hundreds of thousands of rupees over the months that the cranes spend at the village, and even though visitors contribute some of the funds, most of it is from local donations. In the afternoon, the mass of birds diverts its attention to the sand rich in gypsum, grass leaves and roots. By the end of March, it is time for the cranes to return to their breeding grounds in the far north, only to come back by end September with their young to their winter home.

Gala of gods

Two hundred deities descend on the pretty Kullu Valley on Dussehra

HIMACHAL PRADESH

Kullu

Shimla

State and capital:
Himachal Pradesh,
Shimla (220 km)
Convenient access:
Road to Kullu and
other places in the
valley, air to Bhuntar,
rail to Kalka, Shimla
Accommodation:
Budget to high-end
Best season: Year
round. Cold in winter,
pleasant in summer
Also worth seeing:
Bijli Mahadev Temple,
Russian explorer-
painter Nicholas
Roerich's house
turned museum at
Naggar, heli-skiing
(all in the Valley),
Great Himalayan
National Park

In the mid 19th century, Captain R.C. Lee found the wide Kullu Valley an ideal place to introduce apples in India, decades before American varieties were planted in the hills of Thanedar and Kotgarh. He was right in his judgement, for now the fertile fields and side valleys of this long tract of land created by the Beas River ripple with apple orchards, which go a long way in making it one of India's most scenic areas and popular leisure destinations. Besides this and other succulent fruits like pears, plums and apricots, Kullu is also famous for its woollen shawls. Originally made from the hair of locally bred sheep fed on high Himalayan meadows, they are now also woven in angora, pashmina and merino wool. *Pattus* or *pattis,* as they are called, have bright geometrical designs, and worn by the local people with the distinct Kullu cap, add a wonderful dash of colour to the pleasing natural greenscapes that spread in every direction.

As with many of India's former princely states, the early history of Kullu is lost in a morass of myth, conjecture and hearsay. The most popular version is the story of Behangamani, who came to the Valley and was resting by a path when an old lady saw him. He helped her reach a fair that she wanted to visit, and there she revealed herself as the goddess Hirma or Hadimba, who blessed him with a kingdom, now identified as the tract along the upper

Beas. However, the first definitive mention of the place comes from the intrepid Chinese traveller, Hieun Tsang (AD 629-645) who speaks of the kingdom of K'iu-lu-to. The size of the relatively prosperous principality fluctuated through history with victories and losses in war, until after successive periods of rule by Punjab and the British it became part of independent India.

Gods as feudal lords

Though outside influences, such as from Buddhist trans-Himalayan Lahaul, and the neighbouring states of Mandi, Bushair and Suket reached Kullu, most of these winds passed swiftly, leaving only a few forlorn bits behind and, culturally, Kullu remained introvertive. Kulanthipitha's (its earlier name which loosely translates as 'the End of the Habitable World') long seclusion has allowed the area to retain a considerable measure of its traditional charm. Apart from the traditional textiles, one of these is its unique architecture of intricately meshed wooden sleepers and dressed stone. The other is the fascinating corpus of religiosity—a couple of hundred *devtas,* (deities) 'rule' their villages and valleys like benevolent feudal lords, and pass judgement through the *goor* (principal worshipper). There are numerous festivals, which involve these gods, especially the spectacular Dussehra in October. Of the several shrines in the Valley, the

Raghunath Temple, built in the 17th century by Raja Jagat Singh, who had committed a great wrong and wished to atone for it, is closely connected with this most important festival of the valley. Dussehra begins in Kullu when the rest of the country is over with it, and a week of gaiety commemorates the triumph of good over evil. On Kullu's open Dhalpur Maidan (Grounds), Raghunath's chariot is wheeled out of the Temple and the celebrations start with the arrival of the image of the goddess Hadimba Devi from its dark, mysterious abode in neighbouring Manali. Besides her, some 200 deities from all over the area gather to pay tribute to Raghunath. The festival is full of interesting sidelights. For instance, though Jamlu, the enigmatic deity of Malana, is brought down from his village, he does not join in the celebrations. Instead, his worshippers only watch the proceedings from the opposite bank of the Beas. Another deity is carried in by his devotees, who run without pausing through the Maidan and leave in equal haste.

Above left: Draped in
a pattu *with typical
geometrical designs,
a lady sits on the
verandah of a
traditional, wood-
carved house, in the
village of Jagatsukh,
upper Kullu Valley.*
Above right: The
*Dussehra festival
brings together
patron deities of local
villages, who come
down to Kullu in
lively processions
from their homes in
the mountains.*
Facing page: View
*of the valley near
Manali. At the head
of it is the snow clad
wall of the Greater
Himalayas, beyond
which lies the aridity
of Lahaul and
Ladakh.*

Coral reefs and a clear sea

Lakshadweep Islands are a scuba-diving paradise

LAKSHWADEEP ISLANDS

Kerala

● **Kavaratti**

Arabian Sea

Administrative headquarter: Kavaratti

Convenient access: Air to Kavaratti and Bangaram, boat to Kavaratti, thereafter local boats to other islands

Accommodation: Mid-range to high-end

Best season: October to May

Also worth seeing: Kochi town on the mainland

On this far outpost of India, surrounded by hundreds of kilometres of the Arabian Sea, are stretches of shimmering white sand, which are perhaps the country's best beaches. But this is only one facet of the 36 islands, which make up the Lakshadweep chain. Twelve atolls, three reefs and five submerged banks, besides the group of three-dozen islands, provide substantial scuba diving habitat. Manta Point at Bangaram is a well-known station for underwater exploration. One of the attractions in these waters is the 200-year-old wreck of the battleship

Princess Royal, lying 35 metres below the water, complete with four huge cannons, each over a ton in weight. Some of the recovered artefacts from the sunken ship are displayed in the Kavaratti museum. Besides inanimate relics, there is a vast living heritage to mingle with. Immobile yet always growing, creating the atolls that encircle the islands are over 100 species of coral. Reaching up to no more than four metres above the surface of the clear blue sea, these coral formations provide a safe haven for many small varieties of tropical fish. Amongst the 600 species of

reef fish are butterfly, angel, snappers, sharks, surgeon and clown fish. Divers frequently encounter dolphins, manta rays and eels, and Lakshadweep tuna is proclaimed to be one of the best in the world. Hawksbill, green, leatherback and Olive Ridley turtles nest on the islands; and Pitti has been declared a wildlife sanctuary as it is an important nesting place for terns.

Not more than 1,00,000 people live on India's smallest Union Territory, only 10 islands of which are inhabited. A mixture of Indian and Arab lineage, they are overwhelmingly Muslim, and thought to have been converted to the faith by Arab traders. Vasco da Gama was the first European to land here and a Portuguese fort was built in 1498, though the local people soon forced the foreigners off the archipelago. After a period of rule under Tipu Sultan of Mysore, the islands were taken over by the

174

Left: *Kadmat, with its long, sandy coastline, is the sole island with a lagoon on both sides. Apart from Bangaram and Agatti, it is also the only one where foreign tourists are permitted.*
Bottom: *Local inhabitants perform a folk dance.*
Facing page: *Kalpeni Island's small islets of Tilakkam, Pitti and the uninhabited Cheriyam are separated by a calm, clear lagoon.*

Polo to refer to it as the 'Female Island'. Even now, its Maldivian character is evident in the customs and architecture. The Lava dance is a Minicoy tradition.

Kavaratti, the most developed of the islands, has 52 mosques, of which Ujara and Jamath have beautiful woodcarvings. The former's ceiling is crafted in driftwood. Kalpeni has the largest lagoon and a bank of coral deposited by a storm, and Bangaram, Agatti and Kadmat boast the most popular beaches. The craftsmen of Amini Island are especially skilled in making artefacts of coconut shells, and on Bitra, the small shrine of Malik Mulla, an Arab saint, is a local pilgrimage place. As the soil consists of uniformly porous coral deposit on which not much else can grow, most of the total cultivable

land of Lakshadweep is used for coconut. Indigenous construction styles had traditionally used coral stones reinforced with local lime, while roofs were thatched with coconut leaves. However, as coral is the natural barrier against sea-wave erosion, its removal is now prohibited.

British, till Independence brought them back into the Indian fold.

Female Island

Minicoy, the southernmost and the largest of the islands—Bitra, the northernmost, is also the smallest inhabited island in India—and the only one to be fringed with mangroves, has a culture distinct from the rest. Instead of Malayalam, the language of the other nine, it is Mahl, a dialect of Dhivehi and the official language of the Maldive Islands that is spoken here. Oral tradition has it that the original inhabitants of this island are descendants of two Maldivian princesses and the social classes link their lineage to the hierarchy of the crews on their ships: the highest corresponds to the ship owners, the mid rung to the captains and officers, and the lowest to the menial hands. Minicoy's matrilineal social structure prompted Marco

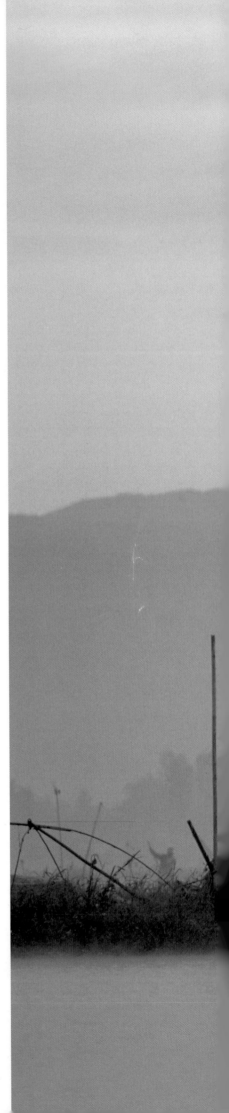

Floating stage of dancing deer

Loktak Lake provides a precarious prop for the nearly extinct sangai

MANIPUR

Imphal

Loktak Lake

State and capital:
Manipur, Imphal
(48 km)

Convenient access:
Road to Loktak, air
to Imphal, rail to
Guwahati, Dimapur

Accommodation:
Budget to mid-range
at Imphal

Best season: October
to February

Also worth seeing:
Bishnu Temple,
Phubala

*Top: Circular, floating
phoomdi (vegetation)
patches give the
Lake its distinctive
landscape.*

*Facing page: Besides
fishing from their
boats, fisherfolk are
often seen sitting
on the phoomdis
outside their huts,
with nets.*

The largest freshwater lake in north eastern India, Loktak is located at the centre of the state of Manipur. Designated a Wetland of International importance under the Ramsar Convention, Loktak is an integral part of the socio-cultural and economic fabric of the region.

Actually a complex monsoonal floodplain system, comprising several smaller lakes called *pats*, which become one continuous sheet of water during the monsoon. Numerous rivers and streams flow into the Lake from the surrounding hills; the two main rivers are the Imphal and the Nambul. A rare ecosystem of floating grass and herb mats, known locally as *phoomdis*, covers the Lake surface. These masses of buoyant vegetation, soil and organic matter at various stages of growth and decomposition host numerous specialised species, besides being useful to the local people in many ways. Loktak is only about a metre deep and, originally, during dry seasons, *phoomdis* temporarily settled onto the lakebed drawing their nutrition from the soil. However, in recent times, forced maintenance of a higher water level does not allow the *phoomdis* to settle, thus reducing the thickness of the layer.

The aquatic vegetation of Loktak numbers over 230 species providing edible produce like the lotus and trapa. The largest single mass of *phoomdis* covers Loktak's 40 square kilometres of its south-eastern corner, which has been declared the Keibul Lamjao National Park. The Park is the last natural refuge of the Manipur brow-antlered deer or the *sangai*, a sub-species of the Thamin or Eld's deer. Reported extinct in 1951 and then rediscovered, the sangai population is currently estimated at about 200. With their splayed-out hooves and horny pasterns, the *sangai* can balance on the shaking, unstable *phoomdis*. Also known as the 'dancing deer' due to its listing gait on the floating mats, the *sangai* is a much loved creature in Manipuri folklore and dance tradition. The deer live in small herds, remain hidden during daylight and come out to feed at dawn and dusk. They can be viewed from boats or from viewing platforms provided in the Park. Amongst the 425 species of animals are otter, civet, wild boar, hog deer, Indian python, sambar and barking deer. The Lake provides refuge to at least 116 species of birds of which 21 migrate from north of the Himalayas.

Distinctive landscape

The Lake is a vital fish habitat and breeding ground for numerous migratory fish species. Outside the Park area, fisher folk build their huts on the *phoomdis*. They also use the *phoomdis* to concentrate fish into the mat's root zones, which they then surround with nets, making circular fish culture zones.

Over 312 square kilometres in area, the huge water body regulates the local climate. It is also the main source of water for hydropower generation, irrigation of agricultural land and drinking water supply for the region. Over 100,000 people on and around the Lake depend on its fish produce—it yields about 1,500 tonnes of fish per year. Loktak's vegetation is used for building huts, weaving, fencing, extracting medicines, handicrafts, and rituals and ceremonies.

The high road from Manali to Leh

A mesmerising drive into trans-Himalayan deserts

Compared to the rest of India, Ladakh is a totally different world. It is a region of craggy rock formations in omnipresent earthy hues of ochres, browns, beiges and greys; and of fluffy clouds that cast moving shadows on the ground. The sun, when out, is strong, the high altitude air thin and though glacial melt flows in streams, it does not provide relief to the land beyond its immediate surroundings. Yet, in this cold harshness is a surreal beauty that stays with visitors long after they have gone, and it would not be an exaggeration to say that those who witness the wildernesses of High Asia, find them quite spellbinding. This is the reason why a handful of people choose to drive, rather than fly into Leh, the heart of central Ladakh, undertaking the gruelling, yet arguably most visually spectacular road journey in India.

are aware of cruising into a world different from the one you started from.

The middle stretch is the remotest

The natural scenery becomes starker. Mountains and ridges thrust up from the bottom of the seabed due to the collision of continental plates 50 million years ago bear many hued patterns. Carpets of scree, ground down by winter glaciers, fan down the slopes, and at various places immense boulder gardens lie sporadically scattered. Wind sculpted towers of sand stand in the gorge of the Tsarap River and enigmatic valleys disappear behind the ranges. Gullies cut across the road by small streams and have amusing names like Whisky, Brandy and Paagal (Mad) Nullah, owing to anecdotes associated with them by drivers over the years. Close to the summits of the big passes is often piercing wind, sleet and remnants of winter snow, and the ubiquitous tattered prayer flags. The ascents themselves are formidable; particularly well known is a series of 21 hairpin bends leading to the Bara-lacha Pass (4,892 metres) called the Gata Loops. Amidst this rugged landscape are huge stretches of flatlands: following the Lunga-lacha Pass (5,059 metres) the road springs upon the Moray Plains extending 50 kilometres at an average height of about 4,700 metres.

Signs of habitation are sparsest on the middle stretch. At Debring, short of the Tag-lang Pass (5,325 metres) are the traditional camping grounds of Ladakh's original people, the Chang-pa nomadic herders, who tirelessly scour the bleak landscape in search of pastures for their yaks, goats and sheep. And if one is lucky, furry marmots popping out from their burrows, and *bharal* (blue sheep) lurking watchfully amongst the rocks and crags may be spotted. Down from the Pass, the going becomes progressively easier. The population increases, tenuous settlements give way to genuine villages, and monasteries appear perched on high cliffs. But despite being accompanied on the last leg to Leh (3,505 metres) with dashes of green cultivation supported by the Indus River, the lunar landscapes of Ladakh continue to keep up their dominating presence.

JAMMU & KASHMIR
HIMACHAL PRADESH

Srinagar • Leh

Manali
• Shimla

States and capitals:
Himachal Pradesh, Shimla (260 km from Manali); Jammu & Kashmir, Srinagar (434 km from Leh)

Convenient access:
Road to Manali, Leh, air to Bhuntar, Leh, rail to Shimla, Jammu

Accommodation:
Budget to high-end in Manali; budget to high-end in Leh; basic tented camps enroute

Only season: July to September

Also worth doing:
Drives from Leh to Srinagar; Leh to Padum, 475 km; Leh to Khardungla Pass, 41 km and Nubra Valley, N; offshoot Manali-Leh road to Tso Moriri, Tso Kar and Pangong Tso Lakes, E

The highway winds through dry, barren moonscapes, bitterly cold deserts, soaring mountains and chilling winds that transport the fine sand of the land into every available crevice and surface. Enroute you might spot a small herd of wild blue sheep, marmots, and the odd trekking caravan.

Over the first pass

The drive begins at Manali (2,050 metres), a small but bustling tourist town in Himachal Pradesh, which lies outside the trans-Himalayan aridity of Ladakh, and within the well-watered realm of the Greater Himalayas. Traffic on this route is sparse even now, except for the climb out of Manali upto the first mountain pass, Rohtang Jot (3,978 metres). The road winds beside the Beas River through alpine vegetation that gives way to sloping meadows. Rohtang is the last outpost for regular tourists, who

head up to frolic in the snow on top of the Pass. On the other side, the terrain loses its lushness, rapidly becoming more desolate as one goes deeper along the Chandra River valley into Lahaul. Once beyond Keylong, the last real town on the route, the road does not dip below 3,000 metres, and from Lahaul onwards, the region's cultural affinity to Tibet—Ladakh forms the eastern edge of the Tibetan plateau—is distinct. As Buddhist *chortens* pass by and people with Tartar features and long robes of coarse cloth watch you pass by, you

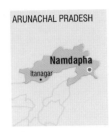
Dark, impenetrable and unexplored

Namdapha is one of the last forest frontiers of the world

State and capital:
Arunachal Pradesh,
Itanagar

Convenient access:
Road to Deban, air to
Dibrugarh, rail to
Tinsukia

Accommodation:
Budget to mid-range

Best season: October
to February

Also worth seeing:
Forest Museum at
Miao, Namdapha eco-
cultural festival in
January-February

*Below: The dandy
Indian Pied hornbill is
one of Namdapha's
few hundred avian
species.*

Nobody quite knows what lies within the depths of Namdapha but many believe that there are a host of species of insects, birds and animals that have still not been seen or identified by modern science. Few places left in the world can make such a claim and Namdapha National Park, encompassing almost 2,000 square kilometres of fascinatingly impregnable jungle, is truly one of Asia's last unspoiled wildernesses. Bordered by contiguous forests spreading in almost every direction, this tiger reserve lies at the tri-junction of India, Myanmar and China, in the remote eastern corner of the Himalayas.

Wide range of wildlife

Namdapha's altitudinal range is impressive—the Park's mountainous terrain rises from about 200 metres in the river valley to above 4,500 metres. Though there are no confirmed sightings of the snow leopard, some believe that along with the tiger, leopard and the rare clouded leopard, it makes up the foursome of big cats that prowl the Park. But there are many other unique animals that form Namdapha's documented faunal wealth. The hoolock gibbon, India's only ape, is one of them; the leaf deer, earlier known to exist only in Myanmar, was recently discovered here; and besides these are the golden cat, marbled cat, Mishmi takin, the red panda and the Namdapha flying squirrel. Of the over 400 species of birds, most well known are the white-winged wood duck, giant and rufous-necked hornbills, peacock pheasant and satyr tragopan.

Because it is virtually impossible to venture into the inner recesses of the Park, visitors usually have access to only a small area in the west near the town of Miao, though one can also enter through Gandhigram at the south eastern edge of the reserve, India's last village in this direction. From here one can walk for several days over a dirt track along the Noa-Dehing River, a tributary of the Brahmaputra, to Deban in the west. Not that the frequented trails around Deban are any less fascinating. Unrelentingly dense and dim, its thick overhead canopy severely restricting daylight, the jungle envelopes you in a wondrous world of its own. The sunlight which manages to reach the forest floor picks out the smaller beings inhabiting the moist, decaying vegetation. These could be any of the 430 species of insects, 10 types of earthworms, five kinds of leeches or several dozen reptiles. A peculiar life form is a parasitical red flower, which emanates a vile stink to beckon pollinating carrion flies. A loop of campsites—the only places which are under the open sky—each offering glimpses into different facets of the forest is networked in a circuit starting from Deban, moving north from the river. At Hornbill, one gets to see its namesake birds, as well as various barbets, woodpeckers and bee-eaters. Butterflies and moths, of which there are 140 identified species, flit around moist patches. Bulbulia is a source of natural hot springs, good for a rejuvenating immersion in soft grey mud. Further on are the Rani Jheel, a small water body, and Camera Point, for sweeping views of the lush jungle.

Lisu tribal guides

The best way to explore Namdapha is with a guide from the local Lisu tribe, one of Arunachal Pradesh's many interesting communities. The Lisus are probably the only people who have been, and still venture, into the mangled interiors of the jungle to hunt and gather food. Traditionally, Lisus sport trophies like hornbill beaks, boar tusks, bear skins and tiger skulls as status symbols and efforts to wean them away from age-old practices of hunting have not yet been fully successful. But with their finely honed instincts and superb jungle-craft, they are the best bet to sense a tiger, identify the rustle of a yellow-throated marten or the distant crash of elephants, or spot a snake before one gets too close to it. Outside the jungle, at Gandhigram, Lisus have a well developed handicraft tradition of fashioning sturdy yet charming cane baskets, bows and arrows, bead jewellery, colourful cloth with distinct patterns, and of course, the formidable *dao*, a multipurpose machete, used to hack a way through the mysterious confines of Namdapha.

Facing page: A tangled mass of ferns, shrubs, bamboo and creepers infests the lower altitudes of the Park.

Above: Camping in the high altitude meadows of the National Park.

Facing page: View of Nanda Devi peak.

The sanctuary of lasting peace

Nanda Devi National Park touches the feet of the Goddess

In the summer of 1934, two Englishmen, Eric Shipton and Bill Tillman, and three Sherpas forced their way through the forbidding gorge of the Rishiganga River to the inner sanctuary of Nanda Devi, the second highest mountain in India. Until then, the 7816-metre peak and its twin, the 7434-metre eastern peak, had been an enigma, thwarting attempts of mountaineers over five decades to break through its protective ring of some of the highest Himalayan mountains, 12 of them over 6,400 metres. Recalling their odyssey, Shipton wrote, 'Return to civilisation was hard but in the sanctuary of the Blessed Goddess we had found the lasting peace which is the reward of those who seek to know high mountain places.' The mountain was finally summited in 1936 by an expedition which included Tillman. At that time it was the highest peak ever climbed in the world.

Upward from the Rishiganga

Nanda Devi is regarded as the Goddess of the Himalayas in the state of Uttarakhand. Almost every peak and river in this high altitude

in place. The larger Park area is, however, open to regulated tourism on carefully designated trails, with accommodation provided at the homes of local villagers. Forests of fir, rhododendron and birch in the Rishiganga gorge give way to scrub juniper and eventually grasses, lichens and mosses, as one goes higher. A total of 323 species of vegetation have been recorded in the Park, whereas the larger Biosphere Reserve hosts 793 species. 14 species of mammals include the Himalayan tahr and black bear, and amongst the 114 bird types, the bluefronted redstart and Indian tree pipit are common.

A ram leads the holy trek

A unique event associated with the mountain is the 12-yearly Nanda Dev Raj Jat, a Hindu pilgrimage with its origins dating back to the ninth century. The 280-kilometres long, 19 day round trek begins in the lower Himalayas, at the village of Nauti (900 metres), traverses heights over 5,300 metres and ends in the high mountains, symbolising the return journey of the Goddess from her parents' home to her abode with Shiva. The journey is led by a four-horned ram, which is born to coincide with the time of the pilgrimage. At the end of the trip, at the base of the Goddess' home on Nanda Ghunghti peak, the ram is bid farewell, to wander away and disappear in the mountains laden with offerings to the Goddess. The next Jat is in the year 2012.

UTTARAKHAND

Dehradun • **Nanda Devi**

State and capital:
Uttarakhand, Dehradun (330 km)

Convenient access:
Road to Lata, air to Delhi, rail to Haridwar, Rishikesh

Accommodation:
Home stays and camping in Park

Best season: April to October for lower altitudes, June to October for higher altitudes (July-August not recommended due to monsoon)

Also worth seeing:
Valley of Flowers

region, referred to as *dev bhumi* (abode of the gods), is named after a deity and almost certainly referred to in the sacred texts. In 1982, a 625-square-kilometre area around the mountain was declared a National Park as part of the larger Nanda Devi Biosphere Reserve. Of this, the inner sanctuary, is the core area (the Valley of Flowers being the other core of the Reserve). Access to the Park is from the villages of Lata and Tolma, near the town of Joshimath, and then through the Rishiganga gorge. Nanda Devi's core area is now closed to protect its fragile

ecosystem. The major reason for this were the negative affects of large trekking and mountaineering expeditions, which caused littering, as well as strip-grazing of the inner sanctum meadows and scented herbs, principal food for musk deer and *bharal* (blue sheep), both in turn the dwindling prey base for the snow leopard. An expedition in 1993, the first group permitted after the ban 11 years earlier, was sent into the inner sanctuary for 52 days to evaluate the possibility of renewed expeditions. They advised that the ban be continued and, as of now, their recommendations are

Above: The Asian elephant is one of three elephant species of the world. One of its four sub species is the Indian elephant, found in Periyar National Park. It is distinguishable from its African cousin by a smaller ear size. Measuring between 2-4 metres at the shoulder, it is also smaller in height, has a more arched back, and two bulges on the forehead.

Park of pachyderms

Elephants rule over Periyar's rich tract of rainforest

Ex-poachers persuaded into the fold of conservation are Periyar's forest guards and guides, and former sandal-wood smugglers are their counter-parts in the adjacent farmlands of mango, jasmine, sunflower and tamarind, nestled in the lee of the Periyar Hills. Because of the integration of these one-time marauders of this South Indian wilderness, Periyar Tiger Reserve is considered one of the biggest success stories of conservation in India.

Periyar's birth pangs took place in the late 19th century when the British constructed a dam across the river of the same name, in the princely state of Travancore (now south eastern Kerala), to create a storage reservoir. The dam created a huge, 26 square-kilometre lake and over time the environs around the lake developed bountiful wildlife and woodlands. Eighty years later the area was notified as one of the 27 Tiger Reserves in the country and, in 1982, a core area of about 350 square kilo-metres became Periyar National Park. Today, the large watery expanse of the lake and the forests around it teem with game, and despite the chugging engines of ferries and boats, it is common to spot a variety of animals, especially herds of elephants.

meadows, and lion-tailed macaques, who restrict themselves to the dense forest canopies. Three types of squirrels, the giant Malabar, large and Travancore squirrels—the last rarely glimpsed—inhabit the Reserve, and the great pied hornbill rules for sheer size Periyar's 320 species of birds, of which many are peculiar to this part of the Western Ghats. Periyar literally flutters with butterflies. About 160 counted species include the Travancore evening brown, a rarity, which was till recently thought to be extinct. The list of 45 types of snakes features some of India's most venomous: king cobra, cobra, Russell's viper, pit viper, krait and the striped coral snake.

2,000 kinds of flowering plants

Surrounded by dense spice plantations and set in the midst of the typical blue-green hills of this region, Periyar boasts of one of the richest tracts of rainforests in the Western Ghats. Marshes proliferate the lower regions, while open grass-lands and *sholas*, from where many small rivulets and streams emerge, dominate the higher, salubrious reaches. Between them, they har-bour 2,000 kinds of flowering plants. A particularly interesting walk traverses the 1,700- metre high, 90 kilometre-long ridge, which overlooks the sprawling plains. Towards the west, a 1,200 metre high plateau drops steeply to the Park's lowest level, the 100 metre deep valley of the Pamba River. And above it all stands Kottamalai, at 2,019 metres, Periyar's highest pinnacle.

State and capital:
Kerala,
Thiruvananthapuram
(267 km)

Convenient access:
Road to Park, air,
rail to Ernakulam,
Thiruvananthapuram

Accommodation:
Budget to high-end

Best season:
September to May

Also worth visiting:
Ancient temples of
Mangaladevi and
Sabarimala, in the
Park's buffer zone

*Below: Protruding
tree trunks help
boatmen navigate
the lake.*

Tracking wildlife on foot

Though the Park is one of the homes of the tiger in India, chances of spotting the elusive cat are slim. Elephants numbering over 900 however, cannot easily keep their presence under wraps, and Periyar, also known as Thekkady after a nearby village, is particularly renowned for sightings of the lumbering beasts. Besides from bamboo rafts, they can be tracked on foot. In fact, Periyar is one of the very few Parks, rich in big game, where escorted walks are allowed. Here, the insightful knowledge of the area and its habitat gathered by the guides through years of stalking wildlife opens up exciting dimensions of the forest. Usually overnight forays covering 20-35 kilometres, these stomps through sticky bogs and leech infested country are worth it for the invariable trysts with elephants and *gaur* (bison), the Park's second largest animal. At Gavi, in the buffer zone, one often comes face to face with the former, as they break and chew bamboo grass, and amble past the forest rest house. Usually seen are also *sambar*, the largest of the Indian deer, and the barking deer, while less common are the Nilgiri tahr, an animal endemic to this part of the country, which roam the high

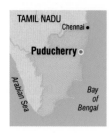

TAMIL NADU
Chennai •

Puducherry •

Arabian Sea

*Bay
of
Bengal*

Union territory:
Puducherry

Convenient access:
Road to Puducherry,
air, rail to Chennai

Accommodation:
Budget to luxury

Best season:
November to March

Also worth seeing:
Mamallapuram,
96 km NE

A preserved piece of France

Puducherry exudes Sri Aurobindo's spiritual philosophy

Early evidence attests the existence of the ancient port of Arikamedu, three kilometres from the capital of the Union Territory of Puduchery— till recently known as Pondicherry, it has now reverted to its original name, which means 'New Village' in Tamil—but the town's strategic history really began when the French East India Company established a trading outpost here in 1673. Thereon, it was occupied and reoccupied a few times by the warring French, Dutch and British, before settling into French hands for a century, till its formal unification with India in 1962. By then it had been stamped with decidedly French character, and although the French may have given up their coastal possession, their presence continues to remain in more ways than one.

local Tamil residents. The right-angled grid plan of the streets makes it difficult to get lost in this town which can still be explored by foot or bicycle.

Sri Aurobindo's Ashram

The Ashram, the focal point of the smaller section, was established in 1926 by the spiritual master, Sri Aurobindo and the Mother (a French citizen, who came to be revered so, working in unison with Sri Aurobindo for an ultimate goal and philosophy). Essentially, Aurobindo propagated 'transformation and perfection of life instead of its rejection' through deliberate spiritual growth leading to a higher level of consciousness. Various departments of the Ashram are engaged in works necessary for the upkeep and maintenance of its 2,000 residents and also

Right: The Matrimandir meditation facility in Auroville is considered the soul of the city. It is supported by four pillars set in the cardinal directions which represent the four forces or attributes of creative evolution. Inside, the meditation chamber is divided into 12 stone-clad 'petals', each with a different symbolic colour.

Facing page: A mix of Portuguese and French styles of architecture, the Church of our Lady of Immaculate Conception is one of the oldest in Puducherry.

The actual town is surrounded by four boulevards of which the one on the east, Goubert Avenue, sits snugly by the side of the sea. Also known as Beach Road, it is the hub of tourist activity, with panoramic views of the sea providing a backdrop for music concerts, walking, snacking and shopping. A canal divides the town into two sections: one third is occupied predominantly by the eclectic mix of people that populate the Sri Aurobindo Ashram, while the other, more commercial, comprises of the

in creative productivity such as handmade paper, perfumes, incense, embroidered goods and marble works. The main Ashram area is the Samadhi, where one can pay respect to the remains of Aurobindo and the Mother.

French influence on places and buildings

What was once known as the White Town because of its French residents still bears French street names like (Rue) Dumas, Romain Rolland, Suffren, La Bourdonnais, Saint

Louis and Saint Gilles. Colonial styled bungalows with arches of heavy bougainvilleas draped over the gates are a common sight. Just as usual are names and structures like the Jeanne D'Arc Park, the Cercle de Pondicherry, Douane (customs) and the statue of Governor Joseph Francois Dupleix (1742-54). Many restaurants too sport French names.

The missionary movement in the 17th and 18th centuries led to the proliferation of highly embellished churches amongst which are

the Church of our Lady of the Immaculate Conception, the Sacred Heart Church with its Gothic spires and stained glass panels and the elegant Romanesque Church of Our Lady of the Angels.

Across the canal, things look very different. There is the hustle and bustle of shops, noisy traffic, and in the various lanes, coffee and fish are the dominating smells. The one thing common to both sides of the waterway seem to be the police in their red kepis, a leftover from the French days.

Auroville, the universal town
Twelve kilometres from Pondicherry is the township of Auroville. Inaugurated in 1968, it was the brainchild of the Mother who wanted to attract representatives of all nationalities to come and live harmoniously in one place. Since then it has grown in both numbers and area. The residents have undertaken enthusiastic experiments with solar power and energy, education, reforestation, architecture, agriculture and small-scale ventures. The soul of Auroville lies in the

temple and meditation chamber called Matri Mandir, which can be seen from a distance because of the gold petals that have been used to cover its massive globe-like edifice. A crystal ball sits at the centre of the inner chamber, around which are arranged white sitting mattresses. This combined with the white pillars and a gently hanging vapour like mist, creates an overall effect of being bathed in the softest of whites.

A desert of many moods

Rann of Kutch is the salty marsh of Gujarat

GUJARAT

Gandhinagar

Rann of Kutch

Arabian Sea

State and capital:
Gujarat, Gandhinagar
(286 km)

Convenient access:
Road to Rann, air, rail
to Bhuj, Ahmedabad

Accommodation:
Budget to mid-range
at Bhuj

Best season:
November to March

Also worth seeing:
Dholavira, Mandvi

Villagers who live in tightly packed mud houses on the edge of the desert say the Rann has a huge population of 'whites', the spirits of men who never returned from the endless desolation. They watch out for them in the quivering mirages and the still night air, and while the eyes of the outsider squinting into the lifeless expanse may not sight these restless phantoms, they might notice the dust kicked up by a galloping herd of *gudhkur* (Asiatic wild asses) on the shimmering horizon. For the Rann of Kutch, flat and white, seemingly uninhabitable, is home to this

chestnut brown beast not found anywhere else in the world.

Once the waters of the Arabian Sea lapped easily over this 52,000-square-kilometre tract of land on the western coast of India, stretching from the edge of the great Thar Desert southward to the Little Rann and the Gulf of Kutch. First a geological upliftment cut off its seawater supply, so that by the time of Alexander the Great it existed as a vast navigable lake. Hundreds of years of silting and a few earthquakes later it had withered into a desert of varying moods. Now in March, it is a

cracked salt flat, while in the searing heat of the long dry season, it becomes parched, with one of the highest annual evaporation rates in the region; temperatures, during this time, can reach 50 degrees Celsius. While the monsoon runs its course, from July to September, the Rann metamorphoses into a salt-clay desert covered by seawater; a shallow salt marsh, with patches of salt-free but sandy higher ground known as *bets*. Several rivers—the Bhambhan, Kankavati, Godhra and Umai from the south, the Rupen and Saraswati from the east, and the Banas from the north

one of the largest flamingo breeding colonies of the world. Besides these, wolves, desert foxes, jackals, the elusive caracal and desert cat are shadowy presences, and *chinkara* (gazelles), *nilgai* (India's largest antelopes), the elegant blackbuck (another Indian antelope) and hyena, tramp its sands. More than 200 avian species, including the lesser florican, houbara bustard, Dalmatian pelican and 13 species of lark live in the seasonal salt marshes. The coastal wetlands support over 40,000 birds. There are also smaller mammals, such as hares and honey badgers, and reptiles like the spiny-tailed lizard, monitor, red and common sand boa, saw-scaled viper, cobra, and the Indian rat snake. Uniquely, the Rann is a combination of desert and wetland habitats.

It is believed by genetic scientists that 60,000 years ago early humans from Africa migrated to Kutch. Today 18 different tribes, each with its own culture live in this region. Amongst these are Bharwad shepherds, Rabari camel and cattle herders, Maldhar buffalo keepers, and Samra and Sindhi Muslim cameleers.

Left: *Flamingoes feed in the shallow waters of the Rann.*
Below: *The Asiatic wild ass once roamed the north-western plains of India from the Satluj to the Indus Rivers. At the Little Rann Sanctuary they number about 2,000. Able to survive on the sparse scrub, these strong beasts can weigh up to 240 kilograms and attain gallop speeds of 70 kilometres per hour.*

east—drain into it during this time. In August, the water is almost knee-high, but by winter it has evaporated, leaving behind salt crust.

The word *rann* comes from the Hindi word *ran*, meaning 'salt marsh', or from the Sanskrit word *ririna* meaning 'a waste'. And yet this bleakness, devoid of clouds and movement harbours diverse life. The *bets* offer a foothold for trees, grass and scrub that provide shelter and food for animals. Three of these, Pung Bet, Vacha Bet and the Jhilandan Bet, are refuge for the wild ass. When it transforms into a marshland, the Rann is taken over by acres of flowering plants, and millions of tall, pink flamingoes, which fly in each year to nest and raise their young in 'cities' of conical mud-nests, turning it into

The mysterious Rupkund Lake

Hundreds of human skeletons remain intact in its waters

Above: Though the numbers have not been completely ascertained, it is believed that a group of 300 to 600 people once perished at the enigmatic Lake, a pilgrimage and trekking destination. Radio carbon dating of the bones found fixed the time period in the ninth century.

Rupkund is not a classical high-altitude lake. In fact, more than a lake, it is a tarn, a small pond-like presence not particularly beautiful to look at. And it would not have attracted more than passing attention if in 1942 a forest guard had not stumbled upon it and its contents: a large number of human skeletons with personal belongings like leather shoes, etc. Today, the lake is a destination for hundreds of trekkers, not just out of macabre curiosity, but also for the challenging yet spectacular Himalayan terrain one has to traverse on the way.

Lying nearly 4,800 metres above sea level, below the right flank of the majestic Trishul peak in the Garhwal Himalayas, Rupkund is not an easy place to reach. It takes at least four days (37 kilometres) of trekking over slippery trails through thick jungles, meadows, and rocky ground to get there. The walk starts from the head village of Lohajang and winds easily in the initial part through cultivated fields, oak and pine forest, up to the Wan village (at an altitude of 2,500 metres). From here a steep ascent through spruce and rhododendron woods takes one above the tree line onto a beautiful spread of *bugyals* (high-altitude

Swept away by a deadly avalanche

The last step of the climb brings you to an edge of a crater within which lies the mysterious water body. Recessed in so dark, bleak a place that the sun shines on it only for a couple of hours—that too on a rare clear day—Rupkund remains frozen for most part of the year, and this is why its hoard of skeletons has survived in almost perfect condition. Several scientific expeditions have been made to the site, though nothing certain has been established regarding the presence of the grim remains, much above the highest permanently inhabitable point in the Himalayas. Various theories propose that they are remains of soldiers, pilgrims, or Chinese travellers. The theory favoured by many, including the local people, is that of Swami Pravana Nand, who worked in the region for a number of years. According to him, the Raja of Kannauj undertook a pilgrimage to Homkund Lake, which lies beyond the Trishul spur above Rupkund. When the group was passing above the lake, the weather took a turn for the worse and an avalanche swept away and buried the entire team. The story seems plausible as the drop from Juerigali, a ledge above the lake over which the trail passes, is a vertical 300 metres.

So pristine is the condition of the bodies that on some bones, shreds of flesh can still be seen. Later, in 2004, a team of Indian and European scientists retrieved jewellery and other vital clues. DNA tests on the bodies revealed that there were two groups of people, a short group (probably local porters) and a taller group who were closely related.

State and capital:
Uttarakhand, Dehradun (284 km to Mundoli roadhead)

Convenient access:
Road to Mundoli or a few km further to Lohajang, thereafter trek. Rail to Haridwar, Rishikesh, air to Dehradun

Accommodation:
None on trek or at Lake; camping enroute

Best season:
April-May, August-September

Also worth seeing:
Day treks to Homkund, Bekhaltal Lakes; serious mountaineering on Trishul

meadows). The next stopover is at Bedni, an (3,400 m) enchanting meadow, lush with plants, flowers and lichens in summer. A small lake here reflects Nanda Ghungti and Trishul peaks. The last halt before Rupkund is at cold and windy Bhagguwasa (4,100 metres), hemmed in by huge mountain walls. On the final three kilometre trudge to Rupkund, one comes across the rare *brahma kamal* (literally 'lotus of the Creator'; a member of the daisy family) wildflower, which is held sacred by the local people and offered at almost all village temples in the higher reaches of the Western Himalayas.

A gleaming jewel of a lake
Chandratal's myriad hues overlook Buddhist Spiti

HIMACHAL PRADESH

Spiti

Shimla

State and capital:
Himachal Pradesh,
Shimla (490 km)

Convenient access:
Road to Spiti (last 6 km
to Chandratal on foot),
air to Bhuntar, Shimla,
rail to Shimla

Accommodation:
Camping at
Chandratal, budget
to mid-range at Kaza

Best season: July and
October (road snow-
bound in winter)

Places on the way to Chandra-tal (4,270 metres) or 'Moon Lake' are just that—places. As a famous signage proclaims: 'Chhota Dara 0 km Population 0'. These 'places' or points actually get peopled temporarily only during summer. During winter it is freezing with layers of snow, and there is no access either to the Lake, or over the spur of the ridge on which it lies. Beyond the ridge is Spiti, which is a high-altitude desert like Ladakh and was closed until recently to foreign tourists.

The first leg of the route to this far northern corner of India is the same as the journey from Manali to Leh. A diversion after the Rohtang Pass takes one on an amazing drive, sometimes through small water-falls, over streams and very 'less' road along the Chandra River, upto the Kunzum Pass (4,550 metres). Nearby, surrounded by the high peaks of Chandrabhaga and Mulikila massifs, nestles the cap-tivating, 8-shaped lake, three kilometres in circumference. What is striking about this glacial melt are its crystal-clear turquoise-blue waters that change hues as the sun arcs through the day. In summer, shepherds bring their flocks to graze on the alpine vegetation on the surrounding moraines and vast meadows, while ruddy shelducks and bar-headed geese find their way

on their own as they have for eons. None are deterred by the strong bone-piercing wind that howls through the trough.

In the 10th century, Spiti along with Lahaul and Zanskar made up the Guge kingdom of western Tibet. By the 18th century, with the disintegration of the Ladakh kingdom, Lahaul came under the rule of the Kullu kings, and by the mid-19th century, the Sikh influence swept over the region. It was wrested from the latter by the British in 1846, and its colonial masters ruled Spiti until India attained Independence

Even now at Kaza, Spiti's only town, there is little presence of the

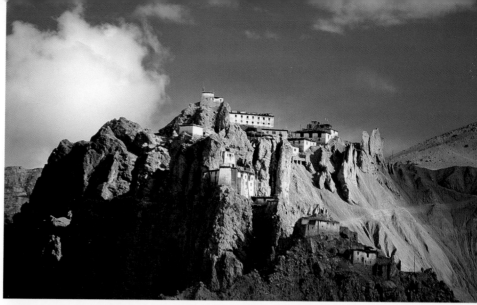

outside world. Adventure enthusiasts, attracted by the myriad opportunities for some of India's best long treks amidst awesome mountain landscapes, are the main visitors. The Pin Valley National Park, one such favoured tramping ground, is home to the endangered Siberian ibex and its ghostly predator, the snow leopard. Besides these two stellar species, the Tibetan wolf, Tibetan gazelle and red fox roam the Park. High altitude birds include the Himalayan snowcock and snow partridge. The harsh but grand scenery is at times punctuated with fields of wheat, barley or paddy, with women and children dressed in bright colours.

Tabo Monastery

Rivers and streams cut grooves in sandy valleys while, occasionally, out of crevices of a distant mountain rises the anthill formation of a village with its parent monastery at the summit. Of these establishments of the Gelugpa monastic order, the over 1000-year-old Tabo is the oldest uninterruptedly functioning monastery in India, with its original decoration—fading frescoes created by Kashmiri artists in its nine temples as well as caves located above—still preserved. Founded by the great translator and teacher, Rinchen Tsang Po at a time when Buddhism was being transmitted from India to Tibet, Tabo contains temples dating from the 10th to the 16th centuries. The main assembly hall of the Tsuglhakhang (Temple of the Enlightened Gods) is surrounded by 33 Boddhisattva statues along with a four-sided figure of Saravid Vairocana, one of the five Dhyani Buddhas. In the Large Temple of Drom-ton, the second biggest, are seated the Sakyamuni, and eight others who represent the Medicine Buddhas. The initiation to monkhood takes place at the Mystic Mandala Temple. The Golden Temple was once painted with gold and another chapel holds a six-metre-tall image of the Maitreya Buddha and a painting of the Potala Palace. Kye is another very old monastery. During the summer Chaam festival, the otherwise quiet environs become a riot of colour, music, and elaborate rituals. Dhankar fortress was once the capital of Spiti, and its monastery today displays a life-sized silver image of the Buddha, besides several frescoes.

Facing page: The pristine waters of Chandratal lie above the treeline.
Above: Tabo monastery and its village, spread out on the plain below. Monasteries are Spiti's most visible man-made structures, located in the tradition of dramatic, isolated settings as in the rest of Buddhist trans-Himalaya.

Vale of houseboats

Srinagar is laced with lakes, gardens, rivers and history

The capital city of Jammu & Kashmir abounds in beautiful natural vistas, and every corner reveals a nugget of history. Nestled in the heart of the Kashmir Valley, on the banks of the meandering Jhelum River, Srinagar goes back to the sixth century. As time passed by, so did monks, armies, kings and travellers of varied faith and fervour, bringing with them a gamut of cultural and artistic influences.

Life on the Dal Lake

At a height of 1593 metres, the old town sprawls on both sides of the Jhelum, which is spanned by seven old *kadals* (timbered bridges). To the east of the city lie the Dal and Nagina Lakes, thickly fringed by woodlands and gardens, and the focus of Srinagar's daily life. Long shallow boats called shikaras (Kashmiri houseboats) ply the lakes and their backwaters, ferrying people, fruits, flowers and groceries.

The famous shikara was invented because members of the Indian Civil Service sojourning in Kashmir in the 19th century were not allowed to construct summer homes by the ruler. Moored on the deepest end of the Dal Lake, these elaborately furnished floating homes provided every comfort, including a personal chef, to the servants of the Raj, and now they continue to offer the same hospitality to tourists. Papier mâché, crewel-embroidered

seventy pillars each made of a single Himalayan cedar tree trunk support the roof. Later 17th century mosques include the Patthar Mosque and Mosque of Akhund Mulla Shah. Hazrat Bal Mosque is, however, the pride of the city and contains the most sacred relic of Kashmir, a hair from the beard of the Prophet Muhammad. Located on the western shore of Dal Lake, it is a brilliant white structure with a slender minaret, in a lakeside setting with a view of snow-capped mountains.

Gardens filled with chinar trees

The natural beauty of Kashmir fascinated the Mughals, who built terraced gardens on the lake shore with fountains, pavilions and watercourses around natural streams. Emperor Jahangir was so delighted by the Valley's spring blooms that he commissioned his artists to paint over 100 pictures depicting them. The Mughals are also credited with introducing the stately chinar (a species of the plane tree). The earliest garden, called Nazim Bagh, or Garden of the Morning Breeze was built by Akbar. Its chinars are over 380 years old. Shah Jahan is said to have planted hundreds of these trees on a rectangular grid. The most famous garden is Shalimar Bagh, built for Empress Nur Jahan by Jahangir in 1616. It contains a black marble pavilion surrounded by fountains of water, and double rows of tiny niches behind sheets of water, in which were placed oil lamps to create a dramatic effect. Other monumental gardens are the Nishat Bagh, the Chashm-i-Shahi and the Pari Mahal.

JAMMU & KASHMIR

Srinagar

State and capital:
Jammu & Kashmir, Srinagar
Convenient access:
Road, air to Srinagar, rail to Jammu
Accommodation:
Budget to high-end
Best season: April to mid October
Also worth seeing:
Temples at Avantipura and Martand. Resort towns of Gulmarg, 58 km W, Pahalgam, 96 km E

Below: The shrine to Shah Hamadan, credited with propagating Islam in Kashmir, was the first mosque built in Srinagar. The Shah, who came here in the 13th century, was originally known as Mir Sayed Ali Hamadni, a name derived from his hometown Hamadan, in Persia. The mosque is sited on the banks of the Jhelum River, between the third and fourth bridge, where he is supposed to have regularly offered prayers.

linen, and richly hued and patterned Kashmiri carpets adorn their interiors.

The Dal and Nagina Lakes span 18 square kilometres, and are linked by a network of backwaters and causeways. Dal Lake is divided into three parts: Lokut or Small Dal, Bod or Large Dal, and Sodura Khon, the western portion, which is the deepest part and the mooring place for houseboats. The two islands on the Dal Lake, Sona and Rupa, are artificial creations, the former just above the waterline so that it seems to be afloat.

The fortress of Hari Parbat on

Sharika Hill, constructed by the Mughal Governor Azim Khan in 1592, dominates the western skyline. Srinagar's numerous mosques and shrines are in the distinct hybrid Kashmiri style of architecture. Built of stone and wood, exquisitely carved in geometric patterns, they are surmounted by a tiered pagoda. Fine examples are the shrine of Makhdum Sahib and the 14th century Shah Hamadan Mosque. At the heart of the city lies the Jami Masjid, first built in 1385, then damaged and rebuilt several times with the original scheme unchanged. Three hundred and

Dense delta of three rivers

The Sundarbans' saline waters are reputed to breed man-eating tigers

The world's largest coastal wetland, the Sundarbans covers about 1,000,000 hectares in the delta of the Ganga, Brahmaputra and Meghna Rivers. It spreads across two countries, Bangladesh and India, with the latter encompassing 40 per cent of the total area. The Ganga and Brahmaputra carry the world's largest load of sediment, which, along with tectonic changes in land gradient and changing hydrology, has created a multitude of small islands amongst a dense network of small rivers, channels and creeks, a habitat ideal for mangrove to thrive in. Ongoing dynamics continue to shape the mangrove's expansion, and with a maximum elevation of about eight metres above mean sea level, they are constantly subject to submergence during high tides and storms.

The Indian Sundarbans is located in the 24-Paragnas District of West Bengal. While the Harinbhanga (Ichamati or Raimongal in Bangladesh) River forms the eastern boundary, the western border lies along the Hoogly River. The islands of Gosaba, Sandeshkali and Basanti form the northern limits and to the south is the sea. The Sundarbans had always been an economic frontier for farmers who attempted to grow rice in the mangroves, and between the 13th and 18th centuries, British regarded the forests as prime timber zones and further promoted agriculture. As a result, vast swathes were rapidly cut down. Later, however, the Sundarbans was recognised as a unique habitat, and following Independence, successive notifications led to the declaration, in 1973, of 2,585 square kilometres as a tiger reserve. In 1984, a core area of 1,330 square kilometres was established as the Sundarbans National Park. The Park consists of 54 small islands, and is criss-crossed by several distributaries of the Ganga and Brahmaputra.

Estuarine crocodiles, horse-shoe crabs and man-eating tigers

Located in a sub-tropical monsoonal region subject to high annual rainfall, severe cyclonic storms and varying salinity gradients that change both spatially and temporally, the Sundarbans hosts unique flora and fauna. It is the largest mangrove system in the world—the name Sundarbans comes from *sundari*, the local name for the most common of the 64 mangrove species found here. Many of the animals, including the Javan rhino, the wild buffalo, hog deer, and barking deer, that once inhabited these forests are now gone. Yet, about 350 species of vascular plants, 250 kinds of fish and 300 species of birds, besides numerous kinds of phytoplankton, fungi, bacteria, zooplankton, benthic invertebrates, molluscs, reptiles, amphibians and mammals exist in the tidal swamp forests, saline mixed forests, brackish water forests and palm swamp forests which constitute the different types of Sundarbans' ecosystems. The creeks are home to the estuarine crocodile, the water monitor, river terrapin and horse-shoe crab, and the beaches are nesting grounds for endangered marine turtles, including the Olive Ridley, green turtle and hawksbill. Rare Gangetic dolphins swim the waters. Heronries abound after the

Right: The Sundarbans tiger is an accomplished swimmer and can survive on fish and crabs.

monsoons, while trans-Himalayan migratory birds come to nest here during the winter.

The Sunderbans harbours some 400 Royal Bengal tigers, known for their ability to hunt in water and swim for several hours. Although their main diet includes spotted deer, wild boar, rhesus monkeys and even crabs and fish, the uniqueness of the habitat is thought to have contributed to an unusual behavioural trend–a man-eating propensity considered a hereditary trait acquired over generations. It is thought that the availability of only saline drinking water and the presence of humans as a natural part of the habitat, as honey and herb gatherers, has a role to play in this tendency.

The Sunderbans' network of water channels are explored by boat cruises on designated routes. Though it is not easy to see a tiger, many other interesting sights pass by: the dense wall of mangroves itself with hetal or tiger bushes and masses of air breathing roots separated from the muddy waters by narrow sandbanks is the endless staple vision. In the foreground one might see water monitors nibbling at floating carrion, hopping, skipping and jumping mudskipper fish, basking crocodiles, schools of dolphins and the odd barking deer emerging from the undergrowth. In the smaller channels, care is taken to keep a safe distance from the shores and stay out of range of hopeful tigers.

Though parts of the Sundar-bans have been declared World Heritage Sites, its biodiversity continues to be threatened by the pressure of more than 1,000 villages, dams and embankments and, of course, global warming which might force the rising sea to permanently swallow this unique ecosystem.

Above: Traditionally, the human population in the Sunderbans has made its living from the ancient forests, foraging for wood and plant food, trapping animals and fishing. During the day local craft function as ferries taking people and cargo across the numerous rivers and mohonas (confluences).

Plantations for the perfect brew

Assam's tea gardens produce strong and smooth teas

Above: Assam's 800 organised tea gardens produce around 475 million kilograms of tea. Women comprise close to half of the total labour force. They are descendants of tribals like the Oraon from Orissa and Jharkhand, the Sonthals from Bengal, and others from Central India, who were brought in by British planters.

Darjeeling tea from West Bengal, may have the fragrance and flavours, but it is actually the plantations of Assam—the world's single largest tea-growing region—which produce the traditional full-bodied Indian tea. Thousands of hectares of neatly serried and clipped, undulating lush green fields, marked with light and shade-facilitating trees, and picturesque red-roofed factories and bungalows are ensconced between the snow-covered eastern Himalayan ranges and the thickly forested hills of the north-eastern states of Nagaland, Manipur, Meghalaya and Mizoram. Spread out over the year, rainfall is plentiful here and the soil has good drainage qualities. In the south flows the Brahmaputra, contributing its waters to the cause. Assam tea is categorised as the first and the second flushes. While the former has a fresh, rich aroma, the second flush produces the more famous 'tippy teas', essentially black tea with gold tips, which creates a sweet and smooth brew. This black tea is far different in taste and colour from the green tea made in China.

Bushes became big business

It all began in the early 1820s, when the Scottish brothers Robert and Charles Alexander Bruce established contacts with the

198

Life at the tea estates

The lifestyle of the *burra* (big) sahib—as tea estate managers are still known—revolves around their *burra* bungalows. Though the occupation may have lost its earlier romance, the latter survive as edifices of old-world graciousness. Built in the 1930s, the sprawling colonial constructions boast up to eight bedrooms, separate kitchen wings, several acres of lawns planted with magnolia, Indian lilac, frangipani, plumaria and other scented blooms, besides a formidable retinue of domestic help. There is also the world of the tea taster, comparable to his Scotch-sampling counterparts. Existing in well-lit but sun-shaded rooms, it demands an accurate analysis of sips from as many as 1,000 porcelain cups of different brews in a day. Out in the fields, the tea-pluckers are generally women, deft fingered to tweak, break and pluck the single leaf and the bud, which makes the best golden and flowering Orange Pekoes. Pruning is usually the task of trained and experienced men, who trim the tea bushes into shape with their long iron blades.

Much of India's well-known wildlife dwells in the vicinity of the luxuriant hill estates of Assam. Virgin natural rainforest in all its hues of green is visible all around and some of the finest mountain vistas and remains of colonial history—clubs, cobbled streets and snooker—endure here. You can ride horse-back through the gardens as the old planters did, or walk through on the lines between the bushes, or on the roads, or wade through the bushes themselves, as the sunlight filters through.

State and capital:
Assam, Dispur
Convenient access:
Road to individual tea estates, air to Guwahati, Jorhat, Dibrugarh, Tezpur, also rail (except to Tezpur)
Accommodation:
Budget to high-end in main towns
Best season:
November to March
Also worth seeing:
Annual winter Tea Festival at Jorhat (dates vary), Kaziranga and other wildlife reserves

Below: The leaf and bud of the robust, malty Assam tea, enjoyed particularly well with milk.

Singhpo tribe, reputed to grow a hitherto unknown species of tea. It was only after a decade that they succeeded in having their discovery certified as tea but events moved fast thereon. British commercial and strategic interests encouraged planters to carve out estates from the dense forests and, by 1862, there were 160 tea gardens in Assam owned by 62 companies. George Williamson, founder of Williamson Magor; Maniram Dewan, the prime minister of the last Ahom king and the first Indian to grow tea on a commercial basis in Assam; Hanuman Bux Kanoi, the largest individual tea producer in India; and later B.M. Khaitan

and the Tata Tea Company were to become legends in the tea industry. In those early years, sensing opportunity, intrepid Marwari traders were gravitating from faraway Rajputana, indelibly soaking their destinies in the brown beverage. The saying went that 'the Marwari can plough a trail where even bullock carts cannot', as the dense north eastern forests. Disease and non existent infrastructure were no deterrent for one of India's most enterprising communities. Eventually, Marwaris were to buy out most British companies and today most of the tea industry is controlled by Marwari families.

TAMIL NADU
Chennai

Toda
settlements

Arabian Sea

Bay
of
Bengal

State and capital:
Tamil Nadu, Chennai
(539 km)

Convenient access:
Road to settlements,
air to Coimbatore, rail
to Udhagamandalam
(formerly
Ootacamund)

Accommodation:
Budget to high-end

Best season: January
to June

Also worth seeing:
Fernhill Palace (now a
Raj-style hotel), The
Botanical Gardens
and St Stephen's
Church (all in
Udhagamandalam)

Settlements of the Todas

Were they a tribe from Israel or descendants of the Pandavas?

Residing in the Nilgiri Hills of South India near the resort town of Ootacamund and Coonoor are a number of tribal communities, of which the most distinctive are the Todas. Toda men and women are tall and attractive, with aquiline features. Both sport long hair, while adult women have tattoo designs on the upper bodies. Their traditional costume is a *puthikuzhi* (colourful cotton shawl), embroidered with woollen designs in red and black, and worn like a Roman toga. Though linked to South Indian dialects, the language of the Todas has no written script.

The origins of these handsome people are obscure. Early colonists speculated that they were the remnants of a lost tribe of Christians who wandered here from Israel; others linked them to the clan of the Pandavas of the epic *Mahabharata*, because of their original polyandrous ways. What-

ever their genesis, they certainly were the oldest inhabitants of this region, as Ootacamund derives its name from the Toda word *udhagamandalam* (village of huts). Traditionally, Todas were pastoralists and their unique culture and religion centres around the water buffalo, which they hold sacred. Their temples were their dairies, occupied by a resident priest and the holy buffalo that provided milk for their religious rituals. Entry to the temple-dairy was restricted to the priest and certain males, but taboo for all women. Till the British developed Ootacamund into a summer resort, the Todas lived in relative obscurity. Contact with civilisation deprived them of their land, and post Independence, social pressures and ecological degradation eroded their traditional way of life. Today, Todas are seeking other sources of income from cottage industries and the sale of their shawls and handicrafts.

Only 1,700 Todas remain now. The community is divided into patriarchal clans usually occupying a single village, ranging in size from one to 19 households. Though some Todas have converted to Christianity, many still practice traditional animist customs relating to birth, marriage and death. Their ceremonies provide a fascinating glimpse into a vanishing way of life.

Huts with tiny entrances

Toda villages are called *munds* and consist of a cluster of oval, wagon shaped structures, three metres high and over 2.5 metres wide. Fashioned out of bamboo fastened by cane, the dwelling is covered with a thatched roof and has stone walls in the front and rear. Its design was probably meant to protect the residents from wild animals—the entrance is a tiny, 90-centimetre high opening, big enough only to crawl through,

Left: The cone-like structure of a Toda temple.
Facing page: Reduced to less than 2,000 individuals, the Todas are a distinct people in terms of customs and way of dressing. Entrances to their huts are as small as a window.

and there are no windows. Tribal motifs decorate the stone façade of the hut, which is surrounded by a small yard enclosed by loose stones. A typical village includes the dairy and a shelter for calves, and is always located near green pastures.

The Valley of Flowers

Hundreds of wildflower species bloom in this paradisical glen

State capital:
Uttarakhand, Dehradun
(320 km)

Convenient access:
Road to Govindghat,
air to Dehradun, rail
to Haridwar

Accommodation:
Budget at Gangharia

Best season: April to
October, snowbound
in winter

Also worth seeing:
Badrinath Temple,
ski slopes of Auli

At least some of Frank Sydney Smythe's weariness must have vanished when he walked into the valley of the Pushpawati stream, on the trudge back from the arduous first ascent of Mount Kamet (7,756 metres). What lay before the mountaineer-writer-photographer and his fellow climbers, the legendary Eric Shipton, and R.L. Holdworth, was a wondrous vista of blooms that inspired him to christen his discovery the 'Valley of Flowers'. That was in 1931, and more than 75 years later the name still holds; in 1982 it was suffixed with 'National Park'. Over this period, the once exclusive domain of

nomadic shepherds set deep in the high reaches of the western Himalayas has attracted many visitors. One of the earliest was the Englishwoman Margaret Lague, a lover of flowers, drawn by the stories of its botanical profusion. While reaching out to pluck one, she slipped off a rock and died, to be buried in the midst of the meadows. Today her tombstone is the only permanent structure in the Valley. It says, 'I will lift mine eyes unto the hills from whence cometh my strength'.

Brahma kamal, the king of Himalayan flowers

What makes the Valley special is

that it is just 10 kilometres long and two kilometres wide (though the Park encloses 87.5 kilometres of surrounding area). The unusual abundance in such a small area is due to its location at the junction of a major Himalayan transition zone: besides being sandwiched by the extreme eastern edge of the Zanskar and the Greater Himalayan ranges, in the north and south, respectively, it is also the meeting place of eastern and western Himalayan flora. The Pushpawati, joined by streams and waterfalls along the way, runs its length. From April to October, climatic and environmental dynamics change on a monthly basis,

offering in hill temples, and also as a balm for bruises and cuts. While the surrounding mountains are obscured during most of the season, a perfectly clear view of the snow-clad heights—Gauri Parbat (6,719 metres) is the tallest finial within the Park, the lower end of which is at 3,250 metres—opens up post monsoon. As winter closes in, the flowers begin to turn brown and peter out until woken once again by spring. Supported by the fiesta of flowers is obviously a large and diverse population of butterflies, but there is bigger Himalayan fauna too: tahr, *bharal* (blue sheep), red fox, seraw and black bear.

The Valley is still not within easy reach. A 15 kilometre trek or pony ride from Govindghat (1828 metres) winds up a steep cobbled pathway amidst mountains covered with oaks, silver birches and pines. Small food stalls along the path provide relief, for it also leads to Hemkund Sahib, a much revered pilgrimage site for Sikhs. At Gangharia, a ramshackle village where the first day's walk ends, the route bifurcates, one leading into the Valley of Flowers and the other towards Hemkund.

Hemkund Sahib, higher up in the mountains

Seven steep kilometres up from Gangharia, the second trail brings one up to the 4,500-metre-high Lokpal Lake, on the banks of which is the shrine. In a verse in the autobiographical *Bichittar Natak*, it is suggested by Guru Gobind Singh, the 10th and last Sikh Guru, that in a previous life he practised spiritual discipline by the side of the Lake, an episode now consecrated by a pentagonal-roofed gurudwara. A small temple nearby is dedicated to Laxmana, the brother of Lord Rama, who is said to have performed austerities here as well. Visitors arriving at Hemkund after the laborious hike are served tumblers of steaming hot, sweet tea by gurudwara *sevaks* (volunteer workers). Devotees consider it customary to take a dip in the ice-cold glacial lake over which a wispy mist usually hangs, periodically lifting to reveal the reflection of the seven surrounding mountain peaks in the crystal clear waters.

Bottom: Hemkund Sahib, the highest gurudwara in the world, was first consecrated in 1936 with the Holy Book of the Sikhs being placed in a small 10-square-metre structure. The current hexagonal structure is designed to bear the weight of heavy snowfall, besides representing an upturned brahma lotus placed by the Creator on the spot where the Guru meditated.
Facing page: Sweeping view of the Valley of Flowers.

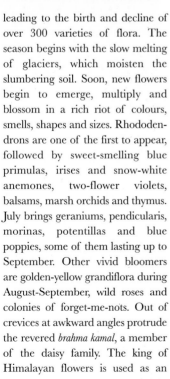

leading to the birth and decline of over 300 varieties of flora. The season begins with the slow melting of glaciers, which moisten the slumbering soil. Soon, new flowers begin to emerge, multiply and blossom in a rich riot of colours, smells, shapes and sizes. Rhododendrons are one of the first to appear, followed by sweet-smelling blue primulas, irises and snow-white anemones, two-flower violets, balsams, marsh orchids and thymus. July brings geraniums, pendicularis, morinas, potentillas and blue poppies, some of them lasting up to September. Other vivid bloomers are golden-yellow grandiflora during August-September, wild roses and colonies of forget-me-nots. Out of crevices at awkward angles protrude the revered *brahma kamal*, a member of the daisy family. The king of Himalayan flowers is used as an

Thunder and spray

Dropping off heights from 20 to 250 metres, these South Indian waterfalls are a spectacle to behold

KARNATAKA & TAMIL NADU

Bengaluru   Chennai

Arabian   Bay of
Sea   Bengal

• Waterfalls

States and capitals:
Karnataka, Bengaluru
(378 km from Jog,
120 km from
Sivasamudram, 420
km from Unchalli);
Tamil Nadu, Chennai
(314 km from
Hogenakkal)

Convenient access:
Road to Hogenakkal,
Jog, Sivasamudra, rail
to Shimoga (Jog),
Bengaluru
(Sivasamudra,
Hogenakkal), air to
Mangalore (Jog),
Bengaluru
(Sivasamudra,
Hogenakkal)

Accommodation:
Budget to mid-range
(Hogenakkal); Budget
(Jog and Unchalli);
none (Sivasamudra)

Best season: July-
August (for high water
volume); otherwise
November to March

Blessed with an immense network of rivers, India has its fair share of waterfalls. Contrary to what one would except, many of these are not on Himalayan streams but are created by rivers of the southern peninsula, flowing off the relatively low uplands of the Eastern and Western Ghats. Some of the more notable ones are Hogenekkal, Jog, Sivasamudram and Unchalli Falls.

Hogenekkal Falls are situated at an isolated location at the confluence of the Chinar and Kaveri Rivers, with only a little village sharing the space. From its origins in the Kodagu region of Karnataka, the Kaveri makes its way to the neighbouring state of Tamil Nadu, weaving in and out of forests and open areas, finally tumbling down in a series of voluminous cataracts at the village of Hogenekkal—the name itself means 'Smoky Rocks' after the misty spray created by the cascading water slamming onto the rocks below—near the town of Dharmapuri. With a drop of only 20 metres, this cataract may not be very high, but it is one of the most picturesque.

Besides standing aside and viewing them, one can journey up close to the base of the Falls. Before it crashes down in masses of white water, the Kaveri spreads over alternating shallow rocky land and deep stretches with strong currents, as it meanders around small islands interspersed with wooded tracts and unusually patterned boulders. Local boatmen take visitors in traditionally crafted circular coracles known as parisals, which are essentially made of light wicker frames with buffalo hide stretched over to keep it waterproof. Everyone wades through the shallow segments of the river while the boatman carries the coracle over his shoulder, only to set it down once there is sufficient depth in the water for everyone to climb back on again. Initially, the coracle is taken near to the edge of the first of the two main waterfall levels accessible by boat. From here one can see the cascade from above and is within range of the sprays. The roar is thunderous

and the views spectacular. If the river isn't in spate, the boatman may decide to take the passengers to the section below, bringing them as close as safety permits. As the proximity increases, so does the turbulence. Along the banks women sell freshly fried fish, masseurs with oils and powders offer their services under shady canopies, and village children dive into the waters for a price.

As the Kaveri approaches the forested hills and lush valleys surrounding the tiny island town of Sivasamudra in Karnataka, it segregates into two channels, which tumble as a series of cascades, 849 metres wide and 90 metres high. These are the Sivasamudram Falls near a group of ancient temples. Pristine but not easily accessible up close, the Falls widen to about 300 metres during the monsoon.

The four streams of Jog Falls

In Shimoga district of Karnataka, the Sharavathi River creates the spectacular Jog Falls (253 metres at their highest), one of the highest in India. At the place it drops, the river splits itself into four separate streams, each of which has been named for their individual characteristics. They are Raja (King), for its serene countenance; Roarer, as it is the loudest section of the Falls; Rocket, owing to the huge volume of water that shoots out from a small opening; and Rani (Queen), named so for the twisting and turning trajectory that is taken to resemble the graceful movement associated with royalty.

Unchalli Falls, originally called Lushington Falls after the British Collector who discovered them in 1845, are the most difficult to get to. Plummeting 116 metres off the top end, they lie on the Aghanashini River, near the town of Sirsi, and are accessible only by a five-kilometre trek.

The single-drop Jog Falls in the monsoon. At its peak in late monsoon, the Sharavathi River pushes water up to 3,400 cubic metres per second down the cataract.

Canyon in the Land of White Copper

The Zanskar River forms an awesome valley on its way to the Indus

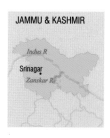

JAMMU & KASHMIR

As you stand on top of the Pensi La Pass, at 4,420 metres above sea level, you can see Drung Dirung glacier's massive, fractured hunk on the south-west, from which drips the essence of the Stod, which later unites with the Tsarap to form the Zanskar River. The valley stretches below, expanding as it extends further, the fledgling stream running through it. It is an awesome sight, and one that not many people see, for Zanskar is one of the last frontiers of India—unmapped and unknown to the world until penetrated by 19th century British expeditions—contiguous to trans-Himalayan Ladakh, yet cut off from it except by way of high mountain passes and sneaking river valleys.

Hemmed in by mountain ranges

The traditional way in from the north is over the Pensi La by road and then one can either trek, or choose to ride the river on rafts and kayaks. The former is a classic 180-kilometre journey for as the Zanskar runs away eastward to seek the Indus, it rams through the heart of the Zanskar Mountain's, carving out a spectacular gorge. On its upper end, however, it is a shallow, rippling stream, chilled to a few degrees above freezing point, running through a beautiful landscape. On one side of the wide valley, the dark wall of the Greater Himalayas is riddled with waterfalls

and glaciers, while on the other side, the pastel-coloured Zanskar range is drier and sandier. Due to its glaciers amid ochre-hued mountains, Zanskar is also known as the Land of White Copper. Almost totally Buddhist, it is dotted with *gompas* (monasteries). These are hundreds of years old, and can mostly be reached only on foot. From the heights of Karsha *gompa*, one can gaze at the entire panorama of the Zanskar plains; Sani is thought to date to the second century; Dzonkhul was the retreat of solitude-seeking hermit masters; and Lingshed, the remotest of all, is accessible only by days of trekking into the heart of the Zanskar Mountains.

Through sheer rock walls

Fortified with the volume of the Tsarap, the Stod gains stature and turns northward. The mountains start closing in and the gorge looms ahead. Once in it, on a raft, one is in surreal isolation, totally removed from the outside world (which, to begin with, is itself considerably removed). Rock spires, in various shades of ochre, shoot up from the surface of the river to heights over 750 metres; it is akin to sitting in the front row of a huge cinema hall, except that the panorama is all around, not just in the front. The staggering scale is put into perspective by a bobbing raft ahead, a tiny speck at the toe of a soaring mountainous mass. Triangular slopes of scree slide into the fluvium and vertical formations of rock rise from under it. No longer are there banks, just a blunt meeting of water and land. Far above, one might spy the ragged thread of a mule caravan making its perilous way along a groove in the cliff. At this stage, the river picks up speed and rapids start forming, and further on, the gorge opens out for about 500 metres and then promptly reconverges, squeezing the effluence into a six-metre gap with sheer rock walls on both sides. Forced into the mouth of the narrow opening the water works up swirls and boils, riding up the walls. This is one of

the most exciting sections of the river trip. A couple of hundred metres later, the walls recede to reveal a scenic spot by a waterfall. The gorge continues, as the River flows over a visually spellbinding section with an archetypal ochre Zanskar mountain rising behind. As it exits the gorge, it is joined by the Markha River, and the first signs of settlements appear; Chiling, on its banks, is a village of traditional goldsmiths and metal workers. Not much lower downstream, it joins the Indus as its largest tributary in India. In winter, this is the starting point of a challenging upstream trek, which winds up the valley to Padum, the administrative head-quarters of Zanskar. At that time of the year the river is a frozen sheet, shot with fantastic patterns of cracked ice. The going is treacherously slippery and bitterly cold nights have to be spent huddled in caves along the way.

State and capital: Jammu & Kashmir, Srinagar (445 km to Padum)

Convenient access: Road to Padum, air to Leh (475 km to Padum), Srinagar

Accommodation: Camping (with own equipment)

Only season: July to early October (for driving, trekking, river journey), January-February for upriver trek

Top left: A frescoed wooden capital in Karsha monastery.
Below: Gorge of the Zanskar.
Facing page: The stream flows through the Zanskar Valley.

Photo Acknowledgements

p.8/9: Corbis; **p.10/11:** left Taj Mohammad, middle Corbis, right Getty; **p.12/13:** Ashok Dilwali; **p.14/15:** left Roli collection, top and bottom Dinodia; **p.16/17:** Corbis; **p.18/19:** left top and bottom Amit Pasricha, right Corbis; **p.20/21:** Corbis; **p.22/23:** Nirad Grover; **p.24/25:** left Usha Kris, right Corbis; **p.26/27:** Dinodia; **p.28/29:** top left and right Getty, bottom left and right Corbis; **p.30/31:** V. Muthuraman; **p.32/33:** Corbis; **p.34/35:** Dinodia; **p.36/37:** Dinodia; **p.38/39:** left Prakash Israni right Roli collection; **p.40/41:** Dinodia; **p.42/43:** Corbis; **p.44/45:** Roli collection; **p.46/47:** Roli collection; **p.48/49:** Dinodia; **p.50/51:** left Roli collection, right Corbis; **p.52/53:** Roli collection; **p.54/55:** Toby Sinclair; **p.56/57:** Dinodia; **p.60/61:** Roli collection; **p.62/63:** Roli collection; **p.64/65:** top left and right Corbis, bottom right Sanjay Singh Badnor; **p.66/67:** Roli collection; **p.68/69:** Roli collection; **p.70/71:** top left and right Roli collection, bottom left Corbis; **p.72/73:** Dinodia; **p.74/75:** Roli collection; **p.76/77:** Corbis; **p.78/79:** Corbis; **p.80/81:** left Roli collection, right Corbis; **p.82/83:** Roli collection; **p.84/85:** top left and right Nirad Grover, bottom right Pallava Bagla; **p.86/87:** V. Muthuraman; **p.88/89:** Malavika Chauhan; **p.90/91:** Corbis; **p.92/93:** Nirad Grover; **p.94/95:** Balan M; **p.96/97:** Dinodia; **p.98/99:** Corbis; **p.100/101:** Roli collection; **p.102/103:** right Dinodia; **p.104/105:** Roli collection; **p.106/107:** left Salarjung Museum, Hyderabad, right Malavika Chauhan; **p.108/109:** Corbis; **p.110/111:** Roli collection; **p.112/113:** Corbis; **p.114/115:** Corbis; **p.116/117:** Corbis; **p.118/119:** Dinodia; **p.120/121:** Toby Sinclair; **p.122/123:** Roli collection; **p.124/125:** V. Muthuraman; **p.126/127:** Corbis; **p.128/129:** Roli collection; **p.130/131:** Nirad Grover; **p.132/133:** Corbis; **p.134/135:** Corbis; **p.136/137:** Dinodia; **p.138/139:** Corbis; **p.140/141:** left Sanjay Singh Badnor, right Nirad Grover; **p.142/143:** left Nirad Grover, right P.C. Dheer; **p.144/145:** left Dinodia, right Nirad Grover; **p.146/147:** Nirad Grover; **p.148/149:** Nirad Grover; **p.150/151:** left Dinodia, right Nirad Grover; **p.152/153:** left Roli collection, right Corbis; **p.154/155:** left Corbis, right Sanjeev Saith; **p.156/157:** top left and right Dinodia, bottom Corbis; **p.158/159:** left Dinodia, right Amit Pasricha; **p.160/161:** Corbis; **p.162/163:** Corbis; **p.164/165:** Dinodia; **p.166/167:** Corbis; **p.168/169:** V. Muthuraman; **p.170/171:** Amrit P. Singh/wildphotos.com; **p.172/173:** left Nirad Grover, right Dinodia; **p.174/175:** Dinodia; **p.176/177:** left Sharatchandra Yanglem, right Corbis; **p.178/179:** Corbis; **p.180/181:** left Rupin Dang/Wilderness Films India Ltd, right Malavika Chauhan; **p.182/183:** Rupin Dang/Wilderness Films India Ltd; **p.184/185:** Dinodia; **p.186/187:** Corbis; **p.188/189:** Amrit P. Singh/wildphotos.com; **p.190/191:** Roli collection; **p.192/193:** left Nirad Grover, right Hashmat Singh; **p.194/195:** Corbis; **p.196/197:** Corbis; **p.198/199:** Dinodia; **p.200/201:** V. Muthuraman; **p.202/203:** left Dinodia, right Nirad Grover; **204/205:** V. Muthuraman; **p.206/207:** Nirad Grover.